The Logic of Law Making in Islam

This pioneering study examines the process of reasoning in Islamic law. Some of the key questions addressed here include whether sacred law operates differently from secular law, why laws change or stay the same, how changing laws are reconciled with fixed foundational texts, and how different cultural and historical settings impact the development of legal rulings. In order to explore these questions, the author examines the decisions of thirty jurists from the largest legal tradition in Islam: the Ḥanafī school of law. He traces their rulings on the question of women and communal prayer across a very broad period of time – from the eighth century to the eighteenth century – to demonstrate how jurists interpreted the law and reconciled their decisions with the scripture and the sayings of the Prophet. The result is a fascinating overview of how Islamic law has evolved and the thinking behind individual rulings.

Behnam Sadeghi has been an assistant professor of religious studies at Stanford University since 2006. His research spans Islamic thought and law in the early and postformative periods. In addition, he has made groundbreaking contributions to the history of the Qur'ān and the *ḥadīth* literature in a series of published essays.

Cambridge Studies in Islamic Civilization

Published titles are listed at the back of the book.

The Logic of Law Making in Islam

Women and Prayer in the Legal Tradition

BEHNAM SADEGHI
Stanford University

CAMBRIDGE
UNIVERSITY PRESS

CAMBRIDGE UNIVERSITY PRESS
Cambridge, New York, Melbourne, Madrid, Cape Town,
Singapore, São Paulo, Delhi, Mexico City

Cambridge University Press
32 Avenue of the Americas, New York, NY 10013-2473, USA

www.cambridge.org
Information on this title: www.cambridge.org/9781107009097

First published 2013

Printed in the United States of America

A catalog record for this publication is available from the British Library.

Library of Congress Cataloging in Publication data
Sadeghi, Behnam, 1969–
The logic of law making in Islam: women and prayer in the legal tradition / Behnam Sadeghi.
pages cm. – (Cambridge studies in Islamic civilization)
Includes bibliographical references and index.
ISBN 978-1-107-00909-7
1. Islamic law – Methodology. 2. Islamic law – Philosophy. 3. Islamic law – Interpretation and construction. I. Title.
KBP144.S227 2012
297.3′82082–dc23 2012012606

ISBN 978-1-107-00909-7 Hardback

Contents

Preface

What makes laws endure or change? When a law changes, how does a tradition of legal interpretation justify the innovation in light of its legal precedents and foundational texts? What is the function of the reasons given for laws? What relationship does law bear to social values? These interrelated questions fall under the heading of philosophy of law, yet it is mainly through the study of history that they can be probed. Answering these questions in different cultural and historical settings is a prerequisite for developing a general theory of law, for it makes distinguishing universal elements from culturally specific parameters possible. In particular, a culturally specific feature of Islamic law is its religious character. One may ask, therefore, whether the fact that Muslim legal traditions invoke sacred authority makes an essential difference to the way the questions posed above are answered. In other words, does sacred law operate in a fundamentally different way from secular law? This book explores these questions through a study of the largest legal tradition in Islam, namely the Ḥanafī school of law.

The book begins by creating a general model of juristic decision making that describes any legal tradition, Islamic or not, in terms of a number of parameters. It does not presuppose that all legal traditions are identical, for the parameters in the model may vary from one tradition to another. A central task of the book is to determine those parameters in the Ḥanafī case. This is achieved through diachronic historical case studies related to laws on women and prayer. The book examines how certain Ḥanafī laws, and the reasons Ḥanafī jurists gave for those laws, evolved from the eighth century to the eighteenth century as reflected in the opinions of some thirty jurists.

Premodern Islamic law as formulated in the four Sunnī legal traditions is sometimes described as the end product of the process of interpreting the foundational texts, namely the Qur'ān and the *ḥadīths* (sayings of the Prophet). Jurists are said to have attempted to *derive* the laws from these sources. This impression owes to the fact that a legal reason (i.e., the reason a jurist gives for a law) often takes the form of a specific interpretation of the Qur'ān and *ḥadīths*, suggesting that the process of interpreting these sources is what generated the law. On this view, these texts represented the starting point of jurisprudence, and the laws its outcome. The transformation of the textual raw material into the laws is said to have taken place through the application of established, recognized methods of interpretation, methods that are described in the classical Islamic genre of legal theory, the *uṣūl al-fiqh*.

The book shows that in fact, at least in the Ḥanafī case, this image must be turned on its head. What is thought to be the outcome of jurisprudence, namely the laws, are actually the starting point for the jurist. The end product, on the other hand, is an interpretation that reconciles the law with the textual "sources," the Qur'ān and the Prophet's sayings. The role of the methods of interpretation, therefore, is not to generate the laws, but rather to reconcile them with the textual sources. The hermeneutic standards governing the process of interpretation can be seen to be so loose as to be inherently incapable of generating laws. They are so flexible that they can be used to reconcile just about any conceivable candidate for the law with the textual sources. Providing maximal indeterminacy, these standards do not constrain the jurist to adopt one possibility (as to what the legal outcome should be in a given matter) to the exclusion of another.

If the binding texts (the Qur'ān and the *ḥadīths*) and the standards of textual interpretation did not determine the laws, the question arises, what did? If the hermeneutic methods imposed no constraint on the laws, does this mean, then, that jurists had a free hand in fashioning the laws as they wished? No, in fact there were severe constraints on the laws. The primary constraint was imposed by the need for legal continuity: normally a law would not change, even if it failed to mirror new social values, as long as it did not become intolerable or highly undesirable. If a person living in the premodern period asked, "Why is this the law?" the correct answer would have been simply, "because this used to be the law," unless this was a new law, in which case the answer would have been, "because the old one became intolerable or highly undesirable due to new social conditions." On this account, present law was a function only of the interaction between past law and new social realities; the reading of foundational sources played no causal role in the evolution of law although it may have played a role in its genesis. This account happens to be a good approximation of the dynamics of secular law, which have been delineated by the legal historian Alan Watson based on his studies in a variety of legal traditions. Thus, at least as far as the fundamental question of how present law relates to past law is concerned, the Ḥanafī legal tradition is similar to secular law notwithstanding its otherwise religious character.

The indeterminacy of the exegetical bridge that linked the laws with the textual sources had important historical ramifications for Ḥanafī jurisprudence. This bridge was constructed of *exegetic rationales*, that is, statements of the type, "this verse abrogates (or qualifies) that one." The flexibility with which exegetical rationales were deployed ensured that any conceivable candidate for the law could be reconciled with the binding texts, and, conversely, that changes in what counted as a binding text did not destabilize the laws. The exegetical bridge did not collapse when the ground shifted on either side of it. When the ground shifted on the side of the laws, for example, when the Ḥanafīs were compelled to change a law due to new social values or circumstances, hermeneutic flexibility allowed them to reconcile the new law with the textual sources, thus enabling legal change. On the other hand, when the ground shifted on the side of the textual foundations, hermeneutic flexibility served the interests of legal continuity by helping to protect the laws from the impact of the changing texts. This happened in the aftermath of the triumph of the Ḥadīth-Folk ideology in the ninth century, when many a *ḥadīth* that at face value contradicted established Ḥanafī laws came to be regarded as binding. This did not force jurists to give up the laws, for hermeneutic flexibility allowed them to neutralize the newly binding texts through interpretation. This episode represented an expansion of the textual basis, but in later centuries there were also contractions. The textual foundations diminished when the Prophetic sayings that had been cited in support of certain laws were disqualified for having been found inauthentic. This did not spell the end of the laws seemingly resting on the disqualified texts. Rather, the laws were furnished new justifications. Hermeneutic flexibility allowed jurists to devise new exegetic rationales to replace those based on the now-lost texts.

The metaphor of a pliable bridge stands for the malleability and revisability of legal reasons and, in particular, of exegetic rationales. Legal reasons (i.e., the reasons jurists gave for the laws) surrounded the laws, forming a protective cushion that absorbed the impact of contrary evidence. The dispensability of legal reasons manifested itself in the historical pattern of the relative stability of laws compared to the reasons given for them. This historical pattern, combined with logical analysis, shows that even though legal reasons logically precede laws, there is an important sense in which they are secondary to the laws: reasons are actually devised to explain existing or newly desired laws. More often than not, they neither cause nor motivate the laws.

The Contribution Made by This Book

Academics are sometimes asked by their colleagues to enumerate concisely the ways in which their contributions differ from those of other researchers. I will do so briefly in the hope that it will be useful for some readers.

First, the broad characterization of juristic thought that I just sketched out and that I will flesh out in this book is largely original, though it certainly resonates with the works of other researchers in some of its particulars. To accept this new picture as a whole is to experience a gestalt shift in which familiar concepts are seen in a new light. For example, techniques such as abrogation, qualification, and analogy that are almost universally described in the academic literature as methods for generating the laws are now seen to operate in the reverse direction, with the laws as their starting point.

Second, the existing academic literature describes premodern methods of scriptural exegesis, but in doing so it normally relies on Muslim works of legal theory, the *uṣūl al-fiqh* genre, a field that was devoted to determining the proper methods of interpreting the Qur'ān and *Ḥadīth*. Scholars usually do not take into account that the principles that premodern legal thinkers expounded in this genre were not always applied in practice. To investigate hermeneutics in practice, one should examine the genres in which the laws were developed and justified, namely those of positive law (*fūrū'*) and legal opinions (*fatāwā*). To my knowledge, this is the first book-length and diachronic study of scriptural hermeneutics in postformative positive law.

Third, as a contribution to Islamic legal studies, this book is methodologically distinct. It is an explicitly framework-driven study. My intention is not to say all that is important about the Ḥanafīs or the legal case studies, nor to engage with every important result reached in recent scholarship. Rather, the study narrowly pursues specific objectives: I approach the legal case studies to investigate the questions generated by the framework devised in Chapter 1, a schema that is well suited to comparative study and the investigation of the causes of continuity and change.

Fourth, in relation to its objectives, not only does the study characterize mainstream methodology in the Ḥanafī school, but also it identifies and describes the few Ḥanafī jurists who did not follow this typical Ḥanafī approach.

Fifth, the framework-driven case studies lead to conclusions elaborated in the final three chapters that enrich some of the ways in which Islamic legal thought is normally understood. These address questions such as the relationship between laws and values, the dynamics and mechanics of legal change and continuity, the concrete ways such dynamics were manifested in Ḥanafī thought over the centuries, and the specific justificatory strategies that made continuity or change possible.

No contribution is without limitations. This book's results could be tested and refined by additional case studies. The conclusions about the role of social values could be further tested and enriched by research into extralegal literature. Important questions related to the case studies other than those treated in this work could certainly be investigated.

Outline of the Book

The first two chapters are introductory in nature. Chapter 1 introduces a general framework for the study of any legal tradition, Islamic or not. This framework underpins the subsequent historical case studies. Chapter 2 introduces, briefly, the Ḥanafī school of law and the legal subject matter of the case studies.

The next three chapters, Chapters 3 to 5, comprise the diachronic case studies at the heart of the book, treating certain laws concerning women and group prayer. They focus on legal reasons, their relationship to laws, and the question of continuity and change.

On the basis of these case studies the last three chapters, Chapters 6 to 8, address broad questions of philosophical and historical interest.

Chapter 6, "The Historical Development of Ḥanafī Reasoning," gives a brief description of the historical trajectory of Ḥanafī legal interpretation in light of the case studies. It describes how the expansion and shrinking of the corpus of binding texts impacted the laws – expansion in the aftermath of the rise of Ḥadīth-Folk ideology, and contraction in later centuries as some *ḥadīth*s that jurists had formerly relied upon were disqualified.

Chapter 7, "From Laws to Values," attempts to explain what one can learn about a society from its laws and legal literature. It emerges that one can learn less than is commonly thought. I argue that law has dynamics of its own that distinguish it from other elements of social reality, and that law is not reducible to the values of a community, essential cultural or religious tenets, or the ideologies of ruling elites.

Chapter 8, "The Logic of Law Making," offers an analysis of the structure of legal reasoning, discussing how legal reasons change in order to accommodate changes in laws. It also characterizes the ways in which exegetic rationales involving qualification, abrogation, and analogy are used to ensure hermeneutic flexibility.

The Appendix establishes the authenticity of the earliest Ḥanafī texts that are used in Chapters 3 to 6.

A Skimmer's Guide

Those who would like to read the conclusions about the nature of legal reasoning without the detailed arguments for them are urged to read the preface, Chapters 1, 7, and 8 and Sections 6.2 and 6.3. (They ought to withhold judgment, however, unless they give the case studies in Chapters 3, 4, and 5 a careful reading.)

Readers who are primarily interested in the laws themselves, for example, because of their interest in gender norms, should read Chapters 2, 3, 4, and 5. For a discussion of what the laws imply about the social values bearing on women and gender, they can read Chapter 7.

Those who are interested in the historical development of the Ḥanafī school of law but not in philosophical questions may read Chapters 2 and 6 and the Appendix.

Readers who are interested only in the first century of Islam will find that Chapters 3, 4, and 5 begin with the formative backgrounds of the legal case studies and that the Appendix concerns the dating of traditions and texts.

Miscellanea

Two authors may use the same word and mean different things by it. And two authors may use different words and by them mean the same thing. Obviously, a word is often used in more than one sense. Since no sense is inherently better than any other, one need not argue over the "right" definition. But authors can minimize confusion by specifying the sense in which they use a key term. When an author does so, it becomes incumbent upon readers to substitute the given definition for every occurrence of the term. I use some terms in technical senses. To make it easier for readers to keep track of them and their definitions, I bring most of them together in the list "Key Technical Definitions."

A note on dates: a *hijrī* year overlaps two consecutive years in the Gregorian calendar. For simplicity, I often give only one of these years.

The lowercase *ḥadīth* refers to an individual report about the Prophet while the uppercase *Ḥadīth* refers to the corpus of such reports.

Acknowledgments

In writing this book, I have benefited immensely from the advice and criticisms of Michael Cook, Hossein Modarressi, and Patricia Crone. I am extremely grateful to them for this and for the numerous other ways they have supported me. I thank Sarah Kistler, Mairaj Syed, Ruth Miller, Karen Bauer, Brent Sockness, Lee Yearley, Christopher Melchert, Vanessa Boren, an anonymous reader, and my students in the Classical Islamic Law seminar at Stanford University for useful comments. I would like to acknowledge my intellectual and personal debts to Kathryn Babayan, Michael Bonner, Sherman Jackson, and Alexander Knysh. The resonance of my work with that of Sherman Jackson will become apparent in the pages that follow. I revised a portion of this work as a Frank H. Kenan Fellow at the National Humanities Center in North Carolina; I thank Geoffrey Harpham and the NHC staff for their support. I am grateful to Marigold Acland of Cambridge University Press for her help in bringing this work to press.

Acknowledgments

[illegible]

Key Technical Definitions

Term	Page number(s)
apparent meaning of the canon	19
canon	13–14
canon-blind law	15
exegetic rationale	27
hermeneutic flexibility	16–19
hermeneutic-methodological approach	16
hermeneutic principle	27
legal effect	166
legal inertia	14
legal principle	166
legal reason	11
postformative	4, 40–1
precedent-blind, canon-blind law	19–20
public reason	147
pure hermeneutic approach	16
received law	14
revisable/revisability	1–2
technical term	13–14
values	14

1

A General Model

1.1. Revisability and Indeterminacy

When a contradiction comes to light in a belief system, the system tends to make adjustments to remove the discrepancy. Some component(s) of the system must be given up and replaced to maintain overall coherence. But which? Let us assume a belief system made up of several components: the body of laws of a legal tradition (*madhhab*); the reasons given for those laws; general legal-methodological principles stipulating what counts as a valid reason; and theological, linguistic, philosophical, and historical tenets. In principle, any of these components might be rejected and replaced. In practice, however, some components are held relatively immune to rejection, as exemplified by the immunity granted in Muslim legal discourse to such "higher level" assumptions, respectively theological and historical, as the authority and authenticity of the Qur'ān. That much is unsurprising. More interesting is the study of what happens to the less immune, more revisable parts of the system, especially such "lower level" components as (1) the laws themselves (e.g., "drinking date wine is forbidden," or "is licit"); (2) the exegetic rationales for the laws (statements of the sort, "this Qur'ānic verse is qualified by that saying of the Prophet," or "this verse is abrogated by that one"); and (3) general legal-methodological or hermeneutic principles governing and disciplining the use of exegetic rationales (e.g., "particular statements qualify general ones," or "a Qur'ānic law is not abrogated by an earlier law").

Historical investigation shows that these three classes are not equally revisable. One may imagine a continuum of revision approaches. At one end of the gamut, one always holds the needed or desired laws absolutely immune and adjusts the rationales for specific laws (and, if need be, modifies even general methodological principles), making the smallest changes necessary to preserve the laws. At the other end of the gamut is the approach that grants no measure of prior immunity or stability to the laws; rather, it always lets stable methodological principles determine the exegetic rationales and the laws. Historical inquiry may clarify where on the continuum between these endpoints a school or an individual jurist is found.

Moreover, just as the class of exegetic rationales as a whole may be found to be more (or less) revisable and historically unstable than the class of laws as a whole, specific types of exegetic rationale may be more vulnerable to revision than others. Different types of exegetic rationale (qualification, abrogation, etc.) are not used equally in the revision process.[1] Where jurists have a choice of two or several methods of getting the job done, they are liable to consistently prefer one type of argument to another. It should be possible, then, to derive a hierarchy of preference. Doing so would be part of reconstructing a school's or a jurist's methodological approach.

The line of inquiry laid out here requires identifying contradictions and examining how they are resolved. How easy is it to find such cases? Any vast and complex system of jurisprudence can be expected to contain contradictions arising from the sheer difficulty experienced by jurists in keeping track, simultaneously, of all principles and rationales and their consequences. Discrepancies of this type may require some effort to detect. Conspicuous contradictions can also arise from specific historical processes. And as a matter of historical fact, Islamic law developed in a way that generated such contradictions on a massive scale.

Islamic law evolved as the judgment of jurists. In the first two centuries of Islam, some of these decisions reflected practices that had always been part of the life of the community, ever since the Prophet Muḥammad had introduced them. Other decisions reflected local customs of non-Prophetic origin: tribal law, personal preference, and ad hoc decisions. These laws of non-Prophetic origin sometimes supplemented the Prophet's laws and sometimes supplanted them.[2] Another important feature of law in

[1] Revision consists of a rejection followed by a replacement. So it is not only the choice of what is rejected that presupposes a methodological approach but also the choice of its replacement.

[2] An example of the latter is the emergence in first-century Medina and Kūfa of the prohibition of women going out to the mosque despite the Prophet's approval of the practice. Mecca and Baṣra, by contrast, preserved the status quo. This subject is treated in a separate work I have under preparation.

this period was that legal opinions clustered along geographic lines. For example, the legal opinions in Baṣra tended to be closer to one another than to those from Medina, and vice versa.

In this early period, law did not primarily derive from the reports about the Prophet (*Ḥadīth*) and his Companions, at least not in the circles from which the earliest surviving legal traditions emerged, namely the Ḥanafī and Mālikī schools of law.[3] Law and such reports had developed in parallel and certainly overlapped, but there were also significant divergences

[3] This need not be explained as a result of the *Ḥadīth* being chronologically secondary to the laws. Rather, the point is that the traditionists (i.e., *ḥadīth* transmitters and scholars) and jurists (*fuqahā'*) formed distinct though overlapping groups: most traditionists were not jurists, and a good many jurists were minor or poor traditionists. The two fields could thus undergo changes independently of each other. Indeed, the earliest jurists would have been aware of only a fraction of the reports in circulation. A Kūfan jurist such as Abū Ḥanīfa worked with a subset of the reports that circulated in Kūfa, including a small number of traditions that originated in other cities. Knowledge of traditions current in other cities reached Kūfa gradually, and on a massive scale only in the second/eighth century. While some sources identify the *Ḥadīth* movement with Medina and the *ahl al-ra'y* with Kūfa, these two authors have argued that both approaches were present in both cities: Joseph Schacht, *Origins of Muhammadan Jurisprudence* (Oxford: Clarendon Press, 1967), 228–57, and 'Abd al-Majīd Maḥmūd, *al-Madrasa al-fiqhiyya li-al-muḥaddithīn* (Cairo: Maktabat al-Shabāb, 1972), 19–79.

Another reason is that many of the earliest jurists of the early regional schools of law, to which the proto-Mālikīs and the proto-Ḥanafīs belonged, did not consider *ḥadīth*s as binding in the forceful and consistent manner that became increasingly common after al-Shāfi'ī. Schacht noted that they preferred the living traditions of their respective cities to *ḥadīth*s. From this, Schacht concluded that they did not always consider the Prophet's *sunna* as binding. Though, he added that eventually some of them came to identify their living traditions with the *sunna* of the Prophet, which they now considered binding; see Schacht, *Origins*, 80. On the other hand, Dutton has argued that Mālik considered the living tradition of his city, Medina, as a better guide to the true normative practice of the Prophet (i.e., the *sunna* of the Prophet): for example, an authentic *ḥadīth* may describe a one-off practice of the Prophet, whereas community practice preserves the truly normative practice of the Prophet. Thus, to the question of whether the *sunna* of the Prophet had always been considered binding, Dutton gives a different answer than Schacht would. Nevertheless, Dutton agrees with Schacht's observation that *ḥadīth*s were not absolutely binding; he just does not completely equate *ḥadīth*s with Prophetic *sunna*. This common ground about the *Ḥadīth*, which is confirmed also by Gurāyā's reading of Mālik's *Muwaṭṭa'* and my reading of al-Shaybānī, is what underpins my statement that law was not primarily based on the *Ḥadīth*. See Muḥammad Yūsuf Gurāyā, *Origins of Islamic Jurisprudence* (Lahore: Muḥammad Ashraf, 1985), 116–20; Yasin Dutton, "*'Amal* v. *Ḥadīth* in Islamic Law: The Case of *sadl al-yadayn* (Holding One's Hands by One's Sides) when Doing the Prayer," *Islamic Law and Society* 3 (1996): 13–40; Yasin Dutton, *The Origins of Islamic Law* (Surrey: Curzon, 1999), 168–77; cf. Hallaq, *The Origins and Evolution of Islamic Law*, 102–21. For a different theory, see M. Mustafa al-Azami, *On Schacht's Origins of Muhammadan Jurisprudence* (Oxford: Oxford Centre for Islamic Studies, 1996).

between them in proto-Ḥanafī and proto-Mālikī quarters.[4] By the third/ninth century, the strengthening of the "Ḥadīth Folk" movement had led to much wider acceptance of Prophetic *Ḥadīth* as a source that trumped any nonrevealed or nontextual source of law. This concession on part of jurists confronted them with contradictions between the existing laws and the *Ḥadīth*. They could no longer ignore *ḥadīth*s that did not fit the law. They were thus faced with a choice: they could clear the legal slate and recreate the law in the image of the *Ḥadīth*; they could preserve the law and explain away the *Ḥadīth*; or they could seek some kind of compromise. Much of the energy and genius of *ḥadīth*-oriented jurists in the following centuries was directed at resolving these contradictions.[5] It is by examining just how jurists in the following centuries went about restoring consistency that one can best uncover their methodological approaches. Part of this task involves determining which components in legal deductions are historically more stable than others.

The two extremes of the range of methodological approaches mentioned previously correspond to differing conceptions of the nature of legal reasoning in the postformative period. (The "postformative period" is defined, for my purposes, as the period after the birth of the Ḥanafī legal tradition in the second/eighth century.[6]) The approach that has hermeneutic principles generate and determine the laws perhaps represents the more usual understanding of Islamic law. According to this conception, represented in Figure 1 (a), the laws logically derive from, or have as their source and starting point, the Qur'ān and the *Ḥadīth*. The jurist's task is to transform the raw materials of the Qur'ān and the *Ḥadīth* into the finished product of the laws (*aḥkām*) that may be readily applied to any circumstance. The transformation is supposed to be effected by fixed hermeneutical methods and legal-methodological principles. The jurist feeds the sources into this methodological machine, turns the crank

[4] For the other schools, the question remains open. Al-Shāfiʿī argued for the absolutely binding quality of Prophetic *ḥadīths*. But it remains an open question whether, in fact, instead of clearing the legal slate and beginning anew with the *Ḥadīth* as his starting point, legal inertia did not compel him to rationalize away the *Ḥadīth* where they disagreed with some of the legal concepts he had inherited. One must examine this question through the chapters on positive law in *al-Umm* rather than through his *Risāla*, which, being on methodology, may conceivably use concrete examples in a selective manner that may not fairly represent the overall character of his jurisprudence.

[5] On the impact of Ḥadīth-Folk ideology, see also Joseph Schacht, *Introduction to Islamic Law* (Oxford: Clarendon Press, 1966), 35–6; Christopher Melchert, *The Formation of the Sunni Schools of Law, 9th-10th Centuries C.E.* (Leiden and New York: Brill, 1997).

[6] See Section 2.1.

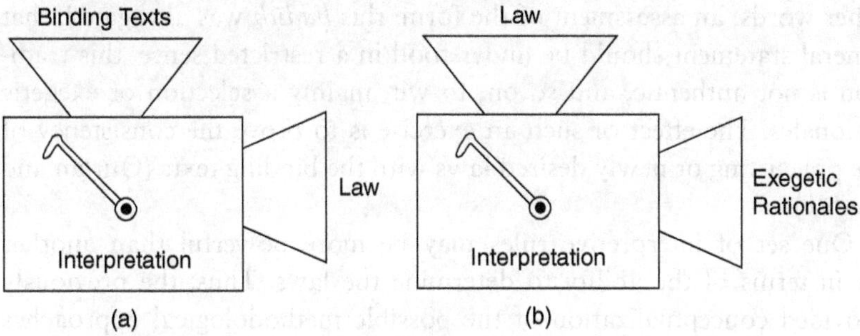

FIGURE 1. Two different conceptions of textual exegesis in legal interpretation.

(performing *ijtihād*), as it were, mechanically processing the sources in accordance with the hermeneutic principles, and finally receives the law at the output. The fallibility and uncertainty of the process and most of the laws it is taken to generate are readily acknowledged, though their subjectivity is not. The process is thought to be objective in the sense that if any other jurist were to turn the crank, the output would be the same or at least within the certified margin of objective uncertainty, thus falling within a bounded set of acceptable legal solutions. The undisciplined, personal discretion of the jurist plays no role. This way of looking at the law allows one to speak of the "discovery" of the law, of "the search for God's law," or of "deriving the law" from the Qur'ān and the *Ḥadīth*.[7]

The other end of the gamut, where the laws are constant or, if they change, they do so not because of hermeneutic/methodological considerations but rather because of extralegal changes such as new social circumstances or needs, corresponds to an altogether different conception of how postformative law operates, represented in Figure 1 (b). Here, the input to the machine consists not only of the Qur'ān and the *Ḥadīth*, but also of the law to be justified – that is, preexisting or newly needed or desired law – which is precisely what the first conception would take to be the end-result of the process. The output consists of a valuation of the textual raw materials that would preserve consistency with the law – in

[7] A more sophisticated development of this position would be to say that a jurist's discretion plays the role of offering laws that serve as hypotheses that may be refuted or confirmed by the evidence. Thus, the testability of the laws makes them responsive and accountable to the evidence of the Qur'ān and the *Ḥadīth*. This would still allow one to speak of the "search" for God's law and its "discovery." It would allow one to speak of an objective margin of uncertainty inasmuch as the evidence and the hermeneutic techniques leave some limited room for maneuver. It would allow one to speak of "deriving" the law from the evidence if one is an inductivist, but not if one is a deductivist.

other words, an assessment of the form: this *ḥadīth* was abrogated, that general statement should be understood in a restricted sense, this tradition is not authentic, and so on; to wit, mainly a selection of exegetic rationales. The effect of such an exercise is to prove the consistency of the preexisting or newly desired laws with the binding texts (Qur'ān and *Ḥadīth*).

One set of interpretive rules may be more powerful than another set in terms of the ability to determine the laws. Thus, the previously provided conceptualization of the possible methodological approaches can be related to the inherent logical capacities of groups of hermeneutic principles to determine the laws. (As defined in the first paragraph, "hermeneutic principles" specify how the different types of exegetic rationales can be used. For example, they may set forth the proper way to use analogy, abrogation, or qualification.) To that end, let us think of a hermeneutic-methodological approach as having a fixed selection of hermeneutic principles. Every jurist has some such principles that are implicit in the way he/she operates, regardless of whether he/she states them explicitly or is even conscious of them. Moreover, it is possible to speak of the hermeneutic-methodological approach of a school of law in a given time interval as an approach that typifies the approaches of the jurists working in that legal tradition in that period. One could then locate different methodologies on a spectrum. At one end of the spectrum, the approach is so stringent that it allows no latitude in what the law must be: a mechanical application of the hermeneutic principles to the textual evidence produces a unique legal outcome. This inflexible, deterministic approach corresponds to the vision of Islamic jurisprudence in which law is the outcome of the process of interpreting the foundational texts. At the opposite end of the spectrum, there is unlimited latitude in the legal outcome; the hermeneutic principles are so flexible that exegetic rationales can be found to show any conceivable law as consistent with the textual sources.[8] Because any and all candidates for the law can be harmonized with the texts, the hermeneutic principles cannot be said to determine any law, and the law cannot be the outcome of the process of interpretation. Interpretation serves to justify the laws rather than determine them. Thus, the test of the hermeneutic flexibility of a hermeneutic-methodological approach is how likely it is that any arbitrarily chosen

[8] This would be an "unfalsifiable" system, to use Karl Popper's term, as no conceivable outcome could be ruled out. See Karl Popper, *The Logic of Scientific Discovery* (London: Hutchinson, 1959).

candidate for a law can be justified within the system. To be sure, neither of these extremes necessarily existed in reality, but every methodology that has existed can be placed somewhere on that spectrum. So, one can study how different jurists' or legal schools' places on that spectrum compare to one another or change over time.

We have just seen how revisability relates to hermeneutic flexibility. However, one does not investigate the two issues in exactly the same way. To learn whether one component of juristic argumentation (e.g., the reasons given for the laws) is more or less revisable/unstable than another component (e.g., the laws), historical investigation suffices: for example, one simply tallies up the laws and the reasons given for them after tracing them over time. The study of hermeneutic flexibility, however, shifts the attention from historical analysis of how the law developed to logical analysis of the methodological approaches, aiming to determine the degree of freedom or flexibility they inherently possess. Historical analysis, of course, is needed to reconstruct a jurist's methodological approach. That is to say, by studying that jurist's reasons, one may be able to determine the hermeneutic principles, if any, inherent therein. But once the methodology is known, in principle no historical analysis is needed to determine the flexibility and capacities of that methodological system. Given knowledge of the methodological approach, the level of flexibility can be determined through logical analysis. Accordingly, one may form a sense of the ways the law could have developed, a sense of the extent of the space of logical possibilities, which (depending on the given methodological approach) may be larger than what history has actually made use of.

What is the best way of reconstructing a methodological approach and, in particular, determining the level of hermeneutic flexibility? What kind of a test case is most suited for the purpose of historical analysis?

To begin answering that question, it helps to consider how the logical structure of a methodological system affects actual legal thought, setting bounds within which historical reality can unfold. A hermeneutically flexible methodology allows jurists to maintain any legal position they advocate by neutralizing seemingly contrary evidence. In particular, the law advocated could be one that the jurist prefers for reasons unrelated to the binding foundational texts – for instance, because it is the established law or because as a new law it would better fit current social conditions and values. But if a methodology rigidly maps the evidence into unique law, leaving little latitude in the choice of the law, then the jurist is typically forced to abandon any legal outcome other than the one determined by the methodology. So, hermeneutic flexibility correlates with the freedom of the jurist to neutralize conflicting textual evidence.

Moreover, as mentioned earlier, maximal hermeneutic flexibility allows jurists to justify any candidate for the law. Generally, the candidates most difficult to justify tend to be those that oppose the apparent meaning of the absolutely binding texts (the canon, for short). These tend to form the toughest test cases of hermeneutic flexibility. Therefore, optimal test cases for baring methodological commitments are those in which the binding texts seemingly clash with a jurist's position, or with what a jurist would have ruled if it were not for the binding texts. Such a confrontation can result from different processes. An obvious one has been explained already, namely the conflict, after the triumph of Ḥadīth-Folk ideology, between the apparent meaning of some Prophetic reports (*ḥadīth*s) on the one hand, and the inertia of the laws of a legal tradition, such as the Ḥanafī school of law, on the other hand. In such a case, the inherited law disagrees with the apparent purport of Prophetic reports. Cases in which the majority position on a point of law changes are also revealing from a methodological standpoint.

1.2. A General Model of Decision Making and Exegesis

1.2.1. *Motivation: The Islamic Case*

According to Joseph Schacht, postformative Islamic jurisprudence was marked by what he called the régime of *taqlīd*, which began setting in around AD 900. In this period, retrospective justification of the early legal positions of the schools summed up the work of jurists; the originality of jurists lay not in the revision of the laws, which were static, but in the process of justifying existing law.

> Even during the period of *taklīd*, Islamic law was not lacking in manifestations of original thought in which the several schools competed with and influenced one another. But this original thought could express itself really in nothing more than abstract systematic constructions which affected neither the established decisions of positive law nor the classical doctrine of the *uṣūl al-fikh*.[9]

The new rigidity characterized not only the legal schools when viewed as wholes, but also even individual jurists. To be sure, there were those who claimed the right to form legal opinions independently from their school's juristic precedents. "But these claims, as far as positive law was

[9] Schacht, *Introduction*, 71–2.

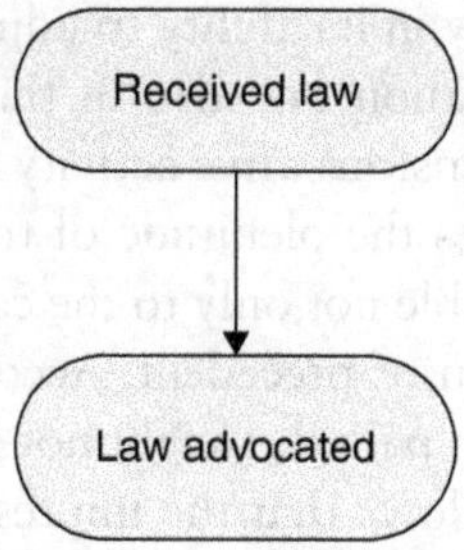

FIGURE 2. Model of postformative decision making: the laws remain as they were before.

concerned, remain theoretical, and none of the scholars who made them actually produced an independent interpretation of the *sharīʿa*."[10] Figure 2 best captures Schacht's theory of legal change.

Inevitably, the result was an increasingly widening gap between the law and the changing social reality.

> Islamic law, which until the early ʿAbbāsid period had been adaptable and growing, from then onwards became increasingly rigid and set in its final mould. This essential rigidity of Islamic law helped it to maintain its stability over centuries which saw the decay of the political institutions of Islam. It was not altogether immutable, but the changes which did take place were concerned more with legal theory and the systematic superstructure than with positive law. Taken as a whole, Islamic law reflects and fits the social and economic conditions of the early ʿAbbāsid period, but has grown more and more out of touch with later developments of the state and society.[11]

Unsupported by detailed diachronic case studies, these views on postformative law represent first impressions. Though first impressions can convey a large kernel of truth, they can also be misleading. After all, notwithstanding some exceptions, postformative Muslim jurists were motivated to minimize their differences with the established precedents of their respective legal traditions. The importance of the precedents and authority of a jurist's legal tradition in Islamic jurisprudence is well-known.[12] In this respect, a Muslim jurist was not fundamentally different from a scholar of Jewish law or an American jurist.[13] For "the creativity

[10] Schacht, *Introduction*, 72.
[11] Schacht, *Introduction*, 75.
[12] See, for example, Wael Hallaq, "Was the Gate of *Ijtihād* Closed?" *International Journal of Middle Eastern Studies* 16.1 (1984): 10–11.
[13] The authority of the past in legal traditions is well-known. That it is a general feature of law, and not just Islamic law, has been noted in the field Islamic legal studies by Sherman

of exegesis consists not only in its ability to adjust to new circumstances not contemplated by the canon but also in the interpreter's claim that there is no innovative or transformative activity involved whatsoever: the interpreter merely elucidates the plenitude of truth already latent in the canon"[14] – a truism applicable not only to the canon, but also, to a lesser degree, to the interpretation of precedent. Accordingly, if a jurist did in fact diverge from the beaten path, he might not have gone out of his way to advertise that fact. It follows that the impression of a basically static law is suspect *ab initio* if not verified by diachronic case studies.

Schacht was right to highlight the salience of retrospective justification. However, his generalization that "none of the scholars" produced an independent interpretation is too sweeping. Others have shown (and this book confirms) that sometimes individual jurists departed from the established school position, and sometimes the school consensus changed.[15] While it is true that retrospective justification constituted a significant part of jurists' work, leaving the matter at that would beg the question of why laws changed or remained the same.

We know that while jurists did retain and justify most received laws, they also abandoned or modified a good number of them. Since the

Jackson, *Islamic Law and the State: The Constitutional Jurisprudence of Shihāb al-Dīn al-Qarāfī* (New York: E. J. Brill, 1996), 80–2 and 73.

[14] Bernard Levinson, *Legal Revision and Religious Renewal in Ancient Israel* (Cambridge: Cambridge University Press, 2008), 16. The author uses the word "canon" in more or less the same sense as I do.

[15] For change in the laws in the postformative period, see, in addition to the examples in this book, for example, the following: Hossein Modarressi, *Kharāj in Islamic Law* (London: Anchor Press, 1983); Baber Johansen, *The Islamic Law on Land Tax and Rent* (London: Croom Helm, 1988); Khaled Abou el-Fadl, *Rebellion and Violence in Islamic Law* (Cambridge: Cambridge University Press, 2001). For more on Schacht's views and a debate about them, see especially the following works of Wael Hallaq and Sherman Jackson: Hallaq, "Was the Gate of *Ijtihād* Closed?"; Wael Hallaq, "*Uṣūl al-fiqh*: Beyond Tradition," *International Journal of Middle Eastern Studies* 16.1 (1984): 3–41; and Jackson, *Islamic Law and the State*, 69–141. Hallaq's essays are reprinted in Wael Hallaq, *Law and Legal Theory in Classical and Medieval Islam* (Cambridge: Cambridge University Press, 2001). More recently, see the following valuable contribution: Wael Hallaq, *Authority, Continuity, and Change in Islamic Law* (Cambridge: Cambridge University Press, 2001).

Jackson's book is exceptionally important, and it remains the most lucid discussion of legal change in the postformative period, though he misunderstands Hallaq. Jackson thinks incorrectly that his own position that the door of *ijtihād* was nearly shut and Hallaq's view that it was open are in genuine contradiction. In fact, they are not. Because the two authors use the word *ijtihād* in different senses, they are not talking about the same door. By *ijtihād*, Jackson has in mind reasoning that bypasses the authority of the legal school, while Hallaq's *ijtihād* subsumes, in addition, reasoning within the framework of the school's precedents.

commitment to received law was not absolute, the question is raised as to why some laws were retained and justified retrospectively while others were not. Consequently, instances in which the law was preserved unaltered require just as much explanation as cases in which it changed. Furthermore, there are cases where the retrospectively justified law is one of several competing options provided by the school's repertoire of legal precedents, raising the question of what guided its selection. In such cases, again, commitment to received law fails to explain why a particular law was retrospectively justified. While many a jurist upheld the idea of commitment to received law, especially when it was ascribed to the founder of the legal tradition, such a norm does not explain the reality of legal continuity and change.

In short, to reject the reality of absolute commitment to received law creates an explanatory gap: a general explanation that accounts not only for change but also for continuity is needed. A satisfactory description of postformative jurisprudence should explain how it came to be that the laws were retained in some cases (and justified) but not in others and why of these two phenomena, the first one, retention, took place on such a significant scale.

Another issue arising from these observations is that of the nature of legal reasons, that is, the reasons jurists gave for the laws they advocated. What was the relationship of such reasons to the laws, be they old laws or new ones? Since the reasons were often based on foundational texts, forming a bridge between the texts and the laws, this question pertains to the nature of exegesis, raising the question of how changing laws related to fixed binding texts. These are indeed the questions with which the present chapter began. Thinking about them with clarity requires a general conceptual framework for inquiry and some terminology.

1.2.2. *A General Model of Decision Making and Exegesis*

I now come to the underlying framework of the book: a model that can be used to study any legal or exegetical tradition that involves the interpretation of a binding foundational text. It turns out to be difficult to discuss the causes of change and continuity with clarity without developing technical terms based on some general model. This has to do with the fact that the causes that may shape the laws are manifold. They can interact with one another in a variety of ways, which means that there are numerous distinctions to be made for which there is no vocabulary in ordinary language. Nevertheless, the complexity of the model ought to

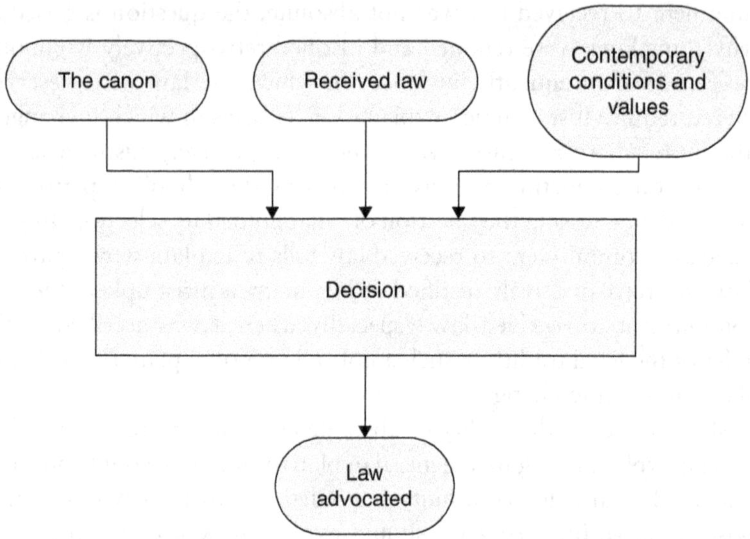

FIGURE 3. The factors shaping a jurist's decision are the inputs. The output is a decision on a point of law.

be kept to the minimum necessary for any given purpose. Accordingly, I offer what I believe is the simplest model necessary for speaking about exegesis, continuity, and change in broad terms. I first develop the model for an individual jurist's decision making and then discuss how it can be extended to describe a legal community. Investigators interested in more specialized issues or higher precision will find that this model needs to be refined for their purposes.

Before devising the model, it helps to be reminded of its purpose. The aim is to enable a discussion of the relationship between a jurist's legal decisions and the factors that shape them. Thus, it must be possible to use the model to give the relationship between certain inputs and outputs as shown in Figure 3. The inputs are the factors that can potentially shape a jurist's legal position. The output is the product of the process, namely the legal decision itself – that is, the jurist's position on the status of an act, object, or state of affairs – for example, whether a specific act is forbidden, a particular kind of contract entails an obligation, a certain situation creates a right, or an act validly fulfills a duty. One may use different shorthands to refer to this output: the legal outcome, the ruling, the legal position, or simply the law. The main factors that can potentially affect the outcome and thus constitute the inputs can be enumerated as follows:

1) The canon (body of absolutely binding foundational texts) and its interpretation.
2) Received law – that is, the legal heritage and precedents, including the known legal decisions of past and present jurists.
3) Present conditions and values
   - Personal attributes of the individual jurist, such as his/her values, personal circumstances, and idiosyncrasies.
   - Present social attributes: circumstances, needs, and values of the larger society.
   - Present disciplinary attributes: tendencies, practices, and circumstances specific to the field of law, community of jurists, or more generally, the law-making class.

The first factor listed here that might shape a jurist's opinion is his or her reading of any absolutely binding foundational texts. In this book, "the canon" is the shorthand used to refer to the body of such texts. By definition, the canon refers to foundational texts that are considered not just authoritative, but absolutely binding. Many a legal tradition around the world today takes a constitution as its canon. In classical Islamic law, the canon included the Qur'ān and accepted reports about the Prophet (*ḥadīth*s), and, therefore, these are the things to which the term "canon" usually refers in this book. Certain Ḥanafīs would have included in the canon also the opinions that the founder of the Ḥanafī legal tradition, Abū Ḥanīfa, had in common with his disciples. Different jurists might disagree over whether a specific text belongs to the canon, that is, whether it is absolutely binding. In the model to be given, what counts is the opinion of the individual jurist whose decision making is being modeled.

The word "canon," of course, is used by different authors in a variety of senses. One definition is not better than any other, though it may be less or more convenient for a particular purpose. In this book I need a shorthand for "absolutely binding foundational texts," and I have chosen the signifier "canon."

This word is thus given a technical definition, like a number of other terms in this book, such as canon-blind law, hermeneutic flexibility, received law, legal reasons, legal inertia, values, postformative, and even "law" in some contexts. Since many readers misunderstand technical definitions altogether, some guidance seems necessary. A technical definition of a term is nothing but a description of the sense in which an author uses the term in a specific work or particular context. It thus instructs readers to interpret the term in a specific way. Accordingly, a reader who remembers a definition for "canon" other than mine and reads it into my uses of the word will surely misunderstand my sentences. Rather, readers should simply substitute "absolutely binding foundational texts" for every instance of "canon" in this book. For example, "the canon shifted" translates into "there was a shift in the choice of texts that were considered absolutely binding." Likewise, "two jurists may draw the boundaries of the canon differently" translates into "two jurists may disagree on exactly which texts are absolutely binding." Technical definitions are usually signaled by sentences of the form "by *x* I mean *y*," "*x* refers to *y*," or "I define *x* as *y*," and they make it incumbent on the reader to substitute *y* for every instance of *x*.

The second factor I listed that may influence the ruling is the jurist's knowledge of the received law. This refers to the decision history – that is, the record of legal precedents within the legal tradition, defined as the known rulings of earlier and contemporaneous jurists. For example, if a jurist's task is to state whether date wine is permissible, the rulings given previously in his school of law on that subject constitute the set of relevant legal precedents. The influence of the received law normally militates against legal change, as jurists often place a premium on diachronic continuity and attach authority to the majority view. Affinity with received law is thus related to legal inertia. "Inertia" here refers to the tendency of the laws to endure over time. The use of the term is not meant to convey passivity: societies enforce the laws that are retained due to legal inertia, and jurists vigorously uphold them and argue for them, often providing new and varying justifications. The issue is the inertia of laws, not people.

The third factor that may conceivably affect a jurist's decisions consists of the values, needs, and circumstances of the jurist at hand, of the community of jurists, and of the larger society at the time of the decision. This category encompasses the force of current social circumstances, institutional realities, social mores, class interests, political pressures, financial motives, the jurist's own values, and the values pervasive in the law-making class, not including the desire for legal continuity or the attitude toward the canon, which are accounted for separately. Here, the word "values" refers to relatively vague and diffuse tendencies, such as "egalitarian" or "patriarchal" attitudes, as opposed to specific and concrete rules such as the laws of marriage or the manner in which inheritance is divided. That "the weak must be protected" may form part of a jurist's or a community's values, but knowing this is one thing, and knowing how it

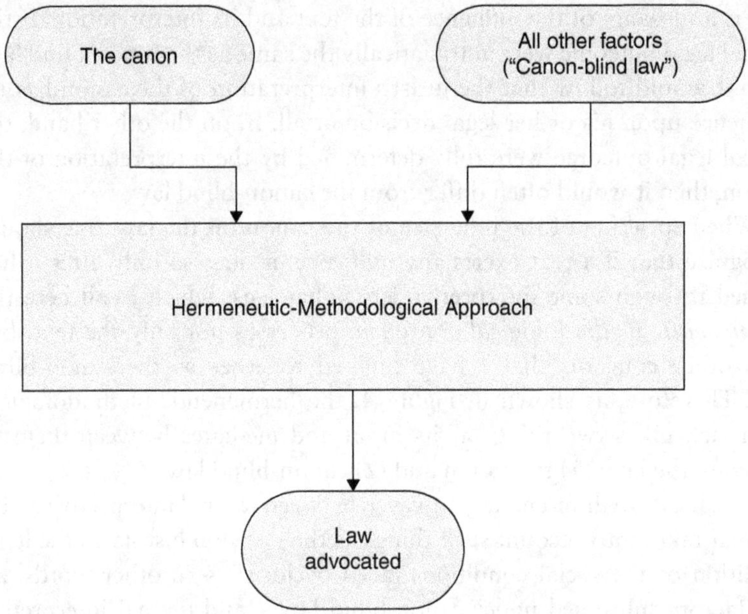

FIGURE 4. An individual jurist's hermeneutic-methodological approach.

is translated into law or handled when it clashes with other values, binding texts, or existing laws is another.

So far, the prototypical model as shown in Figure 3 has the form of an unstructured black box, without any hint of how the inputs may relate to the outcome. The task is to introduce some structure so as to make it easy to compare the roles of the different influences on legal decisions for jurists who may have very different approaches. To that end, one may disentangle the contributions of the different factors by isolating them one by one.

As the first step, I isolate the contribution of the canon from all other factors (see Figure 4). (These other factors are the received law, which exerts a pressure for legal continuity, and present conditions and values at the time the jurist is making his/her decision.) Thus, I define, counterfactually, the *canon-blind law* as the legal position that a jurist *would* have advocated if he/she had been unaware of the evidence of the canon.[16] Canon-blind law, therefore, lumps together factors *other* than the canon. The extent to which the actual legal outcome differs from canon-blind

[16] The definition is counterfactual because the premise of its if-clause is not satisfied in reality, since jurists do know the canon.

law is a measure of the influence of the text and its interpretation. If the actual legal outcome were automatically the same as the canon-blind law, then it would follow that the jurist's interpretation of the canon has no influence upon his or her legal decision at all. If, on the other hand, the actual legal outcome were fully determined by the interpretation of the canon, then it would often differ from the canon-blind law.

When speaking of the influence of the canon on the law, one should recognize that if a text exerts any influence, it does so only after it has passed through some interpretive lens. That lens, which I call here the *hermeneutic-methodological approach*, processes not only the text, but also other concerns that I have lumped together as the canon-blind law. Therefore, as shown in Figure 4, the hermeneutic-methodological approach takes two things as its input and mediates between them to generate the law: (1) the canon and (2) canon-blind law.

One needs to differentiate, however, between textual interpretive activity that takes into account such things as the decision history in the legal tradition or the social conditions faced by jurists – in other words, all the factors subsumed under canon-blind law – and textual interpretive activity that does not depend on such factors, being limited to linguistic knowledge or rules of interpretation that do not take such factors into account. As a shorthand, the latter may be called the *pure hermeneutic approach* (Figure 5). It consists of principles of hermeneutics, if any, whether held consciously and explicitly or not, that do not depend on the jurist's knowledge of the received law or the conditions and values at the time of the jurist. It may capture, for example, procedures of language parsing that do not depend directly on the aforementioned factors. The jurist's pure hermeneutic approach may determine some laws and legal decisions: it may make a certain type of contract invalid or a particular act forbidden. It may also leave some points of law indeterminate or only partially fixed. The legal status of these undetermined cases will be determined by canon-blind law.

The ground has now been laid to define a parameter that is fundamental to the question of how textual exegesis relates to continuity and change, namely *the degree of hermeneutic flexibility*. This parameter is a property of the pure hermeneutic approach. It is a measure of the degree to which a jurist's pure hermeneutic approach determines the laws and legal decisions (Figure 6).

One jurist's pure hermeneutic approach might determine all the legal outcomes in the areas of the law that are treated in the canon. For every act, it will specify its legal status – whether it is forbidden, obligatory, or

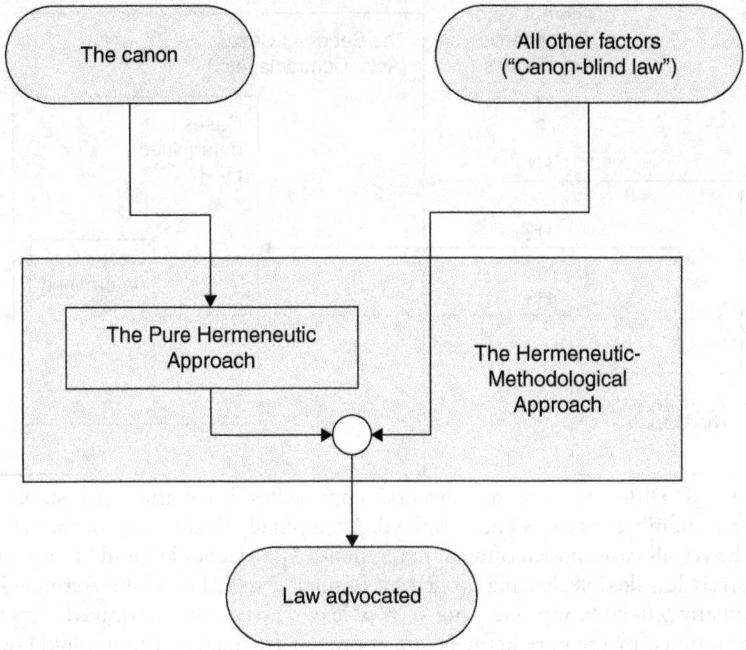

FIGURE 5. The pure hermeneutic approach consists of the jurist's hermeneutic principles and patterns, if any, that deal with the text at the most basic level, prior to consideration of factors such as the decision history or present circumstances and values. Canon-blind law determines the legal status of acts and cases that the pure hermeneutic approach leaves fully or partially undetermined.

something else – and what its legal consequences are. This is a maximally inflexible approach. The upshot of this approach is that the influence of the canon-blind law on the legal outcomes is completely curtailed: factors such as the desire for legal continuity or the need to accommodate new social conditions make no difference to the decisions.

Another jurist's pure hermeneutic approach might determine the status of some acts but leave some others undetermined. This is a relatively more flexible approach. In this situation, the cases left undecided will be determined by the canon-blind law. The upshot is that some laws are decided by a pure reading of the canon and others by such factors as the legal tradition's decision history or current conditions and values.

Yet another jurist's pure hermeneutic approach might be so loose as to be incapable of determining the status of any act. It does not answer any legal question. Therefore, it can accommodate any conceivable legal outcome. It is consistent with murder being permissible and with murder

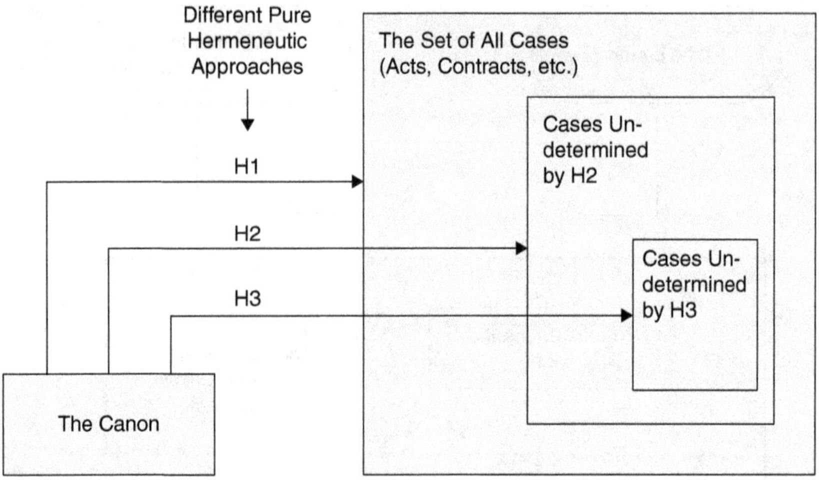

FIGURE 6. Different pure hermeneutic approaches leave the legal status of different numbers of cases undetermined. A maximally flexible approach, such as H1, leaves all cases undetermined, fixing none. Approaches H2 and H3 are progressively less flexible, leaving progressively smaller sets of cases undetermined. A maximally *in*flexible approach (not shown) leaves no case undetermined. Acts left undetermined by the pure hermeneutic approach are fixed by canon-blind law.

being forbidden. This is a maximally flexible approach. The upshot is that the law would be determined completely by the canon-blind law. It would be canon-blind law that would settle the status of murder.

The concept can be illustrated with a simple example. Suppose the canon consists entirely of ten sentences of the form "You shall *X*," where *X* refers to an action. Consider two pure hermeneutic approaches, H_1 and H_2. H_1 states that a You-shall-*X* clause makes *X* obligatory, while H_2 says that *X* could be obligatory, neutral, or forbidden. Clearly H_1 settles the legal status of the ten acts. It is thus maximally inflexible. On the other hand, H_2 does not determine anything, leaving it to canon-blind law to settle the outcomes. It is thus maximally flexible. A pure hermeneutic approach, H_3, that makes all the acts mentioned in the canon permissible is maximally inflexible, as is an approach, H_4, that makes every other act obligatory and the rest forbidden. A pure approach, H_5, that leaves the status of the first five acts indeterminate while making the rest permissible lies somewhere in the middle of the two extremes of maximal flexibility and inflexibility.

It must be clear by now that hermeneutic flexibility comes in degrees, ranging over a gamut, depending on how many cases are left indeterminate, as illustrated in Figure 6. Moreover, the degree of hermeneutic inflexibility is related inversely to the influence of canon-blind law. One may think of these two factors as being on a seesaw: they move in opposite directions, and the peak of one corresponds to the bottom of the other. In sum, one may speak of a hermeneutic-methodological approach as being characterized by a parameter called the *influence of canon-blind law*. The value of this parameter is completely determined by the degree of hermeneutic flexibility and vice-versa.

The pure hermeneutic approach may additionally be characterized by a parameter called the *degree of bias for the apparent meaning of the canon*. It distinguishes a jurist who places a premium on the apparent meaning of the text from one who sets little store by it. Five clarifications are needed: first, to be sure, in many cases there will be no such thing as the "apparent meaning" of the canon, but in some cases there will be – a trivial example being that the Qur'ān apparently does not forbid prayer and does not make adultery or theft obligatory. Second, the apparent meaning of the canon, when it does exist, is generally a probable indication of original intent, not a certain one. Third and related, not following the apparent meaning of the canon does not signify disrespect for the texts or insincerity in exegesis, since many a jurist has internalized the fact that the legal outcome is often different from what one might suspect from an unsophisticated first glance at the binding texts. Fourth, bias for the apparent meaning of the canon can reduce the hermeneutic flexibility of the pure hermeneutic approach. Fifth, in the classical legal terminology, "apparent meaning" (*ẓāhir*) is used in reference to an isolated expression with the understanding that it can be set aside once other statements in the canon have been examined; however, I tend to use the term in reference to all the relevant statements considered together. This concludes, for now, the discussion of the hermeneutic-methodological approach and the canon.

So far, among the influences on the legal outcome, the effect of the canon and its interpretation have been isolated from the canon-blind law. But the canon-blind law is not monolithic, and it may be further analyzed. As shown in Figure 7, the canon-blind law is shaped by two major types of forces that may be separated: the influence of the legal precedents in the form of legal inertia and all other factors.

The prevalence of legal continuity and inertia means that normally the canon-blind law is the same as the received law. Any factor that may overcome legal inertia and upset this normal state of affairs and make the canon-blind law deviate from the received law is subsumed under

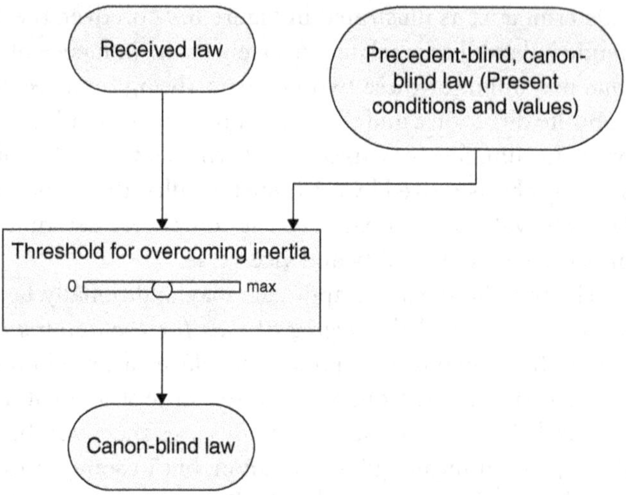

FIGURE 7. The factors shaping canon-blind law.

the heading *precedent-blind, canon-blind law*. More precisely, I define this term, counterfactually, as the legal position that a jurist would have advocated if he/she did not know the decision history *and* the canon. Equivalently, it is what the canon-blind law would be if the jurist did not know the decision history. Thus, the extent to which the canon-blind law differs from the precedent-blind, canon-blind law is a measure of the influence of received law: if canon-blind law is always the same as received law, then legal inertia is absolute, and present conditions, such as new social circumstances and current values, make no difference to the law. On the other hand, if the legal heritage and decision history is trumped by such current realities, then canon-blind law will be the same as precedent-blind, canon-blind law.

It is now possible to summarize, synthesize, and augment the key points by means of Figure 8, which puts the different pieces of the model together. In this schema, the law, or more precisely what a jurist decides the law ought to be, is the output. It is the outcome of the interaction between the canon-blind law and the canon as mediated by the jurist's hermeneutic-methodological approach. The schema, it should be stressed, portrays an individual's mind – the factors in the individual's mind that affect his or her decision. It does not model occurrences outside his or her mind. For example, the canon may have helped shape the decision history of the legal tradition; but this will not be reflected in the diagram since it

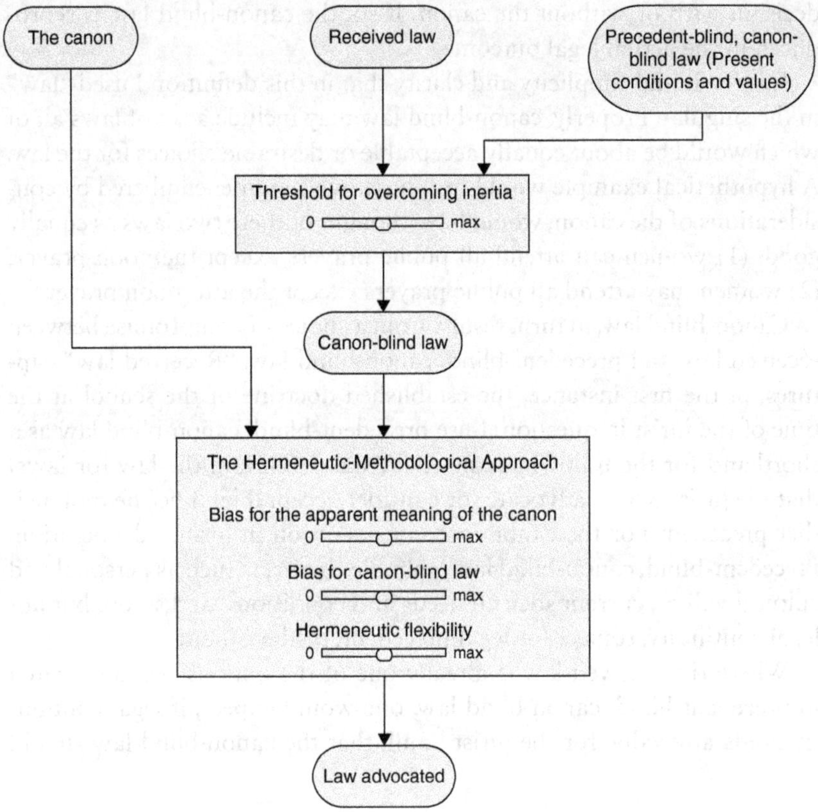

FIGURE 8. A general model of a jurist's decision making.

characterizes not the decision making of the jurist who is being modeled, but that of previous jurists.

I use canon-blind law as no less and no more than a shorthand for the following counterfactual definition: the law that the jurist would advocate if he/she did not take the canon into consideration in his/her deliberation. It is the outcome that would be arrived at without awareness of the canon – the decision that the jurist would reach if the memory of the canon were erased from his/her mind, by surgery as it were. Because jurists generally know the canon, canon-blind law is by definition a counterfactual concept. Nevertheless, often it can be inferred by studying the actual legal decision or the social context. For example, if the jurist's decision goes against the apparent meaning of the canon, in some circumstances that could be a sign that he/she would have reached the same decision with or without the canon. If so, the canon-blind law is reproduced in the actual legal outcome.

It is for initial simplicity and clarity that in this definition I used "law" in the singular. Properly, canon-blind law may include a set of laws all of which would be about equally acceptable or desirable choices for the law. A hypothetical example would be a jurist who, if unencumbered by considerations of the canon, would have thought of these two laws as equally good: (1) women can attend all public prayers except the noon prayer; (2) women may attend all public prayers except the afternoon prayer.[17]

Canon-blind law, in turn, results from a choice or compromise between received law and precedent-blind, canon-blind law. "Received law" captures, in the first instance, the established doctrine of the school at the time of the jurist in question. I use precedent-blind, canon-blind law as a shorthand for the following counterfactual definition: the law (or laws) that the jurist would advocate (or consider acceptable) if he/she took neither precedent nor the canon into consideration in his/her deliberation. Precedent-blind, canon-blind law embodies interests such as personal and cultural values, current societal needs and conditions, and so on, but *not* legal continuity, respect for legal precedent, or the canon.

Where the received law is already one of the options accommodated in precedent-blind, canon-blind law, one would expect, if legal continuity holds any value for the jurist at all, that the canon-blind law should

[17] This formulation, too, is chosen for its simplicity, but a finer model is possible. In particular, it makes much more sense to think of canon-blind law as consisting of a range of candidates with different degrees of desirability, where "desirability" refers to the counterfactual canon-blind state in which the jurist does not know the canon. As a hypothetical example that is inspired by a real case study, suppose the issue is whether women can go out to the mosque to pray; the most desired solution (prior to the consideration of the canon) is that they cannot do so at all (desirability = 10 out of 10), and the least desired one is that they can do so without restriction (0 out of 10). In between the two, there are numerous other possibilities with different degrees of desirability. For example, the solution that only elderly females can go out and only for the daytime prayers may not be ideal, but it is close enough to it (let us say, 9 out of 10) to be perfectly acceptable. Suppose the hermeneutic-methodological approach has a bias for canon-blind law. Suppose, also, that while the system is flexible enough to accommodate the ideal canon-blind law, it can accommodate the nine-out-of-ten solution with much greater ease and logical facility, in the sense that legal reasons can be produced for it in a more straightforward and natural manner. Then, depending on the strength of the bias for the ideal canon-blind law, one may opt for the less than ideal, yet acceptable solution. In other words, one of the parameters of the methodological approach is how the trade-off between justificatory simplicity and the bias for the canon-blind law is decided and how much compromise is deemed acceptable. Moreover, for the sake of simplicity, I have ignored various feedback loops that in reality connect various components of the model.

be the same as the received law. Where there is no relevant received law, as when a completely new situation arises, canon-blind law will be trivially precedent-blind (i.e., it will be the same as precedent-blind, canon-blind law). More interesting is the case of conflict, that is, where received law clashes with precedent-blind, canon-blind law. This can happen, for example, when an old, established law does not match present values or circumstances. In such a case, the interest of continuity would weigh in favor of the received law, while interests other than continuity (i.e., those embodied in precedent-blind, canon-blind law) would weigh against it. How this tension is resolved is an important characteristic of a jurist's decision making. Recognizing the value of continuity for legal traditions, one may think of received law as the default value of canon-blind law.[18] The question is how pressing the other interests (embodied in precedent-blind, canon-blind law) must become before they override the received law. The level of that threshold is an index of a jurist's legal conservatism.

The component labeled "the hermeneutic-methodological approach" concerns the methodology of interpreting the canon. It is governed by many parameters that determine what the jurist finally makes of the canon and the canon-blind law. Among them, three are shown in the figure as sliding scales: the degree of bias for canon-blind law, the degree of bias for the manifest meaning of the canon, and the level of hermeneutic flexibility. Hermeneutic flexibility indicates the degree to which the jurist's hermeneutic method is capable of reconciling an arbitrary candidate for the law with the canon. Thus, a maximally flexible methodology is one that can harmonize the canon with any conceivable candidate for the law, thereby allowing canon-blind law to determine the law. A minimally flexible methodology, on the other hand, always assigns just one legal outcome to the evidence of the canon. A bias toward canon-blind law can be accommodated only if there is enough hermeneutic flexibility.

The degree of bias for the apparent meaning of the canon is not equivalent to the level of hermeneutic inflexibility as it might at first sight appear. This is clear from the definitions given for the two. For example, take a pure hermeneutic approach that makes every conceivable act lawful. Such a methodology is maximally hermeneutically *in*flexible, yet it clashes sharply with the apparent purport of the canon, which apparently

[18] On legal inertia, see Alan Watson, *Society and Legal Change*, 2nd ed. (Philadelphia: Temple University Press, 2001); Alan Watson, *The Evolution of Law* (Baltimore: John Hopkins University Press, 1985).

does declare some deeds unlawful. However, while hermeneutic inflexibility does not entail a bias for the apparent meaning of the canon, the reverse does hold: a bias for the apparent meaning of the canon does tend to increase hermeneutic inflexibility.

As a crude model, the schematization leaves out various factors and relationships. One of the factors, which may be called the "legal-methodological language," subsumes a variety of formal tendencies and constraints with limited bearing on what exactly the law should be in any given case. It can be understood by means of the metaphor of natural language, which offers a range of linguistically valid sentences without pinning down exactly which one we actually say in a given situation. As a concrete example, the legal-methodological language may include a jurist's tendency to eschew subjective, fuzzy criteria in favor of objective, cut-and-dry ones. Another example is the requirement that a Muslim jurist categorize acts as forbidden, undesirable, neutral, desirable, or obligatory. The legal-methodological language constrains the jurist to apply to the act of murder one of these labels, but it does not determine which. This legal-methodological language, if it were shown in the diagram, would be operative at every tier (precedent-blind, canon-blind law; canon-blind law; and advocated law).

How is the model to be used? As it stands, with the various parameters and settings left undecided, the model has limited explanatory power, since most conceivable states of affairs, including contrary ones, can be made to fit into it. For example, in order to obtain the situation described by Schacht that is represented in Figure 2, in which the law simply equals received law, it suffices to consider the threshold for overriding received law as impossibly high, the bias for canon-blind law at the maximum, the bias for the apparent meaning of the canon at the minimum, and hermeneutic flexibility at the maximum. If one disagrees with the Schachtian model, however, one can set the parameters in a different way. For example, for a postformative jurist whose reading of the canon made a difference to his ruling, hermeneutic flexibility will not be at the maximum. Other states of affairs can be accommodated, too, as long as one is able to vary the parameters at will. It is in fixing the settings of these parameters that the historian limits the states of affairs that are consistent with the model, creating a testable theory endowed with explanatory power. The model thus does not predispose the investigator to arrive at a particular characterization. Two historians may use this model to arrive at opposite and incompatible results, or one may use it to describe two different legal traditions with different dynamics. This makes it a suitable framework for inquiry and a useful tool for comparative legal studies.

1.2.3. *From an Individual to a Community*

The model was given for an individual jurist, but a modified version of it can be used to characterize a legal tradition at a point in time. To that end, several of its components would need reformulation. A key modification involves the output, which must be changed from the law advocated by an individual jurist to simply "the law" – that is, the laws espoused by the legal tradition as a whole at a specific moment in time. In the case of a premodern legal school, this would be the legal position of the majority of the jurists in the *madhhab*. In American Constitutional law, it would be the official position of the Supreme Court. The key point is that an individual's decision may or may not represent the legal community, as it may be peculiar, whereas "the law" usually does represent the majority of a law-making class and is consequently potentially less sensitive to the idiosyncrasies of individuals and, in some circumstances, more amenable to prediction and explanation.

The methodological characteristics that the model seeks to describe by parameters such as the level of bias for the apparent meaning of the canon, the degree of bias for canon-blind law, and the degree of hermeneutic flexibility are readily extended to the communal case, but now they represent attributes of the majority of jurists whose decisions count. If there is a typical way in which jurists operate in a given legal tradition, then the model of a typical jurist also characterizes the mainstream of the tradition. The concept of canon-blind law for the community now refers to the law that the law-making class would affirm if its members did not know the canon. Precedent-blind, canon-blind law would be understood along similar lines. The idiosyncrasies of individual jurists would no longer be a factor feeding into precedent-blind, canon-blind law unless the law-making class were an individual – that is, a dictator – in which case there is no need for a communal model to begin with, since the original model of an individual decision maker will suffice. As for the canon, the fact that different jurists may draw its boundaries differently does not necessarily make the concept meaningless for a class of jurists, since they may hold the bulk of the canon in common.

In the case of an individual jurist, one of the parameters is a threshold signifying how easily precedent is overridden by precedent-blind, canon-blind law, for example, by new social circumstances. For a community, this index signifies the inertia of the established laws. It is for the historian to determine how high or low the threshold is for a particular legal tradition at a given point in time. The level of the threshold depends strongly on the institutional specifics of the law-making process and its social context. For example, all other factors being equal, if legal change required the consensus of a group of people rather than a simple majority, that would raise the threshold, making it more difficult for new needs and circumstances to effect legal change. Moreover, a larger law-making class could mean a higher threshold for legal change, since in a larger community more time may be needed for a new opinion to become the majority opinion. In addition, all other things being equal, small law-making and interpretive communities are more sensitive to the idiosyncrasies of individuals and the accidents that brought them to power. Needless to say, all other things are not equal, and the factors affecting the ideological makeup of the law-making class and the degree to which its members are accountable to a social base usually are more decisive than the size of the class.

In summary, the following parameters may characterize an individual jurist:

- The degree of hermeneutic flexibility
- The degree of bias for canon-blind law
- The degree of bias for the apparent meaning of the canon
- The degree of legal inertia

If these parameters have typical values for jurists in a particular legal tradition, then the typical values can be said to represent the mainstream of the tradition rather than just an individual jurist. This book uses case studies to determine these parameters for jurists in the mainstream of the Ḥanafī legal tradition and it also identifies specific jurists who deviate from the mainstream. The Ḥanafī-specific model appears in Section 1.4.1 and includes the Ḥanafī-specific version of the general schema introduced in Figure 8.

1.3. Exegetic Rationales and Degrees of Hermeneutic Flexibility

Theories about the causal relationship between laws and legal reasons – the reasons given for the laws – are closely linked with how textual interpretation is conceptualized. A key factor is the degree of hermeneutic flexibility in the interpretation of the canon. One can assess hermeneutic flexibility by studying the manner in which exegetic rationales are used.

An exegetic rationale refers to a statement of the sort "this verse was abrogated by that verse," "this statement qualifies that one," or "this act is forbidden in analogy to the prohibition in that verse." An exegetic rationale operates on the canon and, when combined with other exegetic rationales and legal principles, entails certain legal effects, such as, for example, the decision that "drinking wine is forbidden." Therefore, exegetic rationales serve as a bridge between the canon and the law advocated. The degree of hermeneutic flexibility reveals in which direction a jurist crosses the bridge, from the canon to the law or the other way, and whether the function of legal reasons is to generate or justify the laws.

Exegetic rationales cannot be deployed in an arbitrary manner. There are certain rules that govern the manner in which they can be used. For example, one may have the rule "Prophetic statement x can be said to abrogate Prophetic statement y only if there is proof that the Prophet said x after y." This rule governs the way in which a particular type of exegetic rationale, namely abrogation, can be used. The collection of all such rules that are applied by a jurist I call his or her *hermeneutic principles*. Hermeneutic principles, in other words, constrain and discipline the use of exegetic rationales. The degree of hermeneutic flexibility is a function of the hermeneutic principles.

Hermeneutic principles may be explicit or implicit. In the genre of classical Muslim legal theory (*uṣūl al-fiqh*), many hermeneutic principles are made explicit. On the other hand, in the genre of positive law (*furūʿ al-fiqh*) many such rules are implicit – one can infer them empirically by the manner in which jurists use exegetic rationales. (For this reason, one might prefer to refer to them as hermeneutic "patterns" rather than "principles.") As could be expected, the hermeneutic principles in the two genres are not always identical. The hermeneutic principles in positive law tend to be laxer than those in the genre of legal theory. In other words, legal interpretation in actuality is more hermeneutically flexible than one might come to expect from the discipline of legal theory.

The key issue here is that the same type of exegetic rationale, such as abrogation or qualification, could be employed, depending on one's hermeneutic principles, in ways leading to varying degrees of hermeneutic flexibility. This section discusses some of the ways in which different hermeneutic principles – that is, different standards for how exegetic rationales may be used – can affect flexibility. I consider, briefly, various possible standards for the use of abrogation, qualification, and analogy.

(1) Abrogation. Classical Islamic jurisprudence held that during the Prophet's lifetime one injunction may have abrogated an earlier one. But unlike modern cases of constitutional amendments, it was not always certain which of two contrary texts abrogated which or in fact whether abrogation was the proper way to explain a discrepancy. If one's methodology puts no limits on the way abrogation can be used, then almost any statement from the Qur'ān or *ḥadīth* conflicting with the canon-blind law can be assumed abrogated. That would make for high hermeneutic flexibility, helping maintain canon-blind law against contrary scriptural texts or reports. On the other hand, other methodologies may require that there be evidence in support of abrogation. Such methodologies will vary in flexibility depending on what standards of evidence they demand. If what is required to claim that a law is abrogated is that there be some *ḥadīth* against it, then hermeneutic flexibility is lessened since if one wants to save a law, before one can dismiss the *ḥadīth* against it as abrogated, one has to find a *ḥadīth* in support of it. There will be some conceivable laws that will not be justifiable in this way, which means that now there is less latitude than in the previous case. But there is nevertheless quite a bit of latitude left, since whenever there are contradictory *ḥadīth*s, one has the discretion to decide which represents the binding law and which the abrogated one. The latitude may be further reduced by removing that discretion; for example, by demanding that a *ḥadīth* that is claimed to be abrogated be proven to refer to a time before that of the *ḥadīth* against it. Another potential source of latitude is in the standards for determining what level of contradiction is needed before one may claim abrogation. If a direct contradiction is required to claim abrogation, that leaves less latitude than if all that is required is that two texts appear contrary in spirit. Even less latitude is left if one demands that there be an early report that explicitly characterizes the rule as abrogated.

(2) Analogy. Inherent to analogical reasoning is a certain amount of hermeneutic flexibility depending on the stringency of the constraints on its use. For example, the absence of an exact rule as to when one has to use analogy, as opposed to when one merely may use it, allows for greater flexibility. Other contributors to flexibility could include the absence of a precise rule to identify what to analogize to (given the choice of several things sharing a feature with the case at hand) and the absence of a way to determine the unique effective cause after one has determined the basis of the analogy. This last can be illustrated by an example: Suppose jurists wish to analogize on the basis of the Qur'ānic prohibition of wine

to determine what other substances are prohibited. They have to determine the attribute of wine that lies behind its prohibition, the "effective cause" (*ʿilla*). Is it that it is mind-altering? Or does it have to do with the sort of intoxication that makes one prone to rowdiness? Or perhaps the fact that it is an intoxicant made of grapes is the crucial factor? The *a priori* list of possibilities is large, and principles may be applied to exclude potential effective causes. The more effectively the rules governing analogy narrow down the effective cause, the less hermeneutically flexible they are.

(3) Analogy combined with qualification. Some jurists feel free to qualify (*takhṣīṣ/taqyīd*) a general statement or term in the canon on the basis of an analogy. Unless regulated carefully, use of this approach moves a jurist toward the flexible end of the spectrum, since if there is a general statement that runs against a canon-blind law, one may "neutralize" it by qualifying it to the point that little remains of its *prima facie* content. That is so because the flexibility often involved in the formulation of analogies enables the jurist to magnify the effect of qualification by extending the range of a qualifying statement.

(4) Qualification. In the case of two *ḥadīth*s, one saying the Prophet said x and the other saying the Prophet said the opposite of x, jurists often take one *ḥadīth* to embody the general rule and the other to apply only to specific circumstances, thus suspending the general rule in cases where those circumstances exist. Unless a methodology lays out in advance a procedure for going about this, there is a great deal of latitude in the legal outcome depending on which statement one takes as the general rule and just how broadly or narrowly one construes the circumstances to which the other statement applies. The degree to which the treatment of these situations is disciplined affects the degree of flexibility.

(5) One may also consider the question of systematization, by which I mean making different parts of the law look as similar as possible. This can be done, for example, by patterning a problem in the law of marriage or divorce on an aspect of the law of sale. One jurist may ruthlessly apply the consequences one would expect from the law of sale in order to work out all the details of the divorce question at hand. Another jurist may accept the patterning but introduce exceptions to it on various grounds, for example, on grounds of what is more convenient or more just. Yet a third jurist may reject the patterning altogether. The first approach leaves relatively little latitude, while the latter two suggest greater flexibility. Although not treated in this book, systematization merits research.

1.4. A Characterization of the Ḥanafīs

1.4.1. *Results*

Despite clear and important variations among Ḥanafī jurists, they operated in a typical way. So, the general model of an individual jurist's decision making from Section 1.2.2 can be used to speak about a typical jurist. That makes it possible to characterize the mainstream of the legal tradition. Obtaining such a characterization requires conducting case studies on points of positive law in order to determine the parameters of the general model (namely the degree of hermeneutic flexibility, the degree of bias for canon-blind law, the degree of bias for the apparent meaning of the canon, and the degree of legal inertia). Based on the case studies in this book, in Chapters 3, 4, and 5, certain conclusions can be supported.

Mainstream Ḥanafī jurisprudence was nearly maximally hermeneutically flexible. It was nearly maximally biased for canon-blind law, and thus the decisions on points of positive law were little affected by the interpretation of the canon. The law advocated was the same as the canon-blind law. Near maximal hermeneutic flexibility made it possible to accommodate canon-blind law even where it clashed with the apparent import of the canon. With the impact of the canon out of the picture, the general model for the Ḥanafī mainstream simplifies to the model shown in Figure 9.

Hermeneutic flexibility refers to the reading of texts, underscoring the wide range of interpretative options afforded by the hermeneutic methods. It does not imply the flexibility of laws. In fact, there were severe constraints on law. The point is that these constraints did not derive from the canon or from hermeneutic techniques. Legal continuity exerted the principal constraining influence; so, canon-blind law (and hence the law) usually consisted of received law. To be sure, legal change occurred: there were deviations from the received law. However, such divergences were not brought about by the reading of the canon. Rather, their causes should be located in pressing changes in the circumstances or values of the community of jurists. That is, the canon-blind law sometimes differed from the received law in favor of the precedent-blind, canon-blind law.

The more usual understanding of the role of the hermeneutic principles as tools for deriving the laws from the canon must thus be abandoned. Hermeneutic principles, as applied in practice, were so flexible as to be inherently incapable of generating the laws. Rather, the canon-blind law formed the real starting point in the process of reasoning. The output

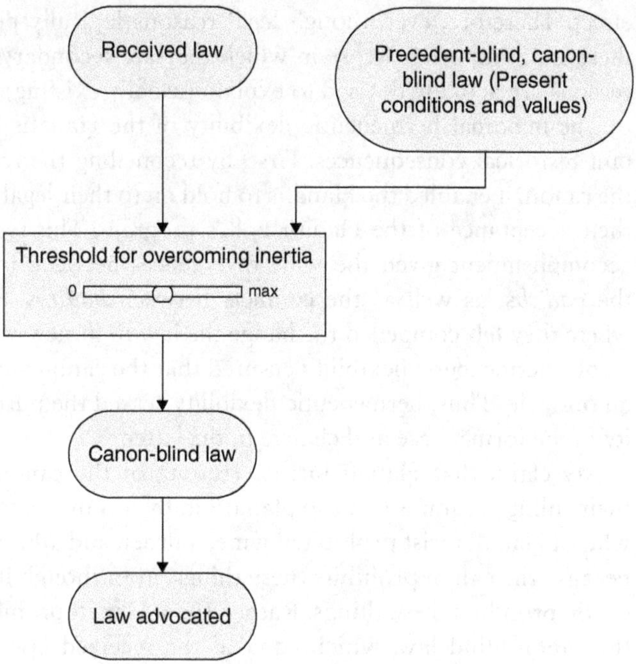

FIGURE 9. Model of a mainstream Ḥanafī jurist's decision making. Due to maximal hermeneutic flexibility, the jurist's reading of the canon plays no causative role in the decision. With the elements related to textual hermeneutics thus eliminated, the general model reduces to this simplified scheme.

of the process in fact consisted of legal reasons, including exegetic rationales, that justified the canon-blind law.

The priority of laws over legal reasons is confirmed by logical analysis showing that juristic arguments leave the laws indeterminate and by the observation of the extensive role of ad hoc justifications. It is also shown by the historical pattern of the relative stability of laws compared to legal reasons: Laws often temporally preceded the reasons cited for them. Different jurists often cited different reasons (and different exegetic rationales) for the same law. Sometimes a jurist was sure of a law but not sure of its underlying reason. Even more striking is what happened when something went wrong with a legal reason, for example, when a statement formerly thought to be an acceptable *ḥadīth* was found to be no such thing or when the reason was found to contradict other legal reasons upheld in the system. When a reason was thus disqualified, the law it supported was not abandoned as one might expect. More typically, jurists would come up with a new and better reason for the same legal effect. Therefore, even though legal reasons logically precede the laws, there is an important sense in which they are secondary to legal effects: reasons are actually devised to explain (usually existing) legal effects.

The maximal hermeneutic flexibility of the Ḥanafīs had two important historical consequences. First, by reconciling the received law with the canon, it enabled the Ḥanafīs to hold on to their legal heritage despite their acceptance of the Ḥadīth Folk's program. This was an important accomplishment given the wide divergences between received law and the *ḥadīth*s, as well as the conflicts between *ḥadīth*s. Second, in cases where they felt compelled to change the law to fit new values or requirements, hermeneutic flexibility ensured that the canon would not become an obstacle. Thus, hermeneutic flexibility served the purpose of continuity in the former case and change in the latter.

My claim that Ḥanafī jurists' reading of the canon did not affect their rulings requires some explanation. By it, I mean, for example, that when a Ḥanafī jurist prohibited wine, murder, and adultery, this was not because the canon prohibits these things, even though it is true that the canon prohibits these things. Rather, these Ḥanafī prohibitions reflected the canon-blind law, which equaled the received law thanks to legal inertia. Jurists upheld the prohibitions not because they were in the canon but because they were the received law and were not overruled by new social concerns (i.e., by precedent-blind, canon-blind law). In other words, the Ḥanafī jurists' prohibitions had two causes: (1) these prohibitions were part of the Ḥanafī heritage, representing the established precedent of the school, and (2) there were no pressing social circumstances or changes of values of such intensity as to outweigh the desire for continuity. Nothing motivated Ḥanafīs to seriously rethink the prohibition of wine, murder, or adultery, as they still found these prohibitions tolerable.

Furthermore, this is not a claim for the irrelevance of the canon to Ḥanafī law. It is abundantly clear, for example, that the fact that the Qur'ān and the Prophet banned wine is the cause for the Ḥanafī prohibition of wine. My claim concerns only the path of causation. This path did not include the postformative Ḥanafī jurists' reading of the canon. Rather, the ban became a legal precedent during the formative period (specifically during the Prophet's lifetime). This precedent endured for over a century and was incorporated into early Ḥanafī law (not every Prophetic precedent was). From this point on, it would endure due to the inertia of the laws of the school and the lack of countervailing changes of values, needs, or circumstances.

These conclusions describe the Ḥanafī mainstream. But there were occasional rebels within the school as well, such as Badr al-Dīn al-ʿAynī and Ibn al-Humām. They appear to have taken a somewhat less flexible approach than the mainstream, giving greater weight to the apparent meaning of the canon.

While this book does not consider the other schools, I offer the conjecture that they were nearly maximally flexible like the Ḥanafīs. Note that this hypothesis does not rule out the possibility that, say, al-Shāfiʿī adopted less flexible methods and conformed more closely to the apparent meaning of the canon. Assuming he did so, that says nothing about the way in which Shāfiʿī jurists in the postformative era operated. The question remains: did members of the Shāfiʿī school adopt al-Shāfiʿī's position on a given question because of their reading of the Qur'ān and *ḥadīth*s, or did they do so because of legal inertia?

The specific legal questions examined include a number of points bearing on women's participation in group prayers: the status of women-only group prayers led by a woman, women's prayer with men, women leading men, whose (if anyone's) prayer is nullified when a woman prays next to or in front of men, and distinctions that depend on the type of prayer, the time of day, the age of the woman, and so on. On some of these points, the apparent meaning of the canon was at variance with the received law, hence with the canon-blind law. Yet jurists successfully maintained the canon-blind law. In cases where they did change the law, it was not the apparent meaning of the canon that motivated this. One knows this because the changes moved the laws even further away from the apparent meaning of the canon, generally toward greater restrictions on women. Since the changes were not motivated by the canon, one can conclude that it was generally social circumstances, possibly changing values, that brought about the changes.

Several points may help ward off potential misunderstandings. First, in establishing hermeneutic flexibility, part of my task is to show that a jurist's interpretation is not the only possible one – in other words, that the legal conclusions do not necessarily follow. The point of such an exercise is not that anything is wrong with the jurist's arguments or decisions or that he should not have supported the law that he did. After all, showing that a law does not follow necessarily from the canon and that alternative interpretations are possible is not tantamount to showing that it is a bad law or that it is irreconcilable with the canon.

Second, lack of bias for the apparent meaning of the canon does not mean that the canon was not considered as binding. It also does not mean that jurists disrespected or disregarded the canon. Nor does it mean that the canon was interpreted in an insincere manner. The competence and sincerity of jurists is not in doubt. The importance of the canon in the act of interpretation is self-evident, and its role in the establishment of public reason is fundamental (Chapter 7).

Third, I am not interested in laying down any prescription about what degree of hermeneutic flexibility is appropriate in jurisprudence. The present work is about the historical reality rather than an imaginary normative utopia. A reader who dislikes hermeneutic flexibility might dismiss Islamic legal practice. Unlike such a critic, I have no firm opinion on the need for hermeneutic inflexibility, and therefore no value judgment is implicit in my work. Moreover, a secular critic who thinks that hermeneutic flexibility delegitimizes Sunnī jurisprudence should consider that it may characterize secular legal traditions as well.

More generally, normative ethics falls outside the scope of this study. This book does not make any argument within law; that is, it does not say that any law is good or bad. It also disregards public policy, theology, and metaphysics; it is concerned solely with legal history, historical interpretation, descriptive ethics, and descriptive (as opposed to normative) philosophy of law.

1.4.2. *Previous Work in the Field*

Studies of postformative legal hermeneutics have almost always been based on Islamic works of legal theory and philosophy, *uṣūl al-fiqh*. In these works, Muslim scholars prescribed rules of interpretation and addressed fundamental questions of epistemology and hermeneutics with great elegance and acumen. On these matters, their thinking is well worth study in itself.[19] However, one cannot assume that these normative and philosophical discussions describe the historical reality of how the

[19] For sources in the English language on the classical Muslim genre of legal theory and philosophy (*uṣūl al-fiqh*), see the following: Bernard Weiss, *The Search for God's Law* (Salt Lake City: University of Utah Press, 1992), which is a highly detailed and clear paraphrase of a classical source; Bernard Weiss, *The Spirit of Islamic Law* (Athens: University of Georgia Press, 2006), which is a good overview of Islamic legal theory in English; Mohammad Hashim Kamali, *The Principles of Islamic Jurisprudence*, rev. ed. (Cambridge: Islamic Texts Society, 1991), which is a survey of theories and positions in the *uṣūl al-fiqh*; Aron Zysow, "The Economy of Certainty: An Introduction to the Typology of Islamic Legal Theory" (PhD diss., Harvard University, 1984); Robert Gleave, *Inevitable Doubt: Two Theories of Shīʿī Jurisprudence* (Leiden: Brill, 2000); and Wael Hallaq, *A History of Islamic Legal Theory* (Cambridge: Cambridge University Press, 1997).

law developed in practice. Aron Zysow has described the relationship between positive law and *uṣūl al-fiqh* aptly:

> This relationship can be fruitfully compared to the relationship between science and philosophy of science ... If you study philosophy, you'll learn that it's a real question: what is the function of philosophy of science? It's clearly not to direct science in most cases. Most scientists aren't studying philosophy of science. In fact, there is a debate whether they would profit from studying it, and the philosophers of science, themselves, are uncertain as to whether it's important for scientists to study it, but they still insist that it's important to get things straight conceptually in philosophy of science.[20]

My subject in this book is not the *uṣūl al-fiqh* genre, but rather actual postformative legal interpretation. As such, I focus on juristic discussions of concrete points of law as found in legal handbooks in the *furūʿ* genre. While there are many studies of concrete points of law, relatively few focus on hermeneutics, and none, to my knowledge, investigate scriptural hermeneutics diachronically.

Among the ideas expressed by other scholars, the views of Sherman Jackson in his article on the *uṣūl al-fiqh* have the greatest relevance and affinity to mine. Jackson states that the methods of Islamic legal theory, the *uṣūl al-fiqh*, did not generate or determine Islamic law, but rather served the function of validating laws. I certainly agree that legal theory in the genre of *uṣūl al-fiqh* did not generate postformative, Sunnī law, but this genre is not my topic. Jackson makes his point explicitly with

[20] Quoted in Bernard Weiss, ed. *Studies in Islamic Legal Theory* (Leiden: Brill, 2002), 414. Zysow then mentions major historical changes in Ḥanafī *uṣūl* with potentially far-reaching consequences for *furūʿ* that in fact left the *furūʿ* completely untouched. For more on the relationship between the genres of legal theory (*uṣūl al-fiqh*) and positive law (*furūʿ al-fiqh*), see Mohammed Fadel, "'*Istiḥsān* is Nine-Tenths of the Law': The Puzzling Relationship of *Uṣūl* to *Furūʿ* in the Mālikī *Madhhab*," in *Studies in Islamic Legal Theory*, ed. Bernard Weiss (Leiden: Brill, 2002), 161–76; Sherman Jackson, "Fiction and Formalism: Toward a Functional Analysis of *uṣūl al-fiqh*," in *Studies in Islamic Legal Theory*, ed. Bernard Weiss (Leiden: Brill, 2002), 177–201; Ahmad Atif Ahmad, *Structural Interrelations of Theory and Practice in Islamic Law* (Leiden: Brill, 2006). Unlike Zysow and me, Ahmad assumes that it would reflect negatively on jurists if it were shown that they did not follow the *uṣūl* prescriptions. This is shown by the word "accuse" in the following sentence: "one need not accuse Muslim jurists of ... separation of theory and practice" (Ahmad, *Structural Interrelations*, 175). To follow up on Zysow's analogy to science: this would be like saying, "One need not accuse scientists of ignoring the prescriptions of the philosophers of science." Some scientists would respond to this with the exaggerated saying apocryphally attributed to Richard Feynman: "philosophy of science is as useful to science as ornithology is to birds." In fairness to Ahmad, there is greater overlap between jurists and legal theorists than between scientists and philosophers, and many jurists studied the *uṣūl al-fiqh*. Nonetheless, positive law and legal theory remained distinct disciplines.

regard to the field of *uṣūl al-fiqh*, and the empirical evidence he gives for it pertains, with one exception, specifically to that genre. For example, he notes that the fact that "there appears to exist no exclusively Mālikī or Shāfiʿī *uṣūl*" does not fit the hypothesis that the *uṣūl* (or *uṣūl* differences) generated the differing laws of these two traditions.[21] My claims, by contrast, concern the hermeneutic principles jurists used implicitly or explicitly and consciously or unconsciously in their discussions of positive law, as found in the legal handbooks in which jurists stated their rulings on concrete legal questions – that is, the *furūʿ* genre. I claim that these principles did not generate the laws. Concerned with practice rather than theory, this is a more far-reaching claim than one about the *uṣūl al-fiqh*. It is less surprising to say that the hermeneutic theories of legal theorists in the genre of legal theory did not generate the laws than to say that the hermeneutic practices of jurists in their works on positive law did not generate the laws.

Furthermore, there is some ambiguity about the scope of Jackson's views about the limited generative powers of hermeneutic principles; it is not clear if he would take them as far as I would. He states, "legal theory cannot be *the* causative and *the sole* source of legal doctrine, since legal theory can neither exclude nor take account of the presuppositions that inform legal interpretation."[22] Again, in the conclusion of his essay, he rejects the "traditional accounts of *uṣūl al-fiqh*" that entail the fiction "that legal theory is *the* exclusive and causative source of legal conclusions."[23] Such language does not deny that the rules of interpretation could have shaped the laws to a significant degree; it denies only that they were "the *sole* determinant."[24] My own view is that in mainstream postformative Sunnī legal interpretation the hermeneutic principles played a negligible role in determining the laws.

Parts of Jackson's essay, however, show that he would probably extend the claim of indeterminacy to the principles governing actual legal reasoning. In other words, he would argue that legal interpretation is (in my terminology) hermeneutically flexible. While I agree with such a thesis and strive to establish it in this book for one legal tradition, the Ḥanafīs, I take issue with the way Jackson arrives at that conclusion.

[21] For the evidence, see Jackson, "Fiction and Formalism," 200, lines 10–16. The exception is his discussion of al-Juwaynī's ruling on whether a Christian or Jew could be an executive vizier (196–9).

[22] Jackson, "Fiction and Formalism," 192. Emphasis mine.

[23] Jackson, "Fiction and Formalism," 200. Emphasis mine.

[24] Jackson, "Fiction and Formalism," 200. Emphasis mine.

Jackson's argument for hermeneutic flexibility seems to depend on a philosophical stance. He takes as his starting point a general theory that holds that "meaning is not discovered but rather fashioned or created by the interpreter."[25] For Jackson, this thesis holds in part because meaning depends on presuppositions made by the reader and because the standards of interpretation "can neither exclude nor take account of the presuppositions that inform legal interpretation," which has the consequence that such standards "cannot be the causative and sole source of legal doctrine." One plausible way in which to understand this argument, though he never quite puts it this way, is to take it as the following philosophical thesis: hermeneutic flexibility is an inevitable attribute of all legal traditions on account of the natures of language, meaning, and interpretation, which entail that meaning is not discovered, but created by the interpreter. I will refer to this as the *premise* or *thesis*.

Jackson's conclusions about Islamic law, and mine as well, would certainly follow if this premise were true. In fact, if the philosophical premise were true, the same conclusion would follow about all real and hypothetical legal systems, not just Islamic law, as long as they were formulated in human language. The thesis would also have implications far beyond law, in all human affairs that involve language. Furthermore, if it were true, there would be little need for empirical, historical work in Islamic law *per se* to establish the final conclusion of indeterminacy; work in linguistics and philosophy would suffice to settle the question. While it would take me too far afield to argue against the thesis in detail, a few words might not be inappropriate.

One way to refute the thesis is to provide a counterexample to its consequences. The relevant consequence, for my purposes, is that legal systems will be necessarily hermeneutically flexible, where "necessarily" refers to an inherent necessity imposed by the natures of language and meaning. So, the premise can be refuted by offering a legal system that is not hermeneutically flexible. It turns out to be easy to construct such a system. Consider the following. Suppose the legal system is one in which every act is assigned one of these two predicates: "forbidden" and "permissible," where these two words are construed in their usual senses. Suppose also that there is a canon, a binding text that needs to be interpreted. Now, suppose that the system has hermeneutic principles that ensure that the text is interpreted in such a way that every act is

[25] He writes that this is a basic premise that underlies New Legal Formalism as expounded by Stanley Fish; Jackson, "Fiction and Formalism," 195.

permissible. (Such principles would be easy to formulate. They could operate like Sigmund Freud's hermeneutic principles for dream interpretation: every dream, even a nightmare, is interpreted as wish fulfillment thanks to principles that, for example, give the interpreter the option to take a thing to mean its opposite.) This yields a completely *in*flexible legal system. There is no indeterminacy.

The reader may object that the hypothetical legal system I just described cannot exist in reality: such a system will not meet any society's needs, it will not serve any purpose, and therefore will never come to be. That is undoubtedly true. But note that according to this objection, if the proposed legal system cannot be, that is because of the constraints of social reality, not because of the nature of language. So, the objection does not affect my demonstration that the system can exist within language and be perfectly meaningful. And if language does not preclude such maximal *in*flexibility, then hermeneutic flexibility is not a necessity of language. And if hermeneutic flexibility is not an inherent linguistic necessity, then one cannot know whether interpretation in a particular legal tradition, say in American Constitutional law or in the Ḥanafī school of law, is hermeneutically flexible prior to having studied that legal tradition empirically.

What, then, shall one make of the thesis that "meaning is not discovered but rather fashioned or created by the interpreter"? While there is a sense in which the interpreter fashions or creates meaning, this thesis does not stop at that proposition; it appears to make a stronger claim, namely that the meaning thus fashioned by the interpreter cannot correspond to something objective that lies outside the interpreter; hence the statement that "meaning is not discovered." On this viewpoint, texts and meaning cannot be granted any measure of autonomy and objectivity. This would entail that what the reader reads into a text has nothing to do with the text itself. In addition, because meaning cannot be discovered, finding out the intention of an author or speaker is out of the question.

Yet, the fact that we read meaning into texts is not incompatible with meaning (when conceived, for example, as authorial intent) also having an objective and autonomous existence and being capable of making a difference in human affairs as an independent variable. One can accept that we read meaning into texts, in the sense that we form conjectures about authorial intent, and simultaneously affirm that one can discover intention, in the sense that such a conjecture can be right. While the discovery of intention is an inherently fallible process, the meanings we read into sentences frequently do correspond with the intentions of their sayers. If they did not, social life as we know it would not exist. If intended meaning were not discoverable, ordinary facts of social life would be inconceivable – for example, the fact that when we order food in a restaurant, what is brought to us usually corresponds to what we expect. Indeed, the human language faculty probably would not have evolved if it were not an effective tool for conveying information about the world and communicating a speaker's ideas and intentions.

Jackson's argumentation is more persuasive when he discusses the way the jurist al-Juwaynī uses the Qur'ān and *ḥadīth*s to argue that Christians and Jews cannot be appointed executive viziers. Here, he argues that al-Juwaynī's interpretation of these sources, while plausible, is not the only plausible reading.[26] This is an important point, and one that shows up repeatedly in my own case studies. However, this shows some hermeneutic flexibility, not maximal or nearly maximal flexibility. What if one took a legal topic on which the evidence of the Qur'ān and *ḥadīth*s is less mixed? Would al-Juwaynī still be able to have his way? To test the limits of flexibility, one must choose test cases carefully, examining instances where the apparent purport of the canon clashes with canon-blind law.

Despite the ambiguities in Jackson's formulations and the lack of convincing justification, his article raises important questions and offers thought-provoking answers. Its attitude is close to mine in so far as it questions the usual view of the nature of *furūʿ* laws, which holds them to be derived from the canon using established hermeneutic techniques.[27]

[26] Jackson, "Fiction and Formalism," 196–9. That one jurist on one legal question is a "narrow data base" is acknowledged in Jackson, "Fiction and Formalism," 200. Mention should be made also of the valuable article of Mohammed Fadel on Averroes. He argues that the interpretation of the canon explains very little as far as the laws concerning collaterals are concerned, and he attributes this to "the ambiguity of the reported proof-texts themselves" (Fadel, "Nine-Tenths of the Law," 165, 172).

[27] For the usual view, see the references cited by Jackson, "Fiction and Formalism," 179, footnotes 4–5; Kamali, *Principles of Islamic Jurisprudence*, 1.

2

Preliminaries

2.1. The Ḥanafī School and the Case Studies

Those case studies best bare jurists' methodological commitments in which the texts pull the jurist in one direction and other incentives, such as the drive for legal continuity, in the opposite direction – in other words cases that pit canon-blind law against the apparent meaning of the canon. It is thus fortuitous that of the three case studies in this book, two meet this criterion. In a third, the connection between the canon and the law is tenuous at best. All three concern women in group prayer. A few introductory words on this subject, and on the Ḥanafī tradition broadly, are in order.[1]

The Ḥanafīs today make up the largest extant school of law. The school has its roots in the jurisprudence of Ibrāhīm al-Nakhaʿī (d. 96/713), a first/seventh-century jurist from Kūfa, a city in Iraq. The legal school is named after Abū Ḥanīfa (d. 150/767), who lived in the same city in the next century, and whose views are authoritative within the school. Ḥanafī legal scholarship thus began in Iraq and spread from there to other places. It centered in Transoxania during the fourth/tenth and fifth/eleventh centuries, and then in Syria and especially Egypt in the seventh/thirteenth century. India would later join Egypt as a major center of Ḥanafī legal scholarship.

By studying concrete points of positive law this book probes postformative jurisprudence. The term "postformative" denotes here the

[1] Noteworthy books on the Ḥanafīs include: Aḥmad b. Muḥammad al-Naqīb, *al-Madhhab al-Ḥanafī* (Riyadh: Maktabat al-Rushd, 2001); Brannon Wheeler, *Applying the Canon in Islam* (Albany: State University of New York Press, 1996).

period beginning with the emergence of Ḥanafī law, that is, the tradition of legal scholarship that derived from the work of Abū Ḥanīfa and in which his name carried authority. This is not inherently any better or worse than any other definition for "postformative." It is chosen simply due to its convenience for a study that focuses on a distinct legal tradition in which a previous jurist's words carry authority. By this definition, for the Ḥanafīs the postformative period began sometime around the middle of the second/eighth century, since the Ḥanafī tradition appears to have been in place by then.[2] The period before that, reaching back to the time of the Prophet, is the "formative period." This distinction provides a shorthand for referring to the period in which a group of jurists reasoned by reference to the opinions of Abū Ḥanīfa and/or by reference to other jurists who did the same.

Calling Ḥanafī jurisprudence a "tradition" highlights its evolutionary character. The laws and the reasons jurists gave for the laws were handed down from one generation to the next even as they accumulated, underwent change, and increased in sophistication. Ḥanafī jurists justifying their positions would rely heavily on the work of their predecessors within their own legal school. Similarly, jurists from the three other Sunnī legal traditions – the Mālikī, Shāfiʿī, and Ḥanbalī schools – would cite authorities from their own traditions. Each legal tradition remained largely distinct over time, distinguished not only by social markers, such as patterns of social association of the scholars affiliated with it, and institutions, but also, and more importantly for our purposes, by legal doctrine. Each school took certain positions on some legal matters that were unique to it and many positions that endured over time. In other words, the schools had distinct legal profiles that exhibited a good measure of temporal continuity.

The subject matter of the case studies is women's participation in ritual prayers held in groups. The daily prayers are obligatory for every believer, male or female, free or enslaved. The prayers may be performed individually or collectively. It is generally considered meritorious to perform these prayers collectively. However, the Ḥanafīs, especially the later ones, did not consider group prayers meritorious for women. The Sunnīs agreed that the Friday noon group prayer is obligatory for men, but not for women. Then there are the two *ʿĪd* communal prayers that are each

[2] Wilferd Madelung, *Religious Trends in Early Islamic Iran* (Albany, NY: Persian Heritage Foundation, 1988), 18–9.

held once a year, and again the Ḥanafīs frowned upon most women's attendance.

Group prayer requires a leader, an imām, and at least one other worshipper. At the beginning of the prayer, the worshipper must consciously resolve to "follow" (*iqtidā'*) the leader. This mental act of resolution (*niyya*) binds the worshipper and the leader in a group prayer. (In order to render into English the technical Arabic terms used for this mental act, I will simply place the verbs resolve and follow in quotation marks.) Thereupon, the worshippers mimic the motions of the leader, resulting in a congregation that moves in unison. The validity of the worshipper's prayer will, for the Ḥanafīs, depend on that of the leader, but not so for the Shāfi'īs. That is, if for any reason the leader's prayer is voided, then so is that of any worshipper "following" him.

A number of questions arise: May women lead men in group prayer? If not, may they pray in the front rows or side-by-side with men? If not, then what happens if they do – is anyone's prayer invalidated? And if they may not pray next to or in front of men, may they join men at communal prayers at all, separated with a barrier or in the back rows? What are the distinctions based on the type of communal prayer (Friday, daily, *'Īd*) and the age of the woman (young or old)? If a woman may not lead men in prayer, may she lead women? In other words, may women hold group prayers together without men or should they instead pray individually?[3] The next three chapters trace the treatment of these questions in chronological order within each subtheme. To appreciate the temporal aspect of the development of legal thought, the reader should use the following timeline comprising most of the scholars considered in this book.

Ḥanafī exegetic rationales were based primarily on the Qur'ān and the *sunna*. As for the Qur'ān, its verses were binding, except for those considered to have been abrogated during the Prophet's lifetime. (See Section 1.3 for abrogation.) As for the *sunna*, this term refers to the normative example of the Prophet. It can be studied by means of a number of sources, chief among them the *Ḥadīth*. A *ḥadīth* is an anecdote about the words or deeds of the Prophet, usually related with a chain of transmission called the *isnād*. The *isnād* is the sequence of the names of persons who related the tradition, one person to the next. Not all *ḥadīth*s were

[3] Though some of its conclusions differ from mine, the following essay mentions a portion of the evidence: Christopher Melchert, "Whether to Keep Women out of the Mosque: A Survey of Medieval Islamic Law," in *Authority, Privacy and Public Order in Islam*, ed. Michalak-Pikulska et al. (Leuven: Peeters, 2006), 59–70.

considered reliable. The judgment on the reliability of a *ḥadīth* usually hinged on the quality of its *isnād* and the reliability of the persons named in it, especially those who lived in the first two centuries of Islam. *Ḥadīth* analysis was, and remains, a technical field with its own specialists. Just as a Qur'ānic law could be abrogated during the Prophet's lifetime, so could a Prophetic norm.

2.2. The Scholars

Here is a list of most of the jurists discussed in this book:

Ibrāhīm b. Yazīd b. Qays **al-Nakhaʿī** (d. 96/715)	Kūfa; born 50/670.
Ḥammād b. Abī Sulaymān (d. 120/737)	Kūfa; transmitter of the doctrines and traditions of Ibrāhīm al-Nakhaʿī; teacher of Abū Ḥanīfa.
Abū Ḥanīfa al-Nuʿmān b. Thābit (d. 150/767)	Kūfa.
Zufar b. al-Hudhayl al-ʿAnbarī (d. 158/775)	Kūfa and Baṣra. Born 110/727. Student of Abū Ḥanīfa. He moved to Baṣra, served as judge and died there.
Abū Yūsuf Yaʿqūb b. Ibrāhīm (d. 182/798)	Kūfa. Traveled to Medina and Baṣra. Born 113/730. He moved to Baghdad. Judge. Author of the *Kitāb al-Āthār*.
al-Shaybānī, Muḥammad b. al-Ḥasan (d. 189/805)	Born in Wāsiṭ ca. 132/750. Student of Abū Ḥanīfa and Abū Yūsuf. Grew up in Kūfa; worked there and in Medina, al-Raqqa, and Baghdad, where he taught al-Shāfiʿī; died in Rayy. Judge. Author of the *Kitāb al-Āthār*.
al-Ṭaḥāwī, Aḥmad b. Muḥammad (d. 321/933)	Egypt; head of the Ḥanafīs in Egypt. Studied with his maternal uncle, al-Muzanī (d. 264/878), the student of al-Shāfiʿī, before studying with the Ḥanafīs.
al-Karkhī, ʿUbayd Allāh b. al-Ḥusayn b. Dallāl (d. 340/952)	Born 260/873. Taught in Baghdad. Head of the Ḥanafīs in his time. Author of *Risāla fī al-uṣūl allatī ʿalayhā madār furūʿ al-Ḥanafiyya*.
Abū al-Layth al-Samarqandī, Naṣr b. Muḥammad b. Aḥmad (d. 373/983)	Samarqand, Transoxania. Author of *Fatāwā al-nawāzil* and *ʿUyūn al-masāʾil*.
al-Qudūrī, Aḥmad b. Muḥammad (d. 428/1037)	He was born and died in Baghdad; head of the Ḥanafīs in Iraq. Author of *Mukhtaṣar*.

(*continued*)

al-Sarakhsī, Muḥammad b. Aḥmad (d. 483/1090–490/1097–500/1106)	From Farghāna, Transoxania, where he lived and worked. Author of *Kitāb al-Mabsūṭ*, a commentary on the *Mukhtaṣar* of Muḥammad b. Muḥammad al-Marwazī (d. 334/945).
al-Samarqandī, 'Alā' al-Dīn Muḥammad b. Aḥmad (d. 552/1157)	Born 488/1095. From Samarqand, Transoxania. Author of *Tuḥfat al-fuqahā'*.
al-Kāsānī, Abū Bakr b. Mas'ūd (d. 587/1189)	From Kāsān, Farghāna, Transoxania. He went to Aleppo in 543/1148, where he taught until his death 44 years later. Student and son-in-law of 'Alā' al-Dīn al-Samarqandī. Author of *Badā'i' al-ṣanā'i'*.
Qāḍī Khān, al-Ḥasan b. Manṣūr al-Farghānī (d. 592/1196)	Transoxania. Author of *Fatāwā Qāḍīkhān.*
al-Marghīnānī, 'Alī b. Abī Bakr (d. 593/1197)	From Marghīnān, in Farghāna, Transoxania, where he lived and died. Traveled for his studies. Author of *al-Hidāya*.
Maḥmūd b. Aḥmad **al-Maḥbūbī** (d. 673/1274)	Known as *al-Ṣadr al-Sharī'a al-Akbar/al-Awwal.* Author of *Wiqāyat al-riwāya*, a summary of *al-Hidāya* to be memorized by grandson, 'Ubayd Allāh b. Mas'ūd al-Maḥbūbī. This book is the object of the commentary of 'Ubayd Allāh b. Mas'ūd al-Maḥbūbī (*Sharḥ al-Wiqāya*) and is quoted in it.
al-Mawṣilī, 'Abd Allāh b. Maḥmūd b. Mawdūd (d. 683/1284)	Born 599/1203 in al-Mawṣil; moved to Damascus; judge in Kūfa; settled in Baghdad, taught and died there. Author of *al-Ikhtiyār li-ta'līl al-Mukhtār*, a commentary on his own *al-Mukhtār li-al-fatwā.*
al-Manbijī, 'Alī b. Zakarīyā b. Mas'ūd (d. 686/1287)	Born in Manbij, Syria; studied there and then moved to Jerusalem. Author of *al-Lubāb fī al-jam' bayna al-sunna wa-al-kitāb*.
al-Nasafī, 'Abd Allāh b. Aḥmad (d. 710/1310)	Born in Sogdiana (Ṣughd), Transoxania. Taught in Kirmān. Author of *Kitāb al-Wāfī*, a commentary on it entitled *Kitāb al-Kāfī*, and a synopsis of the latter entitled *Kanz al-daqā'iq*.
al-Sarūjī, Aḥmad b. Ibrāhīm (d. 710/1310)	Egypt. Syria. Author of *al-Ghāya*, a commentary on *al-Hidāya*.
al-Zayla'ī, Fakhr al-Dīn 'Uthmān b. 'Alī b. Miḥjan (d. 743/1342)	Came to Cairo in 705/1305, where he taught and died. Author of *Tabyīn al-ḥaqā'iq*, a commentary on al-Nasafī's *Kanz al-daqā'iq*.
'Ubayd Allāh b. Mas'ūd al-Maḥbūbī (d. 747/1346)	Died in Bukhārā. Known as *al-Ṣadr al-Sharī'a al-Aṣghar/al-Thānī*. Wrote *Sharḥ al-Wiqāya*, a commentary on *Wiqāyat al-riwāya* of his grandfather, Maḥmūd b. Aḥmad al-Maḥbūbī (d. 673/1274).

al-Kākī, Muḥammad b. Muḥammad (d. 749/1348)	Cairo. Author of *Mi'rāj al-dirāya fī sharḥ al-Hidāya.*
al-Atrāzī, Qiwām al-Dīn Amīr Kātib b. Amīr 'Umar al-Itqānī (d. 758/1357)	Born in Fārāb, taught in Baghdad and Damascus (beginning 747/1346), then went to Cairo and died there.
Jamāl al-Dīn al-Zayla'ī, 'Abd Allāh b. Yūsuf (d. 762/1361)	Lived in Egypt; died in Cairo. Traditionist; namesake and student of al-Zayla'ī, the jurist. Author of *Naṣb al-rāya: Takhrīj aḥādīth al-Hidāya.*
al-Bābirtī, Akmal al-Dīn Muḥammad b. Maḥmūd (d. 786/1384)	Born 710/1310, his *nisba* refers to Bābirt (Abīward) in Bilād al-Rūm; active in Syria and Cairo. Author of *al-'Ināya.*
Abū Bakr b. 'Alī **al-Ḥaddād** [al-Zabīdī] (d. 800/1397)	From Yemen. Author of *al-Sirāj al-wahhāj.*
al-'Aynī, Badr al-Dīn Maḥmūd b. Aḥmad (d. 855/1451)	Born 762/1361 in 'Ayntab (Gaziantep), between Aleppo and Antioch. Studied and lived there and in various places in Syria and then settled down in Cairo; appointed chief judge of the Ḥanafīs in 829/1425. Spoke Turkish. Author of *al-Bināya sharḥ al-Hidāya.*
Ibn al-Humām, Muḥammad b. 'Abd al-Wāḥid(d. 861/1457)	Born 788/1386 in Alexandria. Lived, worked, and died in Cairo. Author of *Fatḥ al-qadīr.*
Mullā Khusraw, Muḥammad b. Farāmurz (or Farāmūz) (d. 885/1480)	Also called Mawlā or Minlā. Ottoman jurist, appointed judge of Istanbul after its conquest. Author of *Ghurar al-aḥkām*, and a commentary on it titled *Durar al-ḥukkām.*
al-Ḥalabī, Ibrāhīm b. Muḥammad (d. 956/1549)	Born in Aleppo, he studied there and in Cairo before moving to Istanbul, where he lived over fifty years. He completed his *Multaqā al-abḥur* in 923/1517. Also, author of *Ghunyat al-mutamallī* on prayer.
Ibn Nujaym, Zayn al-Dīn Zayn b. Ibrāhīm (d. 970/1563)	Born in Cairo 926/1520. Author of *al-Baḥr al-rā'iq*, a commentary on *Kanz al-daqā'iq.*
[Al-Khaṭīb] **al-Timurtāshī,** Muḥammad b. 'Abd Allāh b. Aḥmad (d. 1004/1595)	Born and died in Gaza. Born 939/1532. Went to Cairo four times. Student of Ibn Nujaym. Head of the Ḥanafīs in his time. Author of *Tanwīr al-abṣār.*
Sirāj al-Dīn Ibn Nujaym, 'Umar b. Ibrāhīm (d. 1005/1596)	Egypt. Younger brother of Zayn al-Dīn, his *al-Nahr al-fā'iq* is a commentary on his brother's *al-Baḥr al-rā'iq.*

(*continued*)

Ibn al-'Imād, 'Abd al-Raḥmān b. Muḥammad b. Muḥammad al-'Imādī (d. 1051/1641)	Born 978/1570. Damascus. Author of *Hadiyyat Ibn al-'Imād li-'ubbād al-'ibād.*
al-Shurunbulālī, al-Ḥasan b. 'Ammār (d. 1069/1659)	Born 994/1585; grew up in Cairo from the age of six and died there. Author of *Nūr al-īḍāḥ*, a commentary on it entitled *Marāqī al-falāḥ*, and of the *Ḥāshiya* on Mullā Khusraw's *Durar al-ḥukkām.*
al-Ḥaṣkafī, Muḥammad b. 'Alī b. Muḥammad (d. 1088/1677)	Damascus. Author of *al-Durr al-mukhtār*, a commentary on al-Timurtāshī's *Tanwīr al-abṣār.*
The authors of *al-Fatāwā al-'Ālamgīrīya:* *al-Fatāwā al-Hindīya* (completed 1083/1672)	India. Commissioned by the Mongol ruler Awrangzīb 'Ālamgīr b. Khurram (d. 1118/1706), the *Fatāwā* represents the work of a large group of Indian scholars, overseen by al-Shaykh Niẓām of Burhānpūr (1090/1679). It was composed between 1075/1664 and 1083/1672.
al-Āydīnī, Muḥammad al-Güzelḥiṣārī (d. 1116/1704)	Ottoman. Wrote *Risāla fī dawām al-ḥukm* in 1104/1692.
al-Nābulusī, 'Abd al-Ghanī b. Ismā'īl (d. 1143/1731)	Born 1050/1641; from Damascus, traveled to Baghdad, Egypt, and al-Ḥijāz. Author of *Nihāyat al-murād fī sharḥ Hadīyat Ibn al-'Imād.*
Abū al-Su'ūd, Muḥammad b. 'Alī b. 'Alī al-Ḥusaynī (wrote in 1155/1742)	Egypt. Author of *Fatḥ al-mu'īn*, a commentary, completed in 1155/1742, on Mullā Miskīn's *Sharḥ al-Kanz*, a commentary on al-Nasafī's *Kanz al-daqā'iq.*
al-Ṭaḥṭāwī, Aḥmad b. Muḥammad b. Ismā'īl (d. 1231/1816)	Cairo. Born in Ṭahṭā (also Ṭaḥṭā), near Asyūṭ, Egypt. Author of *Ḥāshiyat al-Ṭaḥṭāwī 'alā al-Durr al-mukhtār* and *Ḥāshiyat al-Ṭaḥṭāwī 'alā Marāqī al-falāḥ sharḥ Nūr al-īḍāḥ.*
Ibn 'Ābidīn, Muḥammad Amīn b. 'Umar (d. 1258/1842 or 1252/1836)	Born 1198/1784 in Damascus; lived in Syria; started out as a Shāfi'ī. Author of *Radd al-muḥtār*, a commentary on al-Ḥaṣkafī's *al-Durr al-mukhtār* and of *Minḥat al-Khāliq*, a commentary on Ibn Nujaym's *al-Baḥr al-rā'iq.*
al-Laknawī, Muḥammad 'Abd al-Ḥayy b. Muḥammad (d. 1304/1887)	Born 1264/1848. India. Traditionist and *faqīh*. Author of *Tuḥfat al-nubalā' fī jamā'at al-nisā'.*
al-Afghānī, 'Abd al-Ḥakīm al-Qandahārī (d. 1326/1908)	Born 1251/1835. Lived and died in Damascus. Author of *Kashf al-ḥaqā'iq.*

2.3. "Undesirable" as a Technical Term

The crucial word "undesirable" (*makrūh, n. karāha*) is ubiquitous in this book. In the usual terminology of Muslim legal theory and philosophy (*uṣūl al-fiqh*), "undesirable" denotes a blameless, lawful category of acts. That is, an "undesirable" deed incurs no punishment from God, though its omission is meritorious. Thus, the term "not preferred" would actually be a more accurate, albeit unwieldy, translation.

On the other hand, in Ḥanafī law manuals (i.e., *furū'* texts) the meaning of the word is often unclear. Its usage seems to vary from author to author. And sometimes the same author seems to use it in different senses or in an ambiguous way. For example, at one point al-Bābirtī refers to two different deeds as being undesirable.[4] Shortly thereafter, he says that refraining from the first deed is obligatory, while refraining from the second is only desirable.[5] This, of course, means that the first deed is forbidden and the second one is lawful – even though both are undesirable. Maybe he consciously shifted the sense of the word from one sentence to the next, or maybe at this stage the concept it referred to was vague in his mind.

Later Ḥanafī jurists had to decide in what sense "undesirable" was used in earlier texts, such as in al-Marghīnānī's *Hidāya*, since these texts were often seen as authoritative, though not as binding. As far as I can determine from this study, they began speaking of two kinds of "undesirability" beginning with Ibn al-Humām: "undesirability *qua* prohibition" (*n. karāhat al-taḥrīm, adj. makrūh taḥrīman*), which simply means prohibition, and "undesirability *qua* blamelessness" (*n. karāhat al-tanzīh, adj. makrūh tanzīhan*), which is basically the undesirability already familiar from the terminology of legal philosophy (*uṣūl al-fiqh*) as described in the first paragraph of this section. The difference is significant, as it is one of legality versus illegality. The ability of later jurists to read the earlier "undesirables" in either way had practical consequences. It gave jurists an additional measure of latitude in the interpretation of the law. It also allowed them to change or fine-tune the school doctrine while maintaining the appearance of fidelity to the true doctrine of the school as represented by the earlier texts. Thus, on occasion, substantive transformations could take place under a veneer of verbal constancy and continuity.

[4] See the quotation in Chapter 4, page 85, footnote 18.

[5] See the quotation in Chapter 4, page 85, footnote 19.

Against my analysis, it may be pointed out that Ibn Nujaym asserts that when earlier jurists use the word "undesirable," it means *qua* prohibition unless expressly specified as *qua* blamelessness.[6] He quotes that view also from al-Nasafī. He adds that Abū Yūsuf asked Abū Ḥanīfa, "When you say about something 'I dislike it,' what do you mean?" Abū Ḥanīfa answered, "prohibition!" These reports possibly embody speculation rather than verified historical fact. They may reflect a later trend that was not shared by all jurists, and it is not clear whether one can project the idea back onto Abū Ḥanīfa.[7] Indeed, Ibn Nujaym himself immediately proceeds to give two examples that seemingly undermine his own view. In the case of the undesirability of cats' saliva, some jurists, like al-Ṭaḥāwī, took it to be *qua* prohibition, while some, like al-Karkhī (d. 340/952), took it to be *qua* blamelessness. And the undesirability of the chicken's saliva was deemed by all to be *qua* blamelessness, not *qua* prohibition. To these examples, I would add that al-Bābirtī argued at length for the permissibility of women-only group prayers, which he, along with jurists before him, deemed undesirable.

In any case, these developments meant that later jurists used two sets of terms, "forbidden" (*ḥarām*, *muḥarram*, *maḥẓūr*, etc.) and "undesirable *qua* forbidden" for the same concept: namely, forbidden. This curiosity called for an explanation. The main explanation offered was that the former implies the certainty of the argument from the canon for prohibition, while the latter implies its probability (*ẓann*).[8] Whatever other value this explanation may have, it is not completely adequate as a description of the historical development of the term. Historically, the use of "undesirable" was rooted in Abū Ḥanīfa's and his students' assertions of the form "I dislike (*akrahu* or *lā yuʿjibunā*) such-and-such a thing." One could not argue merely from the subjective wording of such assertions that they represented nothing beyond personal preference that was independent of the canon; after all, the same form ("I dislike") could also be used to express a preference based on the canon. However, until more

[6] Ibn Nujaym, *al-Baḥr al-rāʾiq sharḥ Kanz al-daqāʾiq* (Beirut: Dār al-Kutub al-ʿIlmiyya, 1418/1997), 1:229.

[7] How Abū Ḥanīfa used the label must be determined through a "horizontal" study of the corpus of his rulings, not through anecdotal evidence cited centuries later.

[8] Ibn Nujaym, *al-Baḥr al-rāʾiq*, 1:433. Characteristically for mature Ḥanafī terminology, al-Nābulusī says that *makrūh* and *wājib* correspond to probable (*ẓannī*) grounds respectively for prohibition and obligation, while *ḥarām* and *farḍ* to certain (*qaṭʿī*) grounds for the same: ʿAbd al-Ghanī al-Nābulusī, *Nihāyat al-murād fī sharḥ Hadīyat Ibn al-ʿImād*, ed. ʿAbd al-Razzāq al-Ḥalabī (Dubai: Markaz Jumʿa al-Mājid, 1414/1994), 577.

studies are conducted to clarify this point, it cannot be ruled out that these assertions at times represented unfettered opinion (*ra'y*) formulated independently of what came to constitute the canon for the Ḥanafīs at a later date.

I now turn to the case studies.

3

Women Praying with Men: Adjacency

3.1. The Formative Background

This chapter explores the relationship between laws and the reasons given for them.[1] It examines the extent to which the reasons jurists cite

[1] This chapter is based on the following Ḥanafī texts – and the quotations in the chapter are from these sources unless specified otherwise: Abū Yūsuf, *Kitāb al-Āthār* (Ḥaydarābād: Lajnat Iḥyā' al-Ma'ārif al-Nu'māniyya, 1355), 47, nos. 238–9 (on passersby), no. 240; al-Shaybānī, *Kitāb al-Āthār*, published as Abū Ḥanīfa, *Kitāb al-Āthār* (Karachi: al-Raḥīm Ākīdimī, 1410), 190–1, nos. 137–40; al-Shaybānī, *al-Jāmi' al-kabīr* (Ḥaydarābād: Lajnat Iḥyā' al-Ma'ārif al-Nu'māniyya, 1356), first page; al-Ṭaḥāwī, *Mukhtaṣar al-Ṭaḥāwī* (Cairo: Dār al-Kitāb al-'Arabī, 1370), 33; al-Ṭaḥāwī, *Mukhtaṣar ikhtilāf al-'ulamā'*, in al-Jaṣṣāṣ, *Mukhtaṣar ikhtilāf al-'ulamā'* (Beirut: Dār al-Bashā'ir al-Islāmiyya, 1416), 1:266, nos. 216–7; Abū al-Layth al-Samarqandī, *'Uyūn al-masā'il* (Baghdad, 1385), 2:28, no. 137; Abū al-Layth al-Samarqandī, *Fatāwā al-nawāzil* (Ḥaydarābād: Shams al-Islām, 1355), 2:28, no. 137; al-Qudūrī, *Mukhtaṣar* (Beirut: Dār al-Kutub al-'Ilmiyya, 1418), 29; al-Sarakhsī, *Mabsūṭ* (Beirut: Dār al-Ma'rifa, n.d.), 1:183–6, 2:78; 'Alā' al-Dīn al-Samarqandī, *Tuḥfat al-fuqahā'* (Damascus: Jāmi'at Dimashq, 1377), 1:145, 228–9; al-Kāsānī, *Badā'i' al-ṣanā'i'* (Egypt: al-Maṭbū'āt al-'Ilmiyya, 1327), 1:159; Qāḍī Khān, *Fatāwā Qāḍī Khān*, printed on the margin of al-Shaykh Niẓām et al., *al-Fatāwā al-'Ālamgīrīya* (Diyār Bakr: al-Maktaba al-Islāmiyya, 1393), 1:91, 95, 130–1; al-Marghīnānī, *al-Hidāya* (Cairo: Dār al-Salām, 1420), 1:147–8; al-Mawṣilī, *al-Ikhtiyār li-ta'līl al-Mukhtār* (Beirut: Dār al-Ma'rifa, 1395), 1:58–9; al-Manbijī, *al-Lubāb* (Jeddah: Dār al-Shurūq, 1983), 1:281–2; 'Abd Allāh b. Aḥmad al-Nasafī, *Kanz al-daqā'iq*, inset text included with al-Zayla'ī, *Tabyīn al-ḥaqā'iq* (Beirut: Dār al-Kutub al-'Ilmiyya, 1420); 'Uthmān b. 'Alī al-Zayla'ī, *Tabyīn al-ḥaqā'iq*, 1:350–7; al-Bābirtī, *Sharḥ al-'Ināya 'alā al-Hidāya*, printed with Ibn al-Humām, *Sharḥ Fatḥ al-qadīr* (Egypt: Muṣṭafā al-Bābī al-Ḥalabī, 1389), 1:357, 359–64; Badr al-Dīn al-'Aynī, *al-Bināya sharḥ al-Hidāya* (Beirut: Dār al-Fikr, 1411), 2:405–18; Ibn al-Humām, *Sharḥ Fatḥ al-qadīr*, 1:359–65; Mullā Khusraw, *Durar al-ḥukkām* (Istanbul: Muḥammad As'ad, 1300), 1:112–13; al-Ḥalabī, *Multaqā al-abḥur* (Beirut: Mu'assasat al-Risāla, 1409), 1:96–7; al-Ḥalabī, *Ghunyat al-mutamallī*, 521–4; Zayn al-Dīn Ibn Nujaym, *al-Baḥr al-rā'iq* (Beirut: Dār al-Kutub

determine or motivate the laws and concludes that such reasons are after-the-fact justifications. The case study concerns the status of group prayers involving both men and women. The legal question is what happens if a woman prays next to or in front of a man, a situation that is referred to as "adjacency" (*muḥādhāt*). One might guess that adjacency either invalidates both the man and the woman's prayers or invalidates neither. Indeed, the schools of Islamic law generally picked one or the other of these two options. The Ḥanafīs, however, took an anomalous position, invalidating only the man's prayer, making for an asymmetric approach that merits scholarly attention. I will refer to this as the "adjacency law." Postformative jurists offered a variety of justifications for the adjacency law, and it turns out that none of them reflected the considerations that had given rise to the law.

The adjacency law has its roots in certain notions about the transmission of ritual impurity that originated in Baṣra in the first half of the seventh century AD.[2] Broadly speaking, in the first century of Islam, there were three main approaches to the question of feminine ritual purity. The majority considered women as ritually pure in the sense that the water they use remains usable for the purpose of ritual ablution or ritual bathing and their walking in front of a worshipper does not affect his or her prayer. This majority approach was symmetric in the sense that a woman contaminated neither women nor men. Another approach,

al-ʿIlmiyya, 1418), 1:617–27, 628–9; al-Timurtāshī, *Tanwīr al-abṣār* (n.p.: Ḥasan Aḥmad al-Ṭūkhī, 1298), 15; Sirāj al-Dīn Ibn Nujaym, *al-Nahr al-fāʾiq* (Beirut: Dār al-Kutub al-ʿIlmiyya, 1418), 1:246–51; Ibn al-ʿImād, *Hadīyat Ibn al-ʿImād li-ʿubbād al-ʿibād*, printed with ʿAbd al-Ghanī al-Nābulusī, *Nihāyat al-murād fī sharḥ Hadīyat Ibn al-ʿImād*, 466, 742; al-Shurunbulālī, *Nūr al-īḍāḥ*, printed with al-Shurunbulālī, *Marāqī al-falāḥ sharḥ Nūr al-īḍāḥ* (Damascus: Dār al-Nuʿmān li-al-ʿUlūm, 1411/1990), 291, 292, 304–6; al-Shurunbulālī, *Marāqī al-falāḥ*, 291, 292, 304–6; al-Shurunbulālī, *Ḥāshiya*, printed with Mullā Khusraw, *Durar al-ḥukkām*, 1:112–13; al-Ḥaṣkafī, *al-Durr al-mukhtār* (Egypt: Muḥammad ʿAlī Ṣubayḥ), 1:96, 100–1; al-Shaykh Niẓām et al., *al-Fatāwā al-ʿĀlamgīrīya*, 1:85, 88; ʿAbd al-Ghanī al-Nābulusī, *Nihāya*, 466, 742–6; Abū al-Suʿūd, *Fatḥ al-muʿīn* (Karachi: H. M. Saʿīd, 1303), 1:210–14; al-Ṭaḥṭāwī, *Ḥāshiya ʿalā al-Durr al-mukhtār* (Beirut: Dār al-Maʿrifa, 1395), 1:245–9, 251; al-Ṭaḥṭāwī, *Ḥāshiya ʿalā Marāqī al-falāḥ* (Egypt: al-Tijāriyya al-Kubrā, 1356), 168; Ibn ʿĀbidīn, *[Ḥāshiyat] Radd al-muḥtār* (Beirut: Dār al-Kutub al-ʿIlmiyya, 1415), 1:609, 616–22; Ibn ʿĀbidīn, *Minḥat al-Khāliq*, printed with Ibn Nujaym, *al-Baḥr al-rāʾiq*, 1:374–80; ʿAbd al-Ḥakīm al-Afghānī, *Kashf al-ḥaqāʾiq* (Karachi: Idārat al-Qurʾān wa-al-ʿUlūm al-Islāmiyya, 1987), 1:54–5.

[2] This paragraph and the next two provide a reconstruction of early Muslim views from scattered pieces of evidence in the *ḥadīth* and *āthār* literature. They summarize the results of a work under preparation on the first 150 years of Islam. Some of the evidence is presented in Behnam Sadeghi, "The Traveling Tradition Test: A Method for Dating Muslim Traditions," *Der Islam* 85.1 (2008): 203–242.

rooted particularly in Mecca, held that a menstruating woman contaminates water and invalidates the prayers of men and women by walking in front of them. This approach was symmetric in the sense that a menstruating woman contaminated both men and nonmenstruating women.

A third approach, popular in Baṣra, held that women contaminate water and break prayers perpetually, that is, regardless of whether they are menstruating or not.[3] Unlike the others, this minority approach was asymmetric: a woman could contaminate men, but not women. Thus, a female passerby would "break" (i.e., invalidate) a man's prayer, and a man's ritual ablution would be invalid if he made use of water already used by a woman for the same purpose. Other women presumably would not be contaminated in this way because, by virtue of being female, they could not be further contaminated. That ritual impurity was the cause of the invalidation of prayers and ablutions is nowhere made explicit, but is confirmed by a variety of indications, including the fact that some key early proponents of this approach referred to female passersby in the same breath as certain other living creatures that they, unlike most other Muslims, explicitly deemed as ritual contaminants.[4]

This last approach became extinct with the spread of the well-known personal schools of law, largely due to the fact that Baṣra itself did not give rise to such a school, or at least not to a successful one. However, the Baṣra-based approach left an imprint that has endured until today, namely the adjacency law. The Baṣra-based approach was also known in Kūfa in the second half of the first century, although it had only a small number of proponents there. It was there that the first-century Kūfan

[3] The existence of this minority group has been noted by Marion Katz in the context of water contamination, though she does not discuss passersby or assign these early views to a place, time, or milieu. See Marion Katz, *Body of Text* (Albany: State University of New York Press, 2002), 149–50.

These rules can be interpreted in two very different ways. First, one might say that this approach was concerned with menstruation, that is, with its potential lingering physical (or spiritual) traces or effects in the entire month, and possibly with the chance that a woman could be menstruating without one's knowledge. The extension of the period of concern to the entire month would then be a cautionary or pragmatic measure. Second, one might say that this approach could have simply held women to be inherently impure independently of menstruation. On this latter approach, a woman's ablution would have made her more ritually pure than before, pure enough for her to pray, but not as ritually pure as a man. In other words, this approach held men and women to different levels of ritual purity. I owe the first interpretation to Hossein Modarressi. I provisionally prefer the second one since the asymmetry it entails seems to fit the evidence of some of the traditions.

[4] Sadeghi, "Traveling Tradition Test," 213–9.

jurist, Ibrāhīm al-Nakhaʿī, took the adjacency law from this approach without, however, borrowing anything else from it. His tendency to pick and choose elements from the three early approaches rather than adopt one of the approaches in its entirety is also illustrated by the fact that he saw no problem in the leftover water from a menstruating woman's ablution but disapproved of her leftover drinking water.

Thus, Ibrāhīm did not hold that female passersby broke prayers. In this respect, Abū Ḥanīfa and al-Shaybānī followed him:[5]

Says Muḥammad [al-Shaybānī]: Abū Ḥanīfa informed us about (*ʿan*) Ḥammād [b. Abī Sulaymān]: about Ibrāhīm [b. Yazīd b. Qays al-Nakhaʿī]: about al-Aswad b. Yazīd [b. Qays, Kūfan, Nakhaʿī, Ibrāhīm's maternal uncle, d. 74/567] that he asked ʿĀ'isha about what breaks prayers. She said: "You Iraqis assert that donkeys, dogs, women, and cats break prayers. You equate us [women] with them? Keep away [passersby] when you can; but nothing breaks your prayers." Muḥammad says: "We accept ʿĀ'isha's position, and that is the position of Abū Ḥanīfa."[6]

Postformative Ḥanafī jurists held on to Abū Ḥanīfa's decision. In this they agreed with the other schools of law, except for the now-extinct Ẓāhirīs.

3.2. Adjacency: The Two-Body Problem

Muḥammad al-Shaybānī, following Ibrāhīm and Abū Ḥanīfa, and prefiguring all later Ḥanafī scholars, held that proximity to a female does not necessarily break a man's prayer. However, again following Ibrāhīm and Abū Ḥanīfa, he took a different view in the special case of a man praying side by side with a woman who prays the same group prayer as he:

Says Muḥammad [al-Shaybānī]: Abū Ḥanīfa informed us from Ḥammād: about Ibrāhīm: he said: "when a woman prays next to a man while both are praying the same prayer, his prayer is voided." Muḥammad says: "We accept that, and that is the position of Abū Ḥanīfa."

There is no problem if the woman who is at the man's side is not praying, and al-Shaybānī approvingly cites, through Abū Ḥanīfa—Ḥammād—

[5] Al-Shaybānī, *Āthār*, 190–1, no. 140.

[6] Similar opinions have been ascribed to ʿĀ'isha through al-Aʿmash (d. 147, Kūfan)—Ibrāhīm—al-Aswad—ʿĀ'isha; al-Aʿmash—Muslim (b. Ṣubayḥ al-Hamdānī, Kūfan, d. 100)—Masrūq (b. al-Ajdaʿ al-Hamdānī, Kūfan, d. 62–3)—ʿĀ'isha; and ʿUrwa—ʿĀ'isha. See al-Bukhārī, *Ṣaḥīḥ* (Istanbul: Dār al-Ṭibāʿa al-ʿĀmira, 1315), 1:130. The opposite view has also been related through her as a Prophetic tradition (Ibn Ḥanbal, *Musnad* (n.p.: Dār Ṣādir, n.d.), 6:84–5). Other authorities, too, have been cited for both sides of the dispute.

Ibrāhīm—'Ā'isha, the report of the Prophet praying with 'Ā'isha asleep at his side while he wore a garment that touched her.[7] He adds:

> It is the same [i.e., harmless], likewise, if she prays next to him a prayer different from his. His prayer is voided only if she prays next to him and they pray the same prayer, with her taking him as the imām or both taking some other person as their imām. That is the position of Abū Ḥanīfa.

Although Abū Ḥanīfa and al-Shaybānī do not deal with the case of a woman praying in front of a man and sharing in the same prayer as him, it is safe to say that they view it, as later Ḥanafī jurists would, in the same negative light as prayers side by side. Al-Ṭaḥāwī puts the matter explicitly. In *Mukhtaṣar ikhtilāf*, he states that in case of adjacency (*muḥādhāt*) with women, the man's prayer is voided if he shares that prayer with her, that is, if they are both part of the same group prayer. He uses the term "adjacency" to refer to the woman standing in front of or next to the man, but not to her standing behind him. All later jurists would use "adjacency" in the same sense. The adjacency rule stated by al-Ṭaḥāwī would remain an unshakable hallmark of Ḥanafī law.

3.2.1. *Partitions and Gaps*

For Abū Ḥanīfa and al-Shaybānī, a gap between a man and a woman did not remove the concern with adjacency, but a barrier did:

> Says Muḥammad: Abū Ḥanīfa informed us about Ḥammād: he said, "I asked Ibrāhīm about a man praying on the eastern side of the mosque and a woman on the western side (*al-rajul yuṣallī fī jānib al-masjid al-sharqī wa-al-mar'a fī al-gharbī*). He disliked (*kariha*) that unless there were between him and her something the size of the rear part of a camel saddle."[8] Muḥammad says: "We do accept that when they share the same prayer, taking the same person as imām."

[7] A remarkably similar tradition is reported of another wife of the Prophet, Maymūna: "the Prophet would stand and pray at night with me sleeping at his side. His garment would touch me when he performed the prostration, though I was menstruating" (see, e.g., Ibn Ḥanbal, *Musnad*, 6:330–2; Ibn Khuzayma, *Ṣaḥīḥ* (Beirut: al-Maktab al-Islāmī, 1412), 2:104; etc.). 'Ā'isha figures in another tradition, sleeping next to the Prophet when he prayed and touching his feet while he performed the prostration; see al-Tirmidhī, *Sunan* (Beirut: Dār al-Fikr, 1403), 5:187, *bāb* 78, no. 3562; al-Ṭabarānī, *al-Mu'jam al-Kabīr* (Beirut: Dār Iḥyā' al-Turāth al-'Arabī, 1984–), 24:23.

[8] *Mu'akhkharat al-raḥl*: This was the part of the saddle one would sit on, as noted in Ibn Manẓūr, *Lisān al-'Arab* (Qum: Nashr Adab al-Ḥawza, 1363), 4:12. In early traditions, this was cited as the ideal size of the object (*sutra*) that a worshipper should place in front of him or her to ward off the interference of passersby.

Some *ḥadīth*s circulating in the first century in Kūfa said that if a worshipper places something the size of the rear part of a camel saddle in front of him, then passersby, including women and other prayer-breaking creatures, do not affect his prayer.[9] Ibrāhīm's borrowing of the distinctive concept of a barrier of this particular size hints that the problem of adjacency was linked to that of the passerby, and specifically proximity to women, and lends further support to the hypothesis that the adjacency law was borrowed from the Baṣra-based approach, which, as mentioned previously, was attested to in Kūfa as well.[10]

But Ibrāhīm's borrowing of the adjacency law does not mean that he shared the Baṣra-based view of women as perpetual (real or potential) ritual contaminators; in fact, his other rulings prove that he did not. There is nothing odd about such ostensible "inconsistency." It is very common for legal traditions to borrow particular laws without all the concomitant laws and presuppositions that are attached to them in the donor legal system. The case at hand is an example of what Alan Watson describes as a borrowing "of surrounding rules but not of the central core of the legal institution because the societal institutions are very different."[11] As he notes, "individual foreign legal rules may be transferred into a system constructed on very different principles."[12] In this case, the borrowing served to fill a gap in Ibrāhīm's fledgling system (answering what happens as a result of adjacency), a gap that the other emerging Muslim legal traditions would fill in different ways.

Thus, the law of adjacency was taken over, but the concerns that occasioned its genesis were forgotten: later jurists would cite altogether different reasons to justify it. Indeed, the values underlying the original law were not only completely forgotten, but also were actually in conflict with the values of postformative jurists, who did not consider women as transmitters of ritual impurity at all. This curious phenomenon underscores that the staying power of a law is often independent of the real or imagined reasons behind it. As Alan Watson has noted, "The historical reasons for the precise contours of the legal institution may well be

[9] Sadeghi, "Traveling Tradition Test," 215–6.

[10] See also footnote 31 on page 64.

[11] Alan Watson, *The Evolution of Law* (Baltimore: John Hopkins University Press, 1985), 75; cf. 66–97.

[12] Alan Watson, *The Nature of Law* (Edinburgh: Edinburgh University Press, 1977), 111; cf. the discussion of borrowing in 99–113; cf. Alan Watson, *Society and Legal Change*, 98–114.

forgotten. Yet people for the most part accept the law they have."[13] The ramifications of this point will be explored further in Chapter 7.

Ḥanafī law retained Abū Ḥanīfa's view that a barrier/partition removes adjacency, but it unceremoniously discarded his view that a gap does not. (It highlights the importance of diachronic investigation that one would not know that the law changed if one did not read Abū Ḥanīfa, as jurists never pointed out that the law actually deviated from Abū Ḥanīfa's view.) So, a man and a woman can pray side by side as long as there is a gap between them. The gap would have to be at least the size of the space taken up by one person standing, that is, a couple of feet, according to al-Zaylaʿī (and, following him, Ibn al-Humām, Mullā Khusraw, Abū al-Suʿūd, and al-Nābulusī). Al-Kākī required a larger gap, enough for nine persons.[14] Thus, in the absence of further evidence, the most likely date for the turnabout in the law is the seventh/thirteenth century or the first half of the eighth/fourteenth century, when both al-Zaylaʿī and al-Kākī lived. Al-Kākī also maintained that a gap of the same size (nine persons) removes adjacency if the woman is in front of the man. Ibn al-Humām and Ibn ʿĀbidīn rejected this view, offering an argument against it.[15]

3.3. Justification: "Keep Them Behind!"

From now on, I will dwell on key features of the law that were already well developed by the time of al-Kāsānī and al-Sarakhsī, two authors whose expositions overlap considerably. Their accounts were broadly prefigured by al-Ṭaḥāwī and Abū al-Layth al-Samarqandī, but I will not map out the development from these earlier authors to their time. I will pay more attention, rather, to the period following them.

[13] The passage is in Watson, *The Evolution of Law*, 73:

> The law created by a society for its use is often by no means a perfect fit. And the historical reasons for the precise contours of the legal institution may well be forgotten. Yet people for the most part accept the law they have. They do not demand perfection. All this is a necessary precondition for one of the strangest of legal phenomena: the prodigious extent of legal borrowing.

[14] Al-Kākī's view is quoted, not necessarily approvingly, by Ibn al-Humām, Ibn Nujaym, and Ibn ʿĀbidīn.

[15] The argument of Ibn al-Humām and Ibn ʿĀbidīn against al-Kākī is flawed. They cite the fact that in the case of three women praying side by side, invalidation propagates backwards all the way to the last row of worshippers (see Section 3.4 on the "multibody problem"). However, this rule was universally acknowledged as a departure (*istiḥsān*) from the pattern of the adjacency law; it was not any more consistent with Ibn al-Humām's treatment of adjacency than it was with al-Kākī's. As an admitted exception, it cannot be used as a counterexample against al-Kākī.

The question is exactly whose prayer is nullified in various configurations of adjacency and why. Al-Sarakhsī writes:

If a woman prays behind an imām who has "resolved" to lead women, and she stands in the middle of the row, then our position, in accordance with *istiḥsān*, is that she invalidates the prayers of the one [i.e., the man] to her right, the one to her left, and the one immediately behind her.

Istiḥsān means abandoning a solution supported by an analogy in favor of a different solution (that may in turn be justified by another analogy or by other evidence, such as a *ḥadīth*). What analogy is being abandoned here? The answer is clarified in the next passage:

Al-Shāfiʿī held that [in this case] no one's prayer is invalidated when a woman is in front of a man, since that would not be worse [lit. stronger] than a dog or a pig standing in front of him, which would not invalidate the man's prayer. And if anyone's prayer were invalidated as a result, it would be more fitting if it were hers, because she is forbidden to go out to attend the communal prayers.

Moreover, the mingling [of men and women] in the row indicates that in the case of funeral prayers or the prostrations mandated upon reciting the Qur'ān (*sajdat al-tilāwa*) a woman's being in the front does not invalidate a man's prayer. It is the same in all prayers.

Thus, al-Sarakhsī discards the analogy with funeral prayers and the analogy *a fortiori* with dogs and pigs. Al-Marghīnānī also refers to an *istiḥsān*, but he discards a different analogy, namely, the inference that the adjacent man's prayer should remain valid like that of the woman. He, too, attributes the analogy to al-Shāfiʿī. Later jurists generally identified the *istiḥsān* in the same manner as al-Marghīnānī. Al-Sarakhsī then goes on to describe how the analogy is abandoned:

To us [Ḥanafīs], however, since he has not taken his legally proper place, his prayer is invalidated ...[16] and [for women] the worst [row] is the first [row] (*wa-sharruhā*

[16] The text reads *fa-tafsudu ṣalātuhu ka-mā law akhkharahā*. This does not make sense and must be a corruption. It appears, based on a comparison with other sources, such as al-Kāsānī (*Badāʾiʿ al-ṣanāʾiʿ*, 1:239), that what ought to be said at this point is: his prayer is invalidated just as if one advanced in front of an imām (al-Kāsānī has *fa-tafsudu ka-mā idhā taqaddama ʿalā al-imām*). The current text could have resulted from a copyist's skipping a line after the words *ka-mā law*. The word *akhkharahā* would then be a corruption of *ākhiruhā*, which would have been part of the tradition *khayr ṣufūf al-nisāʾ ākhiruhā wa-sharruhā awwaluhā*. So, the next line would have picked up in the middle of this tradition, beginning with *ākhiruhā wa-sharruhā awwaluhā*.

The idea is to give a well-known example where an improper position does invalidate one's prayer. This establishes the legitimacy of taking the worshipper's position into consideration as a potential cause of invalidation. Furthermore, it puts the emphasis on the man's action, showing how it can actualize the concept in the *ḥadīth* regardless of what the woman does.

awwaluhā).[17] Properly, men must be in front of women. So, if he stands next to her or behind her, he has not taken his proper place and, also, ignored a requirement (*farḍan min furūḍ*) of prayer. It is his responsibility to make her stay behind during communal prayers. He [the Prophet] said: "Keep them behind where God has kept them" (*akhkhirūhunna min ḥayth akhkharahunna Allāh*).[18] The command to keep them behind is intended to apply to prayer. Therefore, it is among the requirements of a man's prayer. The reason is that prayer constitutes a state of communication (with God). This being so, it is not right that sexual thoughts should cross his mind, which is what usually happens when one faces a woman. Thus, the command to keep them back becomes a requirement of prayer that, if ignored, would invalidate his prayer. However, *her* prayer is not invalidated because the command to keep (women) behind is addressed to men. And he may "keep her behind" by his stepping forward in front of her instead of her staying behind.[19]

Al-Sarakhsī uses the "keep them behind" tradition as Abū al-Layth had and as later Ḥanafīs would. The command in the *ḥadīth* is predictably taken to imply an obligation. Moreover, the binding quality of the demand is linked to the invalidity of a prayer not meeting it. A remarkably mechanical construal of the *ḥadīth*, on the basis that it is addressed to men and not women, is used to argue that the woman's prayer remains valid.[20] This justification would be used by later jurists; but, as will be seen in Section 3.5, eventually an awareness would develop that this "*ḥadīth*" is barely worthy of that label, thus necessitating the creation of complementary justifications. Moreover, questions of authenticity aside, in due course I will discuss whether this tradition in fact explains the origin of the law.

[17] These words are an allusion to a *ḥadīth* to the effect that the best of men's rows is the first of them and the best of women's rows is the last of them. This *ḥadīth* seems admissible if the point is to establish the spirit of the law. However, it does not establish the point conclusively. It can establish at most desirability, not obligation. Secondly, it can be read as being about the relative merits of women's rows compared to one another and the relative merits of men's rows compared to one another. If so, it would not be directly relevant to adjacency. Indeed, later jurists do not use this tradition to establish an obligation.

[18] Literally, "keep them back from places where God has kept them back." Some variants have *ḥayth* instead of *min ḥayth*. Al-ʿAynī cites the view that *min ḥayth* can also mean "because," which would yield "keep them behind, for God has kept them behind."

[19] Following the suggestion of Hossein Modarressi and Michael Cook, I read *tata'akhkhar* for *yata'akhkhar* in this sentence: *wa-huwa yumkinuh an yu'akhkhirahā min-ghayr an yata'akhkhara bi-an yataqaddama ʿalayhā*. Indeed, this reading is confirmed by a parallel in al-Kāsānī that is quite unambiguous: *wa-yumkinuh ta'khīruhā min ghayr an tata'akhkhar hiya bi-nafsihā wa-yataqaddam ʿalayhā*.

[20] A-Marghīnānī cites the same tradition, labeling it well-attested (*min al-mashāhīr*). Al-ʿAynī and Ibn al-Humām point out that it is a saying of the Companion Ibn Masʿūd, not of the Prophet. For more on the tradition, see Section 3.5.

Al-Sarakhsī offers the prevention of sexual thoughts as the point of the rule. One may ask whether the same rationale could not be raised against the Ḥanafī position that women may pray behind men. Consider women praying behind men, who unlike women have to cover themselves only from navel to knees. Are women praying behind men, according to jurists, not as likely to think sexual thoughts as men praying behind women covered from head to toe? Does al-Sarakhsī think women are not sexual? Or does he simply neglect to consider or imagine the situation from the vantage point of women? The latter explanation is more plausible. That is verifiably the right explanation at least in the case of al-Zaylaʿī, who completely agrees with al-Sarakhsī here. Crucially, al-Zaylaʿī does acknowledge that sexual attraction in the case of adjacency is reciprocal between men and women. (This is part of an explanation of why the adjacency of a man to a boy does not bring about invalidation: in this case, sexual attraction, when it exists, is only one way, unlike adjacency to a woman, where it is reciprocal and thus more problematic.) Yet, he fails to see that the reciprocity he acknowledges to exist poses a problem for the justification of the adjacency law. Not so with al-Kāsānī; he is the only jurist, to my knowledge, to point to the reciprocity of sexual desire between men and women to refute the relevance of sexual thoughts to adjacency. There were other jurists who agreed with al-Sarakhsī's rationale,[21] but Ibn al-Humām, al-Ḥalabī, Abū al-Suʿūd, and Ibn ʿĀbidīn

[21] In particular, three books, named by Ibn al-ʿImād and Ibn ʿĀbidīn, must have considered sexual attraction relevant, as they maintained, against the Ḥanafī mainstream, that a man's adjacency to a comely "beardless youth" entails invalidation. The works named are (1) *Jāmiʿ al-Maḥbūbī* (cited by Ibn al-ʿImād and Ibn ʿĀbidīn), (2) *Durar al-Biḥār* (cited by Ibn ʿĀbidīn), (3) and *al-Multaqaṭ* (cited by Ibn ʿĀbidīn). The first one probably refers to *Sharḥ al-Jāmiʿ al-ṣaghīr li-al-Shaybānī* by ʿUbayd Allāh b. Ibrāhīm al-Maḥbūbī (d. 630/1233) (see Kaḥḥāla, *Muʿjam al-muʾallifīn* (Beirut: Maktabat al-Muthannā, n.d.), 6:16; but read ʿUbayd Allāh for ʿAbd Allāh; cf., e.g., al-Dhahabī, *Siyar*, 22:345); the second one to Yūsuf b. Ilyās al-Qūnawī (d. 788/1386, Turkish jurist who moved to Syria), *Durar al-Biḥār* (see Kaḥḥāla, *Muʿjam*, 13:277); and the third one to Nāṣir al-Dīn Abū al-Qāsim Muḥammad b. Yūsuf al-Samarqandī (d. 556/1161), *al-Multaqaṭ* (written 549/1154) (Ḥājī Khalīfa, *Kashf al-ẓunūn* (Beirut: Dār Iḥyāʾ al-Turāth al-ʿArabī, n.d.), 2:1574; Brockelmann gives the wrong date in *GAL*, 1:475). A fourth person probably with the same view is named by Abū al-Suʿūd, namely *al-shaykh al-zāhid* Abū Bakr b. Muḥammad b. Yūsuf b. al-Marʿūsānī, who, Abū al-Suʿūd says, ascribed to al-Shaybānī the view that adjacency to a beardless youth invalidates a man's prayer because it induces sexual thoughts. I have not been able to identify this man. Incidentally, the approach of these four figures implicitly treats homosexual desire (but not homosexual acts) as natural, common, and stigma-free, at least when compared to al-Zaylaʿī and Ibn al-Humām. Al-Zaylaʿī cites the relative rarity of homosexual desire as a reason against adjacency to a boy entailing invalidation, while Ibn al-Humām cites reports on its odiousness and unnaturalness.

expressly reject sexual attraction as a relevant factor. However, they do not exploit the reciprocity of attraction. Rather, Ibn al-Humām and al-Nābulusī's counterexamples include forms of sexual attraction that do not invalidate prayers (namely, toward female corpses or beasts,[22] female passersby, or simply a mental picture of a pretty female), while al-Ḥalabī and Ibn ʿĀbidīn cite cases of attraction-free adjacency where prayers are nullified nonetheless (namely, an old woman or one's mother or daughter). In all of this, it is clear that jurists start with the legal consequences and then speculate about the reasons for them.

An interesting aspect of al-Sarakhsī's remark on "purity of thought" is that he provides the reason underlying the "keep them behind" tradition. Why do so, given that this report, for him, is enough to justify the adjacency law? Could it be that providing this underlying reason serves no purpose as a justification? The answer is that this reason is mentioned here because it allows the suspension of the "keep them behind" principle in another context, the funeral prayer. Al-Sarakhsī writes:

> Thus, the funeral prayer is not invalidated by [a woman] being in front [of a man] since it is not a prayer that strictly constitutes communication with God, but is rather the fulfillment of a right due to the deceased.

The funeral prayer violates the pattern expected from the "keep them behind" principle. To explain the discrepancy, al-Sarakhsī appeals to the rationale behind the principle: the prevention of sexual thoughts during communication with God. Since funeral prayers do not, in the first instance, constitute communication with God, the principle does not apply. In effect, al-Sarakhsī has introduced two ad hoc stipulations – the "purity of thought" rationale and the noncommunicative status of funeral prayers – in order to achieve the needed legal effect: the suspension of the normal consequences of adjacency in the case of funeral prayers.

3.4. The Multibody Problem and the Origin of the Adjacency Law

Before testing the explanatory power of the "keep them behind" tradition, one needs to consider the next question: whose prayer is invalidated by several women praying side by side or by a whole row of them?

One might suppose that this question would be treated as an extension of the two-body problem involving one man and one woman by counting

[22] Ibn al-Humām is not entirely on solid ground here, as jurists generally held that anomalous situations are ignored in the formulation of general principles.

(a)	(b)
m m m m m m m	m m m m m m m
m X F F X m m	m X F F F X m
m m X X m m m	m m X X X m m
m m m m m m m	m m X X X m m
m m m m m m m	m m X X X m m

FIGURE 10. m = male, F = female, X = male whose prayer is invalidated. The top row is the front row.

as invalid the prayer of any man next to or directly behind a woman, as in Figure 10a. (Some jurists, such as al-ʿAynī, would call this an analogy with the case of a single woman.) Indeed, this is the approach taken, but only up to a point. Once the number of the women reaches three, the pattern is broken as a different principle takes over. (Some jurists would say that here the analogy is broken by an *istiḥsān*, for example, al-Kāsānī, al-ʿAynī,[23] and Ibn al-Humām.) The new principle is that when there are "enough" women to qualify as a row, then the prayers of all men directly behind them are voided, not just the ones in the adjacent row behind, as in Figure 10b. In support of this principle, al-Sarakhsī and others quote a tradition of ʿUmar cited both as the latter's own saying (*mawqūf*) and as a saying of the Prophet (*marfūʿ*): "The prayer of one who is separated from the imām by a river, road, or a row of women is not valid."[24] Al-Sarakhsī then explains: "a row of women is like a wall between the imām and a follower, and the presence between them of a big wall without any breach nullifies the validity of 'following.' The same rule extends to the case of a row of women."

The next question is: how many women make a "row"? In other words, how many women does it take to equal the effect of a road, a river, or a solid wall? Al-Sarakhsī and others quote al-Shaybānī as setting the threshold at three, yielding the configurations in Figure 10. This seems to be al-Sarakhsī's preferred solution, and later jurists agree.

[23] Al-ʿAynī calls it an *istiḥsān* within an *istiḥsān*, recalling that the adjacency law itself is an *istiḥsān*.

[24] ʿAlāʾ al-Dīn al-Samarqandī refers to it as a Prophetic tradition: "One who is separated from the leader by a river, a road, or a row of women is not (actually praying) with the leader." I have not found the saying as a *ḥadīth*. Al-ʿAynī calls it weak and unattested. The rule embodied in it exists as a saying of Ibrāhīm – for which, see ʿAbd al-Razzāq, *al-Muṣannaf* (Beirut: al-Majlis al-ʿIlmī, 1970), 3:82, no. 4882 – and of ʿUmar, for which see al-ʿAynī. The *ḥadīth* al-Samarqandī mentions is probably late in origin, as it is not attested in early sources.

(a)	(b)
m m m m m m m	m m m m m m m
m X F F X m m	m X F F F X m
m m X X m m m	m m X X X m m
m m m m m m m	m m m m m m m
m m m m m m m	m m m m m m m

FIGURE 11. Abū Yūsuf – I: respectively with two women (a) and three women (b).

(a)	(b)
m m m m m m m	m m m m m m m
m X F F X m m	m X F F F X m
m m X X m m m	m m X X X m m
m m X X m m m	m m X X X m m
m m X X m m m	m m X X X m m

FIGURE 12. Abū Yūsuf – II: respectively with two women (a) and three women (b).

Al-Sarakhsī and others ascribe two different views to Abū Yūsuf, as shown in Figures 11 and 12. Both treat two and three women as equivalent. In the first view, two and three women are both treated following the pattern in the two-body case, as shown in Figure 11. In the second view, they are both treated as a wall, with invalidation back-propagating to the last row, as shown in Figure 12.

As noted previously, Ḥanafī law settled firmly on the solutions shown in Figure 10.

What all these solutions have in common is their apparent departure from the rationale al-Sarakhsī and most others give for why the men's prayers are invalidated while the women's are not. Recall that his argument resorted to a mechanical reading of the tradition, "keep women behind." A man's prayer is not valid, he argued, if he does not keep the women behind relative to his own position. By this reasoning, however, the prayer of every man standing in the same row as a woman, or in a row further back, should be invalid.[25] In other words, one would expect

[25] Against my point, a reader has argued, "al-Sarakhsī may say that the order addresses only the situation of women standing in front of men or next to them. The distance between the others at the two sides and the woman neutralizes the presence of the latter. For those the same distance behind, the wall analogy prevails. So, there is more than one factor at work here." This objection does not work for the following reason. While eventually many Ḥanafīs did consider a gap (of approximately a couple of feet) as having

mmmmmmm
XXXFXXX
XXXXXXX
XXXXXXX
XXXXXXX

FIGURE 13. A hypothetical solution.

m m m m m m m
m m X F X m m
m m m X m m m
m m m m m m m
m m m m m m m

FIGURE 14. The Ḥanafī solution.

the result to be as in Figure 13. The Ḥanafī solutions, however, are those in Figures 14, 10, 11, and 12.

I would argue that there is a fundamental difference of perspective between Ḥanafī law and the "keep them behind" tradition that is cited in its support. If the tradition were applied to prayer, the crux of the matter would be the relative positions of the male and female worshippers, that is, who is in front and who is behind. The legal consequences one would expect from this approach differ from actual Ḥanafī law, where the operative factor is the concept of "adjacency" (*muḥādhāt*) instead. For example, in Ḥanafī law a barrier/partition or a gap saves a man's prayer from invalidation by a woman in the same row. If the law were based on the *ḥadīth*, a barrier[26] should not make a difference, for a woman standing in the same row is not behind him as the tradition requires. The point is similarly confirmed by the fact that the prayers of the men outside the first "layer" of men immediately surrounding the female are not affected (except when the separate principle embodied in the 'Umar tradition, namely, the "wall" analogy, takes over) (see, e.g., Figure 14).[27]

this effect (for a man and a woman in the same row), this was not the case at the time of al-Sarakhsī, and certainly not the case at the time of Abū Ḥanīfa and his students.

[26] Or a small gap, if one considers later Ḥanafī law.

[27] Some later jurists, such as Ibn al-Humām, say that a man whose prayer is voided effectively turns into a barrier, hence preventing the propagation of invalidity. They use this principle to explain why invalidity does not reach beyond the first layer of men surrounding a woman. However, they do not explain why a barrier must make a difference if "keep them behind" is the operative principle.

Were the law based on the *ḥadīth,* one would expect outcomes like the one in Figure 13 instead, since all the men marked X would have failed to "keep women behind." In short, the tradition is cited where it is consistent with the law and ignored where it is not. And the inconsistencies are big enough to confirm that the law did not derive from the tradition.[28]

In the attempt to move from the concrete ramifications of the two approaches to the broader concepts behind them, one may take a cue from the fact that the "keep them behind" report deals with men and women as groups, whereas the law addresses itself to the individual and his or her immediate surroundings, to two bodies at a time (except when *istiḥsān* takes over in the three-woman case). At its root, the report appears to concern questions of precedence, rank, authority, merit, and leadership.[29]

At first glance, the concern for the individual's purity of thought may seem to fit the law well. It explains, for example, why only the prayers of the men next to and immediately behind a woman are voided. The match, however, is purely coincidental.[30] The law has its origins in the first-century minority view that held that women break prayers due to their transmission of ritual impurity.[31] This "contamination hypothesis" fits the adjacency law at least as well as the purity-of-thought explanation, as it explains all the facts that the purity-of-thought hypothesis explains. For example, the fact that only the immediate layer of male worshippers surrounding a woman is affected follows because that layer

[28] That this *ḥadīth* is not the source of the law is shown in a completely independent way, by an inquiry into early traditions bearing on women's purity, the results of which I summarized on pages 51–3 and in Sadeghi, "Traveling Tradition Test," 213–9.

[29] If *min ḥayth* were understood as "because," that would further support this view, as the translation would become: "Keep women behind because God has kept them behind."

[30] To be sure, the concern for purity of thought must have been a motivating factor for the jurists mentioned on page 59, footnote 21, who held that adjacency to an attractive boy voids a man's prayer. These were jurists who arrived at their conclusion by patterning it on the law that had already been developed for women. Their understanding of the law, therefore, is not evidence for what originated the law in the case of women.

[31] Against my argument, one may point to early reports showing that all passersby are problematic, not just women, implying that concerns other than purity may have made women prayer-breakers. In rebuttal, I would point out that while there are early traditions against walking in front of a worshipper and traditions commanding worshippers to stop passersby, the traditions do not mention the notion of a male, believing passerby breaking prayers. In fact, the things that break prayers according to various traditions from the first century, namely dogs, donkeys, women, or menstruating women, were precisely things that the respective milieus circulating the traditions considered as transmitters of ritual impurity (Sadeghi, "Traveling Tradition Test," 218).

forms a barrier that blocks the contamination from radiating through to the other worshippers. (Indeed, the notion is attested in early Kūfa that a barrier could stop the invalidation occasioned by women and other prayer-breaking creatures passing by.) The contamination hypothesis also explains the curious sexual asymmetry: a woman's prayer is not invalidated by adjacency to a man because men do not radiate ritual impurity, and an adjacent woman does not disturb her prayer either because by virtue of being a woman she cannot be further contaminated. But that is not all: the contamination hypothesis explains aspects of the adjacency law that the purity-of-thought hypothesis does not. For example, it explains why invalidation follows even if the woman praying next to the man is someone to whom he is not sexually attracted, such as his grandmother, mother, sister, or daughter.[32]

In sum, although the adjacency law remained the same through the centuries, the meaning and significance attached to it underwent radical transformations a number of times. This underscores the stability of the laws compared to the meanings attached to them, a matter to be discussed further in Chapter 7.

By now it has become amply clear that when a law and a *ḥadīth* agree, one cannot automatically assume that the *ḥadīth* motivated the law. The question is raised: when is it plausible to assume that a law derives from a *ḥadīth*? A case can be made for instances where the concept shared by the *ḥadīth* and the law is idiosyncratic – that is, it is not widespread or is *a priori* improbable given the legal/cultural context. At first sight, the rule regarding a full row of women would appear to be a good candidate. This ruling is certainly anomalous within the Ḥanafī legal context, as it deviates from the formulation of the issue in terms of adjacency. Have we then come across a law based on *ḥadīth*? Alas, our hopes are dashed. The tradition exists also as a saying of Ibrāhīm, the forefather of the Ḥanafīs.[33] This law, therefore, is rooted in the Kūfan origins of the Ḥanafīs. It is possible that the poorly attested Prophetic version came later.

3.5. New Justifications

What is a jurist to do when the evidentiary carpet is pulled out from under a law? Is the law to be simply abandoned? If the general pattern of the

[32] The purity-of-thought hypothesis faced a number of problems that were noted by some jurists, as discussed on pages 59–60.
[33] See 'Abd al-Razzāq, *Muṣannaf*, 3:82, no. 4882.

dispensability and variability of legal reasons is any indication, the advice to the jurist must be obvious: rationales are easy to come by, so do not get rid of the law; just get a new rationale. Although arguing with the "keep them behind" line of argument was not abandoned, mounting difficulties gradually exposed its inadequacy, necessitating better rationales.

There are obligations and preconditions attaching to an act such as prayer that, if omitted, bring about the invalidation of that act. The Ḥanafīs call such an obligation a *farḍ*. In the eighth/fourteenth century, a major strain of Ḥanafī legal thought required that if omitting an obligation is to bring about invalidation, that obligation must be based on nearly certain (*qaṭʿī*) justifications.[34] If not based on nearly certain grounds, but rather on merely probable (*ẓannī*) grounds, then the precondition remains an obligation, but its omission does not bring about invalidity. This requirement spurred jurists to seek certain grounds for those laws they considered *farḍ*, until eventually, probably due to the failure of the endeavor, the certainty requirement was dropped by Ibn al-Humām in the ninth/fifteenth century.

Thus, in the eighth/fourteenth century, it occurred to al-Atrāzī (quoted by al-ʿAynī), al-Zaylaʿī, and al-Bābirtī that one might object to the adjacency law by pointing out that the "keep them behind" *ḥadīth* is of the so-called *āḥād* category, that is, it is of merely probable authenticity due to having only a few early transmitters. Its authenticity being uncertain, it does not entail invalidity in case of adjacency. They stated this potential objection and proceeded to rebut it in two distinct ways. One approach countered the potential objection by claiming that the *ḥadīth* is actually of the "well-attested" variety (*min al-mashāhīr*), which is a step above *āḥād* in the quality of its *isnāds*, although falling short of the certainty of "universally attested" (*mutawātir*) *ḥadīths* or of the Qur'ān. Indeed, al-Marghīnānī had described the Prophetic tradition as "well-attested," apparently in anticipation of the objection.[35] The other approach (e.g., Zayn al-Dīn Ibn Nujaym, and a statement [by an unnamed jurist?] quoted by al-ʿAynī; cf. Sirāj al-Dīn Ibn Nujaym) still insisted that an indubitable source be quoted, but relaxed the required degree of relevancy; it allowed that an obligation based on uncertain grounds can be lifted to the level of a *farḍ* if it receives loose, circumstantial corroboration from indubitable

[34] See the quotations from al-Atrāzī given by al-ʿAynī.

[35] In addition, apparently, to al-Marghīnānī, this was the approach of al-Atrāzī (quoted by al-ʿAynī), al-Zaylaʿī ("*naqūl innahu min al-mashāhīr fa-jāza al-ziyāda bih ʿalā al-kitāb*"), and al-Bābirtī.

sources, such as the Qur'ān. In this way, the adjacency requirement was said to be a *farḍ* thanks to the support it receives from Qur'ān 2.228: "Men have a degree of advantage above [women]."[36] As Zayn al-Dīn Ibn Nujaym said of the tradition, "even if it be *āḥād*, it clarifies the unclear (*mujmal*)" Qur'ānic passage just quoted.

A remarkable turn of events was about to ensue. The eighth/fourteenth century witnessed renewed interest among some Ḥanafī jurists in the quality of the traditions used in legal discussions. One sees the beginnings of this trend with the jurist al-Sarūjī, who was also a traditionist, in his commentary, *al-Ghāya*, on al-Marghīnānī's *al-Hidāya*, where he traced the traditions cited by the Ḥanafīs and described their *isnāds*.[37] This trend was greatly abetted by the impressive work of the *ḥadīth* scholar Jamāl al-Dīn al-Zaylaʿī, the namesake and student of al-Zaylaʿī the jurist. In his *Naṣb al-rāya*, Jamāl al-Dīn al-Zaylaʿī scrutinized the traditions in al-Marghīnānī's *al-Hidāya*, naming the sources in which they are found, commenting on their *isnāds*, and quoting traditions for both sides of an issue along with *isnād*-critical remarks. His compendium was a work of *ḥadīth*, not law; but it became an indispensable reference work for justification-oriented jurists, who further built on it. The efforts of these jurists culminated a century later in the outstanding *ḥadīth*-conscious legal works of al-ʿAynī and Ibn al-Humām.

Jamāl al-Dīn al-Zaylaʿī's comment on the "keep them behind" *ḥadīth* is quite interesting.[38] So far, the Ḥanafīs had considered the tradition to be a Prophetic *ḥadīth*,[39] and at least four of them considered it to have particularly well-corroborated chains of transmission. However, Jamāl al-Dīn al-Zaylaʿī points out that the tradition appears in collections of traditions only as a saying of the companion ʿAbd Allāh b. Masʿūd, not the Prophet.[40] He then quotes from al-Sarūjī's commentary on al-Marghīnānī,

[36] Qur'ān 2.228: "Women have rights similar to the rights against them according to what is just (*bi-al-maʿrūf*); men have a degree of precedence over them." This clause describes divorce, particularly the procedures of revocation (*rajʿa*), coming immediately after "their husbands have the *better right* (*aḥaqq*) to take them back." Jurists have cited the "precedence" clause as a general principle more often than the "equality" clause that it amends. The question at hand is an example of that tendency.

[37] I have not seen this book. For this characterization, I am relying on the description of the *Ghāya* in Ibn Quṭlūbughā (d. 879/1475), *Munyat al-Almaʿī* (Karachi, 1412), 9, and on the actual quotation from the *Ghāya* given by Jamāl al-Dīn al-Zaylaʿī.

[38] Jamāl al-Dīn al-Zaylaʿī, *Naṣb al-rāya* (Cairo: Dār al-Ḥadīth, 1415), 2:45.

[39] The following scholars did so explicitly: al-Sarakhsī, al-Kāsānī, al-Marghīnānī, al-Mawṣilī, ʿUbayd Allāh b. Masʿūd, al-Zaylaʿī, al-Atrāzī (quoted by al-ʿAynī), and al-Bābirtī.

[40] For the Ibn Masʿūd tradition, see ʿAbd al-Razzāq, *Muṣannaf*, 3:149; Ibn Khuzayma, *Ṣaḥīḥ*, 3:99; al-Ṭabarānī, *al-Muʿjam al-kabīr*, 9:295–6. Al-Suyūṭī says that the tradition

entitled *al-Ghāya*, a passage that captures the dramatic clash of a jurist's easy-going attitude toward the *Ḥadīth* with the more exacting ways of a *ḥadīth* expert:

My teacher (*shaykhunā*) al-Ṣadr Sulaymān[41] used to relate it as: "Wine is the root of abominations (*umm al-khabā'ith*), and women are the snares of the devil. Keep them behind in what God has kept them behind." He referenced the tradition to the *ḥadīth* compilation (*musnad*) of Razīn.[42] This ignoramus also mentioned that it is in the *Dalā'il al-nabuwwa* of al-Bayhaqī. I examined it carefully, but did not find the saying in it either as a Prophetic or as a non-Prophetic tradition. What I found in it as a Prophetic saying was: "Wine is the epitome of sin (*jimā'* or *jammā' al-ithm*). Women are the snares of the devil. And youth is a form of madness." Nowhere in it can be found: "Keep them behind in what God has kept them behind"!

Nor indeed is the tradition ascribed to the Prophet in Sunnī or Imāmī compilations of *ḥadīth*.[43] It is related as a *ḥadīth* only in legal handbooks, mainly Ḥanafī, Imāmī, and some Ḥanbalī ones, and always without an *isnād*. For centuries, jurists had been quoting a *ḥadīth* that was nowhere else ascribed to the Prophet, not to mention praising *isnāds* that simply did not exist. Nor was this tradition an isolated case; Jamāl al-Dīn al-Zayla'ī identifies quite a few more; and in the introduction to his own book, al-'Aynī laments his colleagues' use of unattested reports. All of this not only underscores the historical insulation of legal studies from

is also quoted in the *Musnads* of Sa'īd b. Manṣūr and Musaddad; see al-Suyūṭī, *al-Durr al-manthūr* (Beirut: Dār al-Ma'rifa), 1:258.

41 He is possibly Sulaymān b. Abī al-'Izz (d. 677/1278, a Ḥanafī judge in Egypt and Syria) known as Ṣadr al-Dīn (see Kaḥḥāla, *Mu'jam*, 4:269). The time and place fit: at his death, al-Sarūjī, who moved from Syria to Egypt and served as judge, would have been forty years old. On al-Sarūjī, see Kaḥḥāla, *Mu'jam*, 1:140; al-Ziriklī, *al-A'lām*, 5th ed. (Beirut: Dār al-'Ilm li-al-Malāyīn, 1980), 1:86.

42 Al-Bulbulānī (quoted by Ibn 'Ābidīn) claims that the *ḥadīth* was traced to the book of Razīn b. Mu'āwiya al-'Abdarī (d. 535/1140, a traditionist from Spain who lived in Mecca) "that covers the traditions in the Six Books." The title of that book is *al-Tajrīd* (Kaḥḥāla, *Mu'jam*, 4:155). The tradition is also quoted in Ibn al-Athīr, *Jāmi' al-uṣūl* (Beirut: Dār al-Kutub al-'Ilmiyya, 1418), 11:14, no. 8480, on the authority of the Companion Ḥudhayfa b. al-Yamān, though without an *isnād*, as is typical of this compilation. The text runs: "I heard the Messenger of God say in his sermon: 'Wine is the root of sins. Women are the snares of the devil. And the love of the world is the source of every wrongdoing.' He said: And I heard him say: 'Keep women behind in what God has kept them behind.' " The editor claims, "This is among the additions of Razīn," which fits in al-Bulbulānī's claim. However, al-'Ajlūnī quotes al-Zarkashī as denying that it is found in Razīn's book. See al-'Ajlūnī, *Kashf al-Khafā'* (Beirut: Dār al-Kutub al-'Ilmiyya, 1408/1988), 1:67, no. 1.

43 For the sole possible exception, see the previous footnote. I have not checked Ibāḍī or Zaydī compilations.

ḥadīth studies, but also illustrates just how nonchalantly jurists used to treat the *Ḥadīth*.

Following Jamāl al-Dīn al-Zayla'ī as well as al-'Aynī, Ibn al-Humām avers that the tradition cannot be a valid Prophetic report, "let alone be well attested." He and al-'Aynī point out that with this fact the above two arguments for the adjacency law collapse. His comments are closely echoed by Sirāj al-Dīn Ibn Nujaym.

The "keep them behind" argument thus lost its dominance, but it was not completely supplanted. For example, Mullā Khusraw would repeat the old argument complete with the assumption that the tradition is Prophetic. More astonishing and idiosyncratic is the argument Ibn 'Ābidīn quotes, in seeming approval, in his *Minḥat al-khāliq* from a certain al-Bulbulānī in defense of the Prophetic origin of the tradition. The latter writes that even though *ḥadīth* experts consider it to have an incomplete *isnād* (*munqaṭi'*), the great Ḥanafī scholars have called it "well-attested," and that alone suffices to establish the tradition as a valid Prophetic *ḥadīth*. This is the highest possible expression of confidence in the authority of the school jurists, comparable to Zayn al-Dīn Ibn Nujaym's hard line about deviation from the original school doctrines, a view that I will discuss in Chapter 5.[44] Another approach would be to acknowledge the tradition as non-Prophetic and continue to maintain that it establishes a *farḍ*. Al-Ṭaḥṭāwī did so in his *Ḥāshiyat al-Ṭaḥṭāwī 'alā al-Durr al-mukhtār*, but most jurists did not.[45]

Let us now move to the first alternative justification. There was a different tradition that the Ḥanafīs could put to good use, and this time it *was* a Prophetic report. The Prophet, when praying with Anas, an orphan, and a woman, had placed the woman in the back in a row of her own. Now, on the face of it, there is nothing in the tradition to indicate that it would have been forbidden for the woman to pray next to a man. But that consequence was inferred from the tradition in two distinct ways.

The first Ḥanafī to use this tradition was apparently al-Manbijī, a seventh/thirteenth-century scholar who was more interested in *ḥadīth*s than law proper and who consequently paid some attention to *isnād*s.[46] This explains why he does not even bother to mention the "keep them behind"

[44] See Chapter 5, page 125.

[45] Thus, al-'Aynī and Ibn al-Humām, along with most other Ḥanafīs, do not allow that a Companion tradition may establish a *farḍ*.

[46] For more on this *ḥadīth*-oriented scholar, see Chapter 4, pages 81–2; Chapter 6, page 133.

tradition. Instead, al-Manbijī quotes the *ḥadīth* (found in al-Bukhārī): "Pray as you see me pray!" He concludes that for the Prophet to pray a certain way is tantamount to a command, thus establishing a *farḍ*, that is, a requirement that causes invalidity if it is omitted. This is a peculiar approach, as other Ḥanafīs did not hold that a one-time act of the Prophet establishes an obligation; it would have to be established that he never did it any other way. At any rate, this argument was not used by any other scholar I know of.

Ibn al-Humām exploits the Anas *ḥadīth* in another way. He says it is known to be forbidden for a person to pray in a row all by himself or herself. Therefore, had it been permissible for a male and female to pray side by side, the Prophet would certainly have asked her to join the row of males. That the Prophet did not make this request proves the unlawfulness of adjacency. Needless to say, there are problems with this argument. It does not show why invalidation is brought upon the male but not the female. Moreover, the premise of the argument is that the Prophet would not have tacitly approved a forbidden thing; yet the argument assumes that the Prophet tacitly approved the woman's forbidden act of praying in a row of her own. It would be more natural to infer from the tradition that it is not necessarily forbidden for a woman to pray in a row by herself.[47]

The second alternative justification, given by al-Zayla'ī, al-Bābirtī, and Ibn al-Humām, has more substance and is more complex. It is based on an analogy with the case of the invalidity of female imāms for men, which is taken to be well established. That a woman cannot lead men in prayer, the argument goes, is established by *ijmā'*, that is, consensus, which counts as certain proof in Sunnī legal theory. One can determine the effective cause (*'illa*) behind that prohibition by a process of elimination of potential candidate reasons for the prohibition. Four candidates exhaust the list of potentially relevant factors: (1) some kind of deficiency in women, (2) the unacceptability of women leading prayers in general, (3) the nonfulfillment of a precondition for the validity (of the prayer), and (4) their not taking up the required position (*tark farḍ al-maqām*). The first is ruled out because it is valid to "follow" a wicked person (*al-fāsiq*) or a slave as the prayer leader (so, having a deficiency *per se* does not cause disqualification), the second because a woman may lead women, and the third because the analysis proceeds on the assumption

[47] Incidentally, Ibn al-Humām accepted *āḥād* Prophetic reports for establishing a *farḍ* in matters pertaining to group prayers: *furūḍ al-jamā'a yaṣiḥḥu ithbātuhā bi-al-āḥād li-anna aṣlahā bihā.*

that all the known preconditions are met (*al-mafrūḍ ḥuṣūl al-shurūṭ*), leaving only the fourth possibility.

I will leave aside the fact that this argument, too, fails to explain the sexual asymmetry in invalidation and will focus instead on a methodologically interesting problem. As elsewhere, the use of analogy here introduces an element of indeterminacy, particularly in the determination of the effective cause (*'illa*). The argument, being based on a process of eliminating every candidate except one, depends crucially on the list of four candidate causes being exhaustive. However, other candidate causes can in fact be imagined, some of which cannot easily be dismissed. For example, one may consider that the effective cause of forbidding women to lead men is that such an arrangement puts women in a position of authority over men. Alternatively, one may postulate the effective cause to be the excessive conspicuousness of a female leader, who would have to stand by herself in front of the others. Alternatively, one may posit that there *is* no effective cause for this particular prohibition. (Not every law need have a reason, especially when it comes to rituals of worship.) For the analogy to collapse, it is not necessary that one of these possibilities be proven; it suffices only that one candidate evade disproof, because the argument rests on the disproof of all candidates except one. Such disproof will not be easy to come by, that is, not in the context of premodern juristic methods and standards. For excessive conspicuousness is a reason that the Ḥanafīs themselves offer for forbidding women to lead women, while the banning of women from positions of authority over men constitutes a Mālikī and Shāfi'ī justification for forbidding women to lead men.

3.6. Adjacency: "Willing Out" Female Worshippers

The next topic provides another fascinating illustration of the movement from a particular legal effect as the starting point to general legal principles. While one might suppose that particular statements derive from general ones, in reality reasoning often proceeds in the opposite direction: general principles are adjusted to ensure the needed legal effects; thus, it is the legal effects that have primacy.

We saw that Ḥanafīs agree that a man's prayer remains valid as long as the woman next to him or in front of him is not performing the same communal prayer as him. But the result is different if the woman shares the same prayer; in that case, the prayers of the men next to and behind her are voided, but not hers.

Now, the consequences of adjacency may be a tolerable inconvenience if they affect only a man or two. But what if the woman voids the leader's prayer? A general principle of Ḥanafī law is that the worshippers' prayers are valid *only* if the leader's prayer is valid. Are the whole congregation's prayers then voided if a woman joins the prayer, standing next to the leader after the prayer has started? That would indeed seem to be the consequence of the general Ḥanafī principles. But as might be expected, the prospect that a single woman could so easily ruin everybody's prayer was deemed a problem. The Ḥanafī solution prevents that possibility with an ad hoc stipulation: the woman has not actually joined the prayer unless the leader has "resolved" to lead her. That is, her resolution to join the group prayer can be preempted by the imām's resolution to exclude her from it. She will be "resolving" to join a prayer that she cannot legally be a part of, rendering her prayer invalid from the outset, even if she might go through the motions. Because she is not really partaking in the group prayer, the prayers of the leader and the congregation are saved. This turns the adjacency law on its head: now, the woman's prayer is voided but not the man's.

The solution has, however, the further consequence that women's prayer can be invalidated even if they pray in their mandated position behind the men. It creates, depending on whether the imām includes women in his resolution or not, an all-or-nothing situation where either every woman's prayer is valid regardless of whether she is adjacent or not or it is invalid regardless. This could mean the complete exclusion of women from the group prayers. Some jurists felt uncomfortable with this far-reaching consequence of the "willing out" principle, so they introduced an ad hoc amendment: the imām's decision to "will in" women is necessary for the validity of a woman's prayer if she is adjacent to a man, but not if she is not. So, women who pray behind the men (or in the same row with a barrier or gap) have nothing to worry about. Other jurists did not accept this, holding to the "all or nothing" solution.[48] There were also those (the narrow majority according to Ibn al-Humām, but the minority according to Ibn Nujaym) who exempted the Friday and the two *Īd* prayers, not requiring the act of "willing in" for the validity of the women's prayers.[49] Al-Sarakhsī quotes their viewpoint as follows:

> [They argue:] "Here, the principle of necessity is on her side. For she cannot pray the *'Īd* and Friday prayers on her own, and may not find another imām to

[48] The two views are reported by al-Marghīnānī and later scholars.

[49] Among others, Qāḍī Khān and the Indian scholars who wrote *al-Fatāwā al-'Ālamgīrīya* supported this position.

'follow' ... so we rule her 'following' of him to be sound in order to ward off harm from her, unlike in other prayers."[50]

The Ḥanafīs accepted the "willing out" solution with the exception, as al-Ṭaḥāwī and others point out, of Zufar.[51] On the other hand, the Shāfiʿīs and Mālikīs did not accept the principle that the leader may "will out" a female worshipper.[52] That is what one would expect from them. Since for them a woman did not void anyone's prayer,[53] they had no use for the remedy provided by the principle. Moreover, the Ḥanafīs did not apply the "willing out" principle to funeral prayers.[54] So, again, the principle is applied only where adjacency would have annoying consequences, confirming that it was generated in order to avoid those consequences.

This case is an eloquent example of how "higher level," more general, legal principles can be repeatedly adjusted to achieve intended outcomes at the "lower level" of specific, concrete legal effects. This scheme is the reverse of the idea that, historically, specific legal effects flowed from more general principles. In this case, one sees that a specific outcome is the starting point, namely, the inability of a woman to void a congregation's prayers. This outcome is the opposite of what would follow from previously accepted general principles, which are: (1) the adjacency rule and (2) the congregation's dependence on the leader's prayer. To avert the troubling consequence of combining these principles, an entirely new general precept is introduced; namely, that the leader can "will out" a woman if he so wishes. This amendment is ad hoc in the sense that its only function is to achieve this specific outcome. Thus, here, the movement is from the (desired) legal effect to the general legal principles rather than the other way around.

It comes across very clearly that pragmatic considerations and intuitive notions of what would be sensible and reasonable guided the deliberations of jurists, rather than rigid adherence to either the received legal principles or to some hermeneutical algorithm that would mechanically

[50] Al-Zaylaʿī and Ibn Nujaym explain the necessity quite differently: because of the crowdedness and lack of space, a woman may need to stand next to the imām. This appears to involve a misunderstanding and misstatement, as the matter in question is not specifically about a situation where there is adjacency. Al-Sarakhsī's explanation is far more coherent.

[51] Al-Ṭaḥāwī writes: "Concerning a woman joining men's prayer in the absence of an intention that she be led: our colleagues except Zufar hold that her participation is not valid unless he "resolves" [to include] her. Mālik, Zufar, and al-Shāfiʿī held that it is valid" (al-Ṭaḥāwī, *Mukhtaṣar ikhtilāf*, 266, no. 217).

[52] Al-Ṭaḥāwī, *Mukhtaṣar ikhtilāf*, 266, no. 217.

[53] Al-Ṭaḥāwī, *Mukhtaṣar ikhtilāf*, 266, no. 216.

[54] Abū al-Suʿūd cites a consensus on this point.

generate law once fed the relevant Qur'ānic and *ḥadīth* texts and the legal precedents of the school eponym.

3.7. Conclusion

This examination of the reasons given for the adjacency law has shown that they did not determine the law. The interpretations jurists put on the texts were not the only possible ones. Hermeneutic flexibility was on full display. The starting point in the process of interpretation was the canon-blind law. In keeping with legal inertia, the canon-blind law was usually the same as the received law. That there was a fair amount of legal inertia is supported by the fact that the adjacency law was maintained and defended even though the concerns that originally gave rise to it had long disappeared and even though some consequences of the law turned out to be inconvenient. These unacceptable consequences were dealt with by introducing new legal principles to amend the adjacency law rather than by giving it up.

The secondary status of the legal reasons compared to the adjacency law is confirmed not only by the fact that they did not determine the law, but also by their relative instability: while the adjacency law endured, the reasons given for it were variable and fluid, and they postdated the law. Moreover, when a reason was disqualified, as happened to the "keep them behind" report, this did not bring about the collapse of the law that ostensibly rested on it; rather, new reasons were devised. The implications of this case study will be further explored in the last three chapters.

Excursus: Women Leading Men

Abū Ḥanīfa and his disciples do not say whether a woman may lead a man in prayer.[55] They would clearly invalidate the man's prayer in such a

[55] All the references in Chapter 3, page 50, footnote 1, are relevant to the present section. Here are passages that directly refer to women leading men: al-Ṭaḥāwī, *Mukhtaṣar al-Ṭaḥāwī*, 33; al-Qudūrī, *Mukhtaṣar*, 29; Qāḍī Khān, *Fatāwā Qāḍī Khān*, printed in the margin of al-Shaykh Niẓām et al., *al-Fatāwā al-ʿĀlamgīrīya*, 1:88; al-Marghīnānī, *Hidāya*, 1:146–7; al-Mawṣilī, *Ikhtiyār*, 1:58; al-Nasafī, *Kanz al-daqā'iq*, see the inset text included with al-Zaylaʿī, *Tabyīn al-ḥaqā'iq*; ʿUthmān b. ʿAlī al-Zaylaʿī, *Tabyīn al-ḥaqā'iq*, 1:352, 357; al-Bābirtī, *ʿInāya*, printed with Ibn al-Humām, *Fatḥ al-qadīr*, 1:357, 362; al-ʿAynī, *Bināya*, 2:342–4; Ibn al-Humām, *Fatḥ al-qadīr*, 1:357, 360; Mullā Khusraw, *Durar al-ḥukkām*, 1:109; al-Ḥalabī, *Multaqā al-abḥur*, 1:97; al-Ḥalabī, *Ghunyat al-mutamallī*, 516; Zayn al-Dīn Ibn Nujaym, *al-Baḥr al-rā'iq*, 1:628–9; al-Timurtāshī, *Tanwīr al-abṣār wa-jāmiʿ al-biḥār*, 15; Sirāj al-Dīn Ibn Nujaym, *al-Nahr al-fā'iq*, 1:251;

situation if it involved adjacency. What if there were no adjacency in the technical sense, for example, if a partition or gap separated the female leader from men? They do not say; however, the law was soon elaborated upon more precisely, and that possibility was ruled out. Al-Ṭaḥāwī, like the Ḥanafīs after him, holds: "The prayer of a man who takes a woman or a hermaphrodite as his imām is not valid" (*Mukhtaṣar*). Most jurists framed the rationale against women leading men in terms of their mandated position behind men, that is, through the "keep them behind" rationale (Section 3.3), for example, Abū al-Layth al-Samarqandī, al-Mawṣilī, al-Zayla'ī, al-Bābirtī, al-Marghīnānī, Ibn Nujaym, Mullā Khusraw, and al-Shurunbulālī. They did not address the partition issue. In addition to ignoring the partition question, this rationale suffers from the same problem that plagued the adjacency law, namely, the difficulty of establishing a *farḍ*. Eventually, however, some jurists would claim *ijmā'* (consensus) for the law (e.g., al-Zayla'ī, al-Bābirtī, Ibn al-Humām, and Sirāj al-Dīn), thereby placing the law on a relatively surer footing.

al-Shurunbulālī, *Nūr al-īḍāḥ*, printed with al-Shurunbulālī, *Marāqī al-falāḥ sharḥ Nūr al-īḍāḥ*, 290; al-Shurunbulālī, *Marāqī al-falāḥ sharḥ Nūr al-īḍāḥ*, 290; al-Ḥaṣkafī, *al-Durr al-mukhtār*, 1:101; al-Shaykh Niẓām et. al., *al-Fatāwā al-'Ālamgīrīya*, 1:85; Abū al-Su'ūd, *Fatḥ al-mu'īn*, 1:215; al-Ṭaḥṭāwī, *Ḥāshiyat al-Ṭaḥṭāwī 'alā al-Durr al-mukhtār*, 1:249; al-Ṭaḥṭāwī, *Ḥāshiyat al-Ṭaḥṭāwī 'alā Marāqī al-falāḥ*, 166; Ibn 'Ābidīn, *[Ḥāshiyat] Radd al-muḥtār*, 1:609, 621–2; Ibn 'Ābidīn, *Minḥat al-Khāliq*, printed with Ibn Nujaym, *al-Baḥr al-rā'iq*, 1:381; al-Afghānī, *Kashf al-ḥaqā'iq*, 1:55.

4

Women Praying with Women

4.1. The Formative Background

Opposition to women leading other women in prayers of any kind – obligatory or supererogatory – originated in Medina sometime in the first century AH.[1] On the other hand, the opposite view that allowed

[1] This chapter is based on the following Ḥanafī texts – and the quotations in the chapter are from these sources unless specified otherwise: Abū Yūsuf, *Kitāb al-Āthār*, 41, no. 212; al-Shaybānī, *Kitāb al-Āthār*, published as Abū Ḥanīfa, *Kitāb al-Āthār* (al-Shaybānī's recension), 208, no. 217; al-Ṭaḥāwī, *Mukhtaṣar al-Ṭaḥāwī*, 33; al-Ṭaḥāwī, *Mukhtaṣar ikhtilāf al-'ulamā'*, in al-Jaṣṣāṣ, *Mukhtaṣar ikhtilāf al-'ulamā'*, 1:305, no. 263; al-Qudūrī, *Mukhtaṣar*, 29; al-Sarakhsī, *Kitāb al-Mabsūṭ*, 1:133, 187; 'Alā' al-Dīn Samarqandī, *Tuḥfat al-fuqahā'*, 1:229; al-Kāsānī, *Badā'i' al-ṣanā'i'*, 1:141, 157; al-Marghīnānī, *al-Hidāya*, 1:145–6; al-Mawṣilī, *al-Ikhtiyār*, 1:59; 'Alī b. Zakarīyā al-Manbijī, *al-Lubāb fī al-jam' bayna al-sunna wa-al-kitāb*, 1:278–9; al-Nasafī, *Kanz al-daqā'iq*, see the inset text included with al-Zayla'ī, *Tabyīn al-ḥaqā'iq;* 'Uthmān b. 'Alī al-Zayla'ī, *Tabyīn al-ḥaqā'iq*, 1:348–9; al-Kākī, *Mi'rāj al-dirāya fī al-sharḥ al-Hidāya* (Princeton: Islamic Manuscripts), ms. Garrett no. 97Y; al-Bābirtī, *Sharḥ al-'Ināya*, printed with Ibn al-Humām, *Sharḥ Fatḥ al-qadīr*, 1:352–4; Badr al-Dīn al-'Aynī, *al-Bināya*, 2:395–401; Ibn al-Humām, *Sharḥ Fatḥ al-qadīr*, 1:352–4, 356; Mullā Khusraw, *Durar al-ḥukkām*, 1:107; al-Ḥalabī, *Multaqā al-abḥur*, 1:94–5; al-Ḥalabī, *Ghunyat al-mutamallī*, 519; Zayn al-Dīn Ibn Nujaym, *al-Baḥr al-rā'iq*, 1:614–16; al-Timurtāshī, *Tanwīr al-abṣār*, 15; Sirāj al-Dīn Ibn Nujaym, *al-Nahr al-fā'iq*, 1:244–5; Ibn al-'Imād, *Hadīyat*, printed with al-Nābulusī, *Nihāyat al-murād fī sharḥ Hadīyat Ibn al-'Imād*, 602; al-Shurunbulālī, *Nūr al-īḍāḥ*, printed with al-Shurunbulālī, *Marāqī al-falāḥ sharḥ Nūr al-īḍāḥ*, 302–3; al-Shurunbulālī, *Marāqī al-falāḥ sharḥ Nūr al-īḍāḥ*, 302–3; al-Shurunbulālī, *Ḥāshiya* [on Mullā Khusraw's *Durar al-ḥukkām*], printed with Mullā Khusraw, *Durar al-ḥukkām*, 1:107; al-Ḥaṣkafī, *al-Durr al-mukhtār*, 1:99; al-Shaykh Niẓām et al., *al-Fatāwā al-'Ālamgīrīya*, 1:85; 'Abd al-Ghanī al-Nābulusī, *Nihāyat al-murād*, 602–4; Abū al-Su'ūd, *Fatḥ al-mu'īn*, 1:208–9; al-Ṭaḥṭāwī, *Ḥāshiyat al-Ṭaḥṭāwī 'alā al-Durr al-mukhtār*, 1:245; al-Ṭaḥṭāwī, *Ḥāshiyat al-Ṭaḥṭāwī 'alā Marāqī al-falāḥ sharḥ Nūr al-īḍāḥ*, 166; Ibn 'Ābidīn, *[Ḥāshiyat] Radd*

such prayers was widespread, being attested in Baṣra, Kūfa, Mecca, and possibly Medina.[2] This permissive position found expression, for example, in reports that the female Companions 'Ā'isha, Umm Salama, and Umm Waraqa had led prayers. Iraq also gave rise to an intermediate position, one allowing group prayers of women in the case of supererogatory prayers, for example, those held in the month of Ramaḍān, but presumably not in the case of the daily obligatory prayers. This seems to have been the view of the first-century Kūfan jurist Ibrāhīm al-Nakha'ī. Although most of Ibrāhīm's positions came to enjoy the support of Abū Ḥanīfa, this one did not. The position that gained Abū Ḥanīfa's support and consequently became a part of Ḥanafī law was one of opposition to both obligatory and supererogatory female group prayers. In this, the Ḥanafīs agreed with the Mālikīs, who simply took over the old hardline, Medinan position, but disagreed with the Shāfi'īs, who considered female group prayers desirable. Postformative Ḥanafīs faced the problem of justifying their position in the face of the considerable number of early Companion reports in favor of female leadership. They did so by positing that the permissibility of female group prayers had been abrogated. Moreover, the Ḥanafī position shifted gradually from disapproval to outright prohibition. Two Ḥanafī scholars, however, rejected the school consensus, namely al-'Aynī and al-Laknawī, while Ibn al-Humām expressed reservations about it.

I argue that in mainstream Ḥanafī jurisprudence the reading of the textual evidence about the Prophet's Companions did not affect the laws. The reasons jurists gave for the school's positions were after-the-fact justifications and did not determine the laws. I also examine the methods used to reconcile Ḥanafī laws with binding texts.

4.2. Formation of the Standard Position: Abū Ḥanīfa to al-Marghīnānī

Al-Shaybānī quotes a tradition through Abū Ḥanīfa—Ḥammād—Ibrāhīm—'Ā'isha that "she used to lead women in the month of Ramaḍān, standing in their midst."[3] Abū Yūsuf relates through the same *isnād* that

al-muḥtār, 1:609–10; Ibn 'Ābidīn, *Minḥat al-Khāliq*, printed with Ibn Nujaym, *al-Baḥr al-rā'iq*, 1:372–4; 'Abd al-Ḥakīm al-Afghānī, *Kashf al-ḥaqā'iq*, 1:53–4; al-Laknawī, *Tuḥfat al-nubalā' fī jamā'at al-nisā'* ('Ammān: Mu'assasat al-Risāla, 2002).

[2] Sadeghi, "The Traveling Tradition Test," 227–37.

[3] Al-Shaybānī, *Āthār*, 208, no. 217. The tradition does not appear in al-Khwārazmī, *Jāmi' al-masānīd* (Ḥaydarābād: Majlis Dā'irat al-Ma'ārif, 1332).

'Ā'isha "used to lead women for supererogatory prayers (*taṭawwu'an*), standing in the middle of the row."[4] Al-Shaybānī adds, "We would not like (*lā yu'jibunā*) a woman to lead, but if she does, she must stand in the middle of the row with the women, as 'Ā'isha did. That is the position of Abū Ḥanīfa." (The mention of supererogatory prayers appears in only one of the transmissions from Abū Ḥanīfa.) Remarkably, al-Shaybānī and Abū Ḥanīfa report a practice of 'Ā'isha and then unceremoniously rule against it.

Al-Ṭaḥāwī adds that it is better (*afḍal*) for women to perform individual prayers than group prayers in which a woman leads. But if they do pray in the latter manner, then the leader must stand in the middle of the row.[5] The use of the word "better" (*afḍal*) in legal contexts usually implies the permissibility of the less preferred act. Al-Ṭaḥāwī, therefore, rules for permissibility. Moreover, he does not speak of undesirability. There is thus a verbal difference between him and Abū Ḥanīfa and al-Shaybānī. The latter two went against the tradition they had quoted. A century after them, however, al-Ṭaḥāwī adopts a position that is not one of verbal opposition to the *ḥadīth*, but that nevertheless includes a nod to Abū Ḥanīfa's unfavorable attitude toward the prayers – a verbal compromise, in other words. In this, he apparently differed from other Ḥanafīs, who maintained the negative language of Abū Ḥanīfa. He reports that his Ḥanafī colleagues "dislike it" outright, but also "hold that if she leads them, she must stand in the middle of the row."[6] This is what one may call the classical Ḥanafī position. A century later, al-Qudūrī states it as follows: "It is undesirable (*yukrahu*) for women to pray together without men (*waḥdahunna jamā'atan*). If they do so, then the imām stands in their midst."

With al-Sarakhsī, one begins to see some hints of justification. He explains that women are not to perform the calls to prayer, the *adhān* and *iqāma*. The first reason he gives for this touches on women's group prayer:

> These two are *sunnas*[7] of *group* prayers, and women's group prayers were abrogated because of the misdeeds (or temptation) their gatherings entail.[8] Thus, if

[4] Abū Yūsuf, *Āthār*, 41, no. 212.

[5] Al-Ṭaḥāwī, *Mukhtaṣar*, 33.

[6] Al-Ṭaḥāwī, *Mukhtaṣar Ikhtilāf*, 305, no. 263.

[7] This term refers to required elements of prayer of which the omission does not necessarily invalidate the prayer, in contrast to *rukn*.

[8] The text runs *wa-jamā'atuhunna mansūkha li-mā fī ijtimā'ihinna min al-fitna*. Unfortunately, al-Sarakhsī does not clarify the nature of the misdeeds referred to as *fitna*.

they perform a group prayer, then they pray without the *adhān* and *iqāma*, due to the *ḥadīth* of Rayṭa,[9] who said, "We were a group of women in the presence of ʿĀʾisha. She led us in prayer, standing in our midst [i.e., within the row of worshippers]. She prayed without the *adhān* or *iqāma*."[10]

He adds that if women do perform group prayers with the *adhān* and *iqāma*, then their prayer is nonetheless valid. He touches on women's group prayers also in a different context. After having just described the manner of prayers of persons without enough clothes to cover themselves, he adds:

The case [of naked people], with regard to location, is like the case of women's prayer. It is better that women pray individually. If, however, they pray as a group, their imām must stand in their midst. But if the imām stands in front of them, that is permissible. The same is the case with naked people.

The comparison of women to naked people is of interest. Al-Sarakhsī's discussion of naked people is concerned with minimizing exposure. For example, the imām stands within the row rather than in the front so that the glances of others may not fall on his nakedness. Implicitly, therefore, that is also the rationale behind the similar rules for women. Preferably, women must isolate themselves in prayer, even from other women, notwithstanding their being covered from head to toe as is normally required of free women in prayer even in the absence of men.

A century later, al-Kāsānī and al-Marghīnānī restate the classical position and go a step further. Unlike al-Sarakhsī, who by means of the comparison to naked people merely hinted at the rationale behind the female imām's placing, al-Kāsānī and al-Marghīnānī make the rationale explicit. After mentioning that ʿĀʾisha and Umm Salama had stood within the row, al-Kāsānī adds: "The principle governing women is that they be covered, and they are better covered this way." Al-Marghīnānī reasons similarly.

A *ḥadīth* disseminated by al-Wāziʿ b. Nāfiʿ, a transmitter thought to be unreliable, in the Jazīra in the second/eighth century states that there is no good in the group prayers of women, because when they get together they "talk and talk." For this tradition, see Sadeghi, "Traveling Tradition Test," 232–4. There is nothing to indicate that this is what al-Sarakhsī had in mind, but the tradition does raise the possibility that the misdeeds referred to as *fitna* in this context may go beyond sexual temptation.

[9] Read thus for Rābiṭa.

[10] Al-Sarakhsī, *Mabsūṭ*, 1:133. The second reason he gives is that "the muezzin exposes himself by climbing to the highest point and raises his voice for the *adhān*, while women are barred from that due to fear of temptation (*al-fitna*)." The reason is not conclusive. It may be noted that this reason addresses the *adhān*, not the *iqāma*. Besides, it is not required that the muezzin be one of the group or of the same gender. (I owe these points to Hossein Modarressi.)

While al-Kāsānī supports the standard, disapproving position, he also highlights the permissibility. He states plainly, "Women may pray in a group, so it would be permissible if a woman were to lead the prayer." This affirmation is significant in light of the eventual Ḥanafī shift toward prohibition.

Interestingly, aside from al-Sarakhsī's mention of abrogation, jurists so far have not spelled out a canon-based justification of the law. They certainly have not dealt at any length with the contrary evidence of the canon. Al-Kāsānī and al-Marghīnānī are the first to take up this task. And a challenging task it is, considering that the law goes back to a decision of Abū Ḥanīfa that he frankly acknowledged as a departure from 'Ā'isha's practice, which presumably reflected a Prophetic norm.

As both al-Kāsānī and al-Marghīnānī point out, the Shāfi'īs consider such prayers desirable. Al-Kāsānī writes: "Some *ḥadīths* are related about it [in support of female group prayers], but they had to do with the beginnings of Islam [i.e., the beginning of the Prophet's mission] and were abrogated thereafter." He provides no evidence for this assertion from the canon, as indeed there is none. Al-Marghīnānī makes a similar argument, but his wording betrays its speculative character: "['Ā'isha's] performance of group prayers is interpreted (*ḥumila*) to pertain to the beginning of Islam."

We see that an ad hoc appeal to abrogation is used to protect the school's doctrine from falsification by contrary evidence. With all evidence for female group prayers or prayer leadership thus disqualified, the sting is taken out of the Shāfi'ī argument for desirability. But, needless to say, to neutralize the Shāfi'ī proof of desirability is not to prove undesirability. To produce such proof, the best al-Marghīnānī can do is to say that female group prayer "entails the commission of a forbidden thing, namely the imām's standing in the midst of the row." Should anyone raise the objection that 'Ā'isha and others stood within the row, al-Marghīnānī would surely remind them that the practice was abrogated, as would later commentators. But, again, al-Marghīnānī cannot produce evidence for abrogation. His argument may harmonize the law with the canon, but it does not show that the Ḥanafī interpretation is better than the alternative.

Clearly, al-Marghīnānī starts with the goal of supporting the canon-blind law, to wit, forbidding female group prayers and leadership, and then makes as many adjustments as needed in the system to preserve that "outcome." In particular, the reports about the Companions did not fit Ḥanafī law, so they had to be explained away by appeal to abrogation. In this case, the antecedence of the law to the reason given for it involves a time gap of more than two centuries.

4.3. Justifying the Standard Position: Al-Marghīnānī to al-Bābirtī

Al-Sarakhsī's, al-Marghīnānī's, and al-Kāsānī's presumption of abrogation became the standard Ḥanafī position. But a justification for it from the canon was still lacking. In the seventh/thirteenth and eighth/fourteenth centuries, the scholars al-Manbijī, al-Kākī, al-Atrāzī, and al-Zayla'ī rose to the challenge by attempting to find indirect evidence against female group prayers from the Qur'ān and the *Ḥadīth*.

Al-Manbijī's treatment in his book, *al-Lubāb*, is the earliest and therefore the least sophisticated attempt at solving this problem. He cites a *ḥadīth* that I will soon discuss under al-Zayla'ī. It basically states that it is better for a woman to pray in her room, or home, than elsewhere. He also cites Qur'ān 33.33, which asks the Prophet's wives to stay home, taking the injunction to apply to all women and saying that it is not compatible with women going out to group prayers. He appears to equate women-only group prayers with leaving home, a problematic assumption that would not be held by later writers, except al-Atrāzī.

More interesting is his treatment of the *ḥadīth* about how the Prophet appointed a woman, Umm Waraqa, to lead the prayers of her household, even assigning a muezzin for her. He says: "In its *isnād* is found [al-Walīd b.] 'Abd Allāh b. Jumay' al-Zuhrī. Although Muslim has quoted his traditions, some have expressed reservations about his reliability (*fīhi maqāl*). However, if the tradition is sound, then it is interpreted to apply to the beginning of Islam, when women could go out to the mosques and pray with men in all prayers."

This comment highlights an interesting process. Al-Walīd is like many other transmitters quoted in the prestigious *ḥadīth* collections of al-Bukhārī and Muslim in that one finds both positive and negative assessments of him by the early *ḥadīth* critics.[11] In al-Walīd's case, the positive reviews outweighed the negative ones, and he was even quoted by

[11] Al-Dhahabī, in his *Mizān al-i'tidāl* (Beirut: Dār al-Ma'rifa, n.d.), a dictionary of transmitters who received negative comments, lists many who were quoted by al-Bukhārī and Muslim. In a later work, he lists one hundred more transmitters, many of them quoted by al-Bukhārī and Muslim, who received negative comments, yet whom al-Dhahabī believes are reliable. See al-Dhahabī, *Risāla fī al-ruwāt al-thiqāt*, printed with Ibn Quṭlūbughā, *Munyat al-alma'ī*, 76–96.

Muslim, whose traditions were usually not questioned by Sunnī jurists.[12] Jurists often quoted traditionists of less repute than al-Walīd without a second thought. *Isnād* criticism was an unusual practice among Ḥanafī jurists through the seventh/thirteenth century, and they commonly cited "weak" or even *isnād*-less *ḥadīth*s. But the Umm Waraqa tradition was something of a problem for Ḥanafī law, so there was an incentive to make an issue of the doubts recorded about al-Walīd. Ḥanafī jurists (other than al-Manbijī and al-Kākī) generally did not give in to that temptation, perhaps thinking that to do so would be to throw stones in a glass house. Thus, they preferred to neutralize the *ḥadīth* by other means.

Al-Manbijī stands out among the Ḥanafīs in that here and elsewhere in his book, he criticizes the *isnād*s of traditions going against the received law. This is because al-Manbijī's book is not a law manual. Rather, as its introduction and contents make clear, it is an apologetic work devoted to refuting accusations that Ḥanafī law deviates from the *Ḥadīth*. He appears to be more a student of the *Ḥadīth* than of law, and the only other book with which he is credited is on the *Ḥadīth*.

Al-Kākī attacks permissibility with some arguments that, while original, are arguably not as strong as those of his contemporaries and that I will therefore discuss in a footnote. It appears that he begins with the received law and then contrives justifications.[13] Here, one sees again that

[12] See the entry on al-Walīd in Ibn Ḥajar, *Tahdhīb* (Beirut: Dār al-Fikr, 1404).

[13] Al-Kākī writes: "if their group prayer had been lawful (*mashrū'*), then it would have been undesirable to abandon it, and its practice would have spread like men's group prayers." He adds that leading group prayers belongs to rites of worship that are unique to men, such as saying the Call to Prayer (*adhān*), sermons, Friday prayers, and the *'Īd*s. The female imām's advancing in front would increase her exposure, which is forbidden given that God tells women to "not reveal their adornments" (Qur'ān 24.31), while her staying behind is forbidden because neither the Prophet nor any Companion did it that way. As for the *ḥadīth* of Umm Waraqa, her practice was at the beginning of Islam, and, besides, the main transmitter of the report was controversial. Al-Kākī's arguments are not conclusive. He argues on the basis of Qur'ān 24.31, but it concerns modesty in front of unrelated men, men who need not be present during women's group prayer. Besides, even with such men, the verse exempts "adornment save such as is outward," implying that women's presence with men *per se* is not an issue. Al-'Aynī and al-Laknawī refute the other points. Al-'Aynī points out that the lawfulness of a thing does not necessarily make it undesirable to refrain from it. "If the lawful thing (*al-mashrū'*) were an obligation, then its omission would be forbidden; if it were desirable (*sunna*), then omission would be undesirable (*makrūh*), and if recommended (*nadb*), omission would be permissible but not undesirable." As for the other two points (the Umm Waraqa tradition and the practice of the Prophet), see the discussion of al-'Aynī in Section 4.4. Al-Laknawī adds other arguments to refute al-Kākī. For example, he points out that by al-Kākī's reasoning, the group prayer of discerning boys near puberty (*al-ṣibyān al-mumayyizīn al-murāhiqīn*)

a law remains stable while the arguments for it vary greatly. Let us now proceed to the more substantial arguments of al-Atrāzī and al-Zayla'ī.

Al-Atrāzī writes that the practice had been "abrogated when women were commanded to behave in a dignified manner and remain in their homes (*al-waqār wa-al-qarār fī al-buyūt*) " (quoted by al-'Aynī). Here, he alludes to Qur'ān 33.33. The relevance of this verse is not immediately discernible, as it is not clear why women's maintenance of dignity in their homes should preclude group prayer.[14] One might connect this verse to group prayers by arguing that its spirit requires women's isolation even from other women, which is incompatible with group prayer. Even so, if one takes this connection to group prayer to be a plausible one, it is clear that this would not be the only plausible interpretation of the verse: it involves reading quite a bit into the text. But if one does take this reading to be the correct one, one could still just as easily consider this broad and vague principle of feminine seclusion to be qualified by the reports endorsing women's prayer leadership, which are by comparison specific and direct. Finally, the verse is part of a long passage addressed to the wives of the Prophet. In the light of the fact that the passage itself indicates that stricter standards apply to them than to other women, it is not necessary to follow al-Atrāzī in extending its contents to all women. In making these various assumptions, al-Atrāzī interprets the Qur'ān in the light of Ḥanafī law rather than the other way around.

Al-Zayla'ī discusses a *ḥadīth* that to him indicates the abrogation of women's group prayers:

> Women's group prayer is undesirable (1) because of [the Prophet's] statement, "A woman's prayer in her room (*bayt*) is better than her prayer in her quarter

should be forbidden since it is not widespread, yet Ḥanafīs permit it. He also uses traditions indicating that at the time of the Prophet women prayed in group prayers with men in order to argue that women had, therefore, no need to hold their own group prayers, and this could explain why their group prayers were not widespread, thus "from its lack of prevalence [at the time of the Prophet, when they could attend group prayers with men] prohibition does not follow, especially for eras in which women are barred from Friday and group prayers [with men]."

[14] The most relevant part of Qur'ān 33.33 runs, "*wa-qarna fī buyūtikunna.*" Among the Seven Reciters, this is the way in which 'Āṣim and Nāfi' read the text, and it means, "Stay in your houses!" The other reciters read it as "*qirna*," yielding, in the words of al-Ṭabarī, "in your houses comport yourselves with dignity and calm" (*kunna ahl waqār wa-sakīna fī buyūtikunna*). Al-Ṭabarī expresses a preference for the latter reading on grammatical grounds. Al-Qurṭubī argues that it could mean "stay," too, in addition to the previously mentioned meaning. See al-Ṭabarī, *Jāmi' al-bayān* (Beirut: Dār al-Fikr, 1415), 22:5–6; al-Qurṭubī, *Tafsīr* (Beirut: Dār Ihyā' al-Turāth al-'Arabī, 1405), 14:178; 'Abd al-Laṭīf al-Khaṭīb, *Mu'jam al-qirā'āt* (Damascus: Dār Sa'd al-Dīn, 1422), 7:283–4.

(*ḥujra*), and her prayer in her *mukhda*ʿ is better than her prayer in her room," and (2) because it entails one of two forbidden things (*maḥẓūrayn*), either the leader's standing in the middle of the row, which is undesirable, or the stepping forward of the leader, also undesirable in the case of women. So their case becomes like that of naked people, for whom group prayers are not lawful (*lam yushra*ʿ) at all. ...[15]

[If they pray as a group, the leader stands in the middle] because ʿĀ'isha did so at a time when women's group prayer was (still) desirable. But then the desirability was abrogated. [The leader stands in the middle] also because she is forbidden to be conspicuous, especially in prayers, which is why a woman's praying in her house is better, and why during prostration she keeps her torso low, leaving no gap between her stomach and her thighs. The leader's advancement would increase conspicuousness, which is undesirable.

It is easy to see that for al-Zaylaʿī, too, Ḥanafī law determines the understanding of the *ḥadīth* rather than the other way around. He provides two arguments, which I have numbered in the body of the quotation:

Al-Zaylaʿī's first argument relies on a *ḥadīth* to the effect that it is better for a woman to pray in the *mukhda*ʿ than elsewhere, *mukhda*ʿ meaning a small room within a larger room, as in a walk-in closet, or a storeroom according to the dictionaries.[16] Other variants of the tradition refer, instead of *mukhda*ʿ, to "the depths of her room [or house]" (*qa*ʿ*r baytihā*) or the darkest corner in it. Al-Zaylaʿī does not clarify what bearing the *ḥadīth* has on the question of group prayers, but Ibn al-Humām would later explicate the views of those who cite this tradition and its variants: the *mukhda*ʿ is understood to mean storeroom, and, therefore, it "does not provide enough room for group prayers, as is the case with the depths of her room [or house] or the darkest spot."

Al-Zaylaʿī's use of the tradition involves a number of assumptions. First, regardless of the nature of the linkage between *mukhda*ʿ and praying alone in al-Zaylaʿī's mind, one thing is clear. For his argument to work, the *ḥadīth* must be understood as discouraging prayers anywhere but in the *mukhda*ʿ. But to say that A is better than B is not, in general, to say that B is bad. The *ḥadīth* could easily be construed as consistent with either the desirability (in different degrees) or permissibility of women's prayer in places other than a *mukhda*ʿ. (Indeed, the tradition goes on to indicate that praying anywhere in her bedroom (inner room of the house) is better than in her quarter (*ḥujra*, i.e., outer room), suggesting that praying outside the *mukhda*ʿ in her room may not be bad after all.) Secondly,

[15] He continues: "Therefore, [calling out] the *adhān* is not lawful for them, being a call to group prayers. Had it not been for the undesirability of their group prayers, it would have been lawful."

[16] Ibn Manẓūr, *Lisān al-ʿArab*, 8:65.

if one goes by Ibn al-Humām's explication, it is not certain that, if there is enough room for a woman to pray in a *mukhda*ʿ (which may be a closet or storeroom), there will not always be enough room left for another one to join her. If one does grant al-Zaylaʿī these two points, thereby accepting his view that this *ḥadīth* discourages prayers outside a *mukhda*ʿ, it is still not clear why it should not be reconciled with the reports about ʿĀ'isha and others through qualification rather than abrogation. For example, one could take it as a general rule that women must pray inside the *mukhda*ʿ, but make an exception (qualification) in the case of group prayers.

Al-Zaylaʿī's second argument does not offer any evidence directly against women's group prayers. Rather, he argues from the general principle that women must not be conspicuous during prayers. He is able to support this general principle with two examples: the preference for women praying in their homes rather than elsewhere, and women's crouching posture during the prostrations. He infers from this principle that the female prayer leader is confined to the middle of the row, a less conspicuous position. In other words, he treats the leader's location in analogy to women's posture and to the preference for praying at home.[17] Having thus ruled out the position in front, the position in the middle of the row remains the only possibility. But that position, al-Zaylaʿī posits, was ruled out by abrogation, which at this point is taken for granted rather than argued for. Thus, this is not really a proof that women should not pray in groups. At most, it shows that *if* women were to pray in groups, the leader would have to pray in the middle of the row.

Al-Bābirtī offers a somewhat similar argument.[18] Al-Kākī and al-Bābirtī also add a new thought that again amounts to working back from the received Ḥanafī position.[19]

[17] One can set forth the components of the analogy as follows. Conspicuousness during prayers is the effective cause for the discouragement of women from praying outside their homes or performing prostrations with elevated torsos. The same effective cause is present in the case of a female leader who advances beyond the row of worshippers. Hence in this case the same result (i.e., discouragement) obtains. Incidentally, al-Zaylaʿī's analogy may fall short of one of the requirements mentioned in the *uṣūl al-fiqh* for a proper analogy, due to the vague and indeterminate nature of conspicuousness as an effective cause.

[18] Al-Bābirtī writes:

> [Women's group prayer] is undesirable (*yukrah*) because their leader stands either in front of them or in the middle of them. The former entails an increase in exposure, which is undesirable (*makrūh*). The latter entails that the imām leave the proper position of the imām, which is undesirable (*makrūh*). Group prayer is a desirable act (*sunna*), and it is better to refrain from a desirable act than to commit an undesirable one.

[19] Al-Bābirtī writes:

> It may be asked: "Here, two forbidden things (*ḥurmatān*) come into conflict: increase of exposure if one steps forward, and leaving the proper position (of the imām) if

After al-Marghīnānī, the standard Ḥanafī view was that female group prayers had been abrogated. But there was a problem with al-Marghīnānī's statement that 'Ā'isha's leadership must have taken place "in the beginnings of Islam." Al-Sarūjī[20] refutes al-Marghīnānī's formulation, pointing out that only in the last nine years of the Prophet's life would 'Ā'isha have been old enough to lead prayers, so that she could not have done so "in the beginnings" of Islam. This is not to say that al-Sarūjī denies abrogation. He writes, "one may say that 'Ā'isha led prayers when women still used to attend group prayers," that is, before the abrogation. Al-Bābirtī, who also accepts abrogation, defends al-Marghīnānī's wording: "It is possible that what is meant by 'the beginnings of Islam' is the period before the abrogation, so it is a 'beginning' relative to the period following it."[21] So, al-Bābirtī has stretched the meaning of "beginning" to potentially

> one stays in the middle (of the row). Why do you give more weight to the factor of exposure than to the factor of leaving the proper position?" I would answer that avoidance of exposure is an obligation (*farḍ*), whereas keeping to the proper position is a desirable thing (*sunna*). Without a doubt, the obligation preponderates.

Here, he works his way back from the intended outcome (of women not stepping forward) to (1) lack of exposure being obligatory rather than merely desirable and (2) nondeviation being desirable but not obligatory. The redistribution of assessments has an interesting consequence: it contradicts al-Marghīnānī's judgment that deviation is forbidden, and it also implies women's group prayers to be permissible (while undesirable). Al-Bābirtī indeed defends permissibility independently of this point (see Section 4.8.2, "Did Abrogation Remove Permissibility?"). His implicit departure from al-Marghīnānī is significant, given the zeal he otherwise displays in defending Marghīnānī's formulations. On the other hand, the departure is not surprising. I will show that it would prove difficult to be consistent and precise at the same time without deviating from the apparent meaning of al-Marghīnānī's statements.

20 Quoted by Ibn al-Humām and by Jamāl al-Dīn al-Zaylaʿī, *Naṣb al-rāya*, 2:41.

21 The full text of the discussion in al-Bābirtī is as follows:

> The statement [of al-Marghīnānī] that "['Ā'isha's] prayer in a group is interpreted to pertain to the beginnings of Islam" – this statement answers the point that is raised, namely that: if women's leadership is undesirable, then how is that 'Ā'isha did it? The reason for it is that she did so in the beginnings of Islam, when it was permissible as a desirable practice (*sunna*) and she would stand in their midst; but then its desirability was abrogated without its permissibility being abrogated. According to the consensus, if women pray as a group, that is permissible, whether the imām stands in the front or in the middle, since the preconditions for permissibility have been met. But the better option (*al-afḍal*), due to the preferability of greater concealment, is that she stay in the middle.
>
> Here, there is room for discussion on a few points. (1) The Prophet lived in Mecca for thirteen years, and then married 'Ā'isha in Medina. So, how could one assent to his [al-Marghīnānī's] statement that "her prayer in a group is interpreted to pertain to the beginnings of Islam"?
>
> The answer to (1): It is possible that what is meant by "the beginnings of Islam" is the period before the abrogation, so it is a "beginning" relative to the period following it.

include any point of time prior to the Prophet's death. Clearly, what he says al-Marghīnānī may have meant is not what al-Marghīnānī meant. Al-Bābirtī could have defended the law without endorsing al-Marghīnānī's wording: all that matters to the legal outcome is that abrogation took place; it is irrelevant whether it took place as early as al-Marghīnānī put it. The fact that, in addition to defending the law, al-Bābirtī goes to some trouble to absolve al-Marghīnānī of error shows that he is also interested in safeguarding al-Marghīnānī's authority. This confirms the high stature of al-Marghīnānī among the Ḥanafīs.

4.4. The Maverick: Badr al-Dīn al-'Aynī

4.4.1. *Arguing from Tradition*

Writing in the ninth/fifteenth century, al-'Aynī was the first and until recent times sole Ḥanafī jurist to jettison the Ḥanafī position and actually support the desirability of women's group prayers. In rebutting al-Atrāzī, who a century earlier had called women's group prayer a misguided innovation (*bid'a*), al-'Aynī quotes traditions indicating that at the time of the Prophet, Umm Waraqa, Umm Salama, and 'Ā'isha led women, the latter two standing within the row of worshippers, in addition to quoting a favorable report from Ibn 'Abbās:[22]

(1) Abū Dāwūd, *Sunan* [the tradition of al-Walīd b. 'Abd al-Allāh]: Umm Waraqa had been reciting the Qur'ān. She asked the Prophet to let her have a muezzin for her household. The Prophet agreed and commanded her to lead the prayers of her household.

(2) 'Abd al-Razzāq, *al-Muṣannaf*— Ibrāhīm b. Muḥammad—Dāwūd b. al-Ḥuṣayn— 'Ikrima—Ibn 'Abbās: "Women lead women, standing in their midst."

(3) Ibn Abī Shayba—Sufyān b. 'Uyayna—'Ammār al-Duhnī—a woman of his clan named Ḥujayra: "Umm Salama led our prayers, standing in the middle of the women."

(4) Ibn Abī Shayba—Wakī'—Ibn Abī Laylā—'Aṭā'— 'Ā'isha: she used to lead women, standing in their midst.

(5) 'Aẓma (read Rayṭa) al-Ḥanafiyya: "'Ā'isha led us," standing in their midst in the required daily prayers (*al-maktūba*).[23]

[22] For the various traditions cited by al-'Aynī, see especially Jamāl al-Dīn al-Zayla'ī, *Naṣb al-rāya*, 2:38–41. For Jamāl al-Dīn al-Zayla'ī, see Chapter 3, page 67.

[23] This tradition is found in al-Dārquṭnī. Not much is known about Rayṭa al-Ḥanafiyya. She is identified as "Kūfan, successor, fair transmitter" in al-'Ijlī, *Ma'rifat al-thiqāt* (Medina: Maktabat al-Dār, 1405), 2:453, no. 2335.

(6) Al-Shaybānī—Abū Ḥanīfa—Ḥammād—Ibrāhīm—'Ā'isha that "she used to lead women in the month of Ramaḍān, standing in their midst."

(7) Al-Ḥākim, *al-Mustadrak*: 'Abd Allāh b. Idrīs—'Aṭā'—'Ā'isha: she used to say the *adhān*, stand, and lead women, standing in their midst.

Al-'Aynī cites these traditions to argue against undesirability, adding to them two other reports from Ibn Ḥazm's *al-Muḥallā* that 'Ā'isha and Umm Salama respectively led sunset and afternoon prayers. And against the view of the Kūfan jurists al-Sha'bī and al-Nakha'ī that women can worship in groups for supererogatory prayers only, he points out that the fifth tradition explicitly involves the obligatory daily prayers.[24]

It was implicit as early as al-Marghīnānī that the reason the leader is forbidden from standing in the middle of the row is that the Prophet (and his Companions) never deviated from standing in the front. Al-Kākī and, later, Ibn al-Humām would make this reason explicit. [25] However, al-'Aynī appeals to the traditions attesting female prayer leaders to rebut al-Marghīnānī's view that it is forbidden for the leader to stand in the middle of the row. He adds that "one may hold that it is forbidden in the case of men. For if [the prohibition] had been categorical [i.e., for both genders], then the group prayers [of the women] would not have been allowed." He thus notes that the Prophet's permission that a female leader pray within the row of worshippers means that doing so is permissible. This is the commonsense reading of the evidence, the apparent import of the canon.

Al-'Aynī is committed neither to al-Marghīnānī, nor even to the founders of the school. He becomes the first Ḥanafī to cast doubt on the idea that women-only prayer was abrogated – Ibn al-Humām and the nineteenth-century jurist al-Laknawī being the other exceptions – and the only one prior to al-Laknawī to deny abrogation outright and defend desirability. He writes that the *ḥadīths* he quotes show that female leadership was not limited to the beginning of Islam and that therefore there could be no question of abrogation.

4.4.2. *The* Isnāds *of the Traditions*

Al-'Aynī comments on *isnāds*, not a regular practice among the Ḥanafī jurists. On the Umm Waraqa tradition, he reacts to the following

[24] He could have also adduced the first tradition, as the appointment of a muezzin points to the daily required prayers.

[25] For al-Kākī, see page 82, footnote 13.

criticism by al-Kākī: "As for the traditions of Rāyiṭa [read Rayṭa] and Umm Waraqa, they concern the beginning of Islam or the teaching of girls [rather than actual prayers]. Besides, the traditionists have criticized the *ḥadīth* of Umm Waraqa."[26] The last sentence alludes to the doubts raised about al-Walīd b. 'Abd Allāh, the main transmitter of the Umm Waraqa tradition. Al-'Aynī responds, "Muslim has quoted him [i.e., has quoted al-Walīd in his prestigious *ḥadīth* collection], and that suffices as far as his probity and truthfulness are concerned."[27]

Al-'Aynī discusses also the *isnād* of one other tradition:

If one cites [against my view] the tradition of Asmā' bint Abī Bakr, which is quoted by Ibn 'Adī in *al-Kāmil* and by Abū al-Shaykh al-Iṣbahānī in the book *al-Adhān,* that the Prophet said, "the *Adhān*, the *Iqāma*, Friday prayers, and ritual purification[28] (*ightisāl*) are not incumbent on women (*laysa 'alā al-nisā'*). And a woman shall not step in front of them (to lead them), but, rather, shall stand in the middle of them" – then I will answer: in its *isnād* there is al-Ḥākim [read al-Ḥakam] b. 'Abd Allāh. Ibn Ma'īn said, "He is not fair, nor trustworthy." Al-Bukhārī reportedly said, "Ignore him!" Al-Nasā'ī reportedly said, "His *ḥadīth*s are ignored." Ibn al-Mubārak considered him weak. And Ibn al-Jawzī, in his book *al-Taḥqīq*, rejected (*ankara*) this *ḥadīth*. The tradition is not known as a Prophetic statement. Rather, it is something reported of al-Ḥasan al-Baṣrī and Ibrāhīm al-Nakha'ī.

In any case, the tradition does not directly discourage group prayers. Rather, it could be used to buttress al-Kākī's point that conspicuous rituals of worship tend to be in the purview of men.

4.4.3. *Summing up al-'Aynī*

Al-'Aynī's position fits the apparent meaning of the canon. After all, if half a dozen reports describe a certain practice, with some placing it in Medina, while no report from the Prophet, a Companion, or a Successor hints at abrogation, then the appearance is that there was no abrogation. That noted, it must also be stressed that just as his opponents do

[26] The manuscript of al-Kākī's book has *aw ta'līman li-al-jawāz* ("or by way of disclosing permissibility") and the printed text of al-'Aynī that quotes al-Kākī has *aw ta'alluman li-al-jawāz*. I consider both corruptions of *aw ta'līman li-al-jawārī*.

[27] After a few lines, al-'Aynī adds: "If one makes an objection that Ibn Baṭṭāl has said in his book, 'al-Walīd b. ['Abd Allāh b.] Jumay' and 'Abd al-Raḥmān b. Khallād are of unknown quality,' I will answer that Ibn Ḥibbān named them in (the book of) *Fair Transmitters* (*al-Thiqāt*). Therefore, the tradition is sound." For Ibn Baṭṭāl, read Ibn Qaṭṭān; cf. Jamāl al-Dīn al-Zayla'ī, *Naṣb al-rāya*, 2:40.

[28] This refers to the supererogatory ritual purification for Friday prayers.

not prove that abrogation took place, al-ʿAynī does not prove that it did not.[29] Although al-ʿAynī's thesis was in keeping with the apparent meaning of the canon, he did not prove it conclusively. But then who has the burden of proof? Though in theory the burden of proof may fall on the party claiming abrogation, in practice it falls on whoever goes against the standard school doctrine.

Could one conclude that al-ʿAynī actually applied a somewhat less hermeneutically flexible methodology than his colleagues, one with a greater bias for the apparent meaning of the canon? Or, did he differ from his colleagues merely in that he started with a different canon-blind law, being no different from them in devising interpretations in order to justify that position? To put the question differently, does his disagreement with the other Ḥanafīs stem fundamentally from a different hermeneutic approach? The proper way to answer that question is to study a larger part of his work to see whether he displayed somewhat consistent methodological proclivities. Did he, for example, abandon Ḥanafī law also in other cases of flagrant contradiction with the *Ḥadīth*? Not having conducted the required survey, I cannot answer the question with certitude. However, on the basis of the introduction al-ʿAynī wrote for his work, I conjecture that indeed he differed methodologically from other Ḥanafīs at least to a degree. Al-ʿAynī's *al-Bināya* is a commentary on al-Marghīnānī's *al-Hidāya*, a book on which more commentaries were written than any other Ḥanafī text. In its introduction, al-ʿAynī sets out to explain how his commentary differs from those of others:

> However, I consider the foundation of this discipline to be the Qur'ān and the established (or apparent) *sunna* (*al-sunna al-ẓāhira*), in that, where possible, it should not deviate from the two texts [i.e., Qur'ān and *Sunna*] in favor of the texts from the exponent of the discipline [i.e., al-Marghīnānī or Abū Ḥanīfa] (*ʿalā annahu lā yuʿdal ʿan-al-naṣṣayn ʿind-al-imkān bi-al-naṣṣ al-wārid ʿan ṣāḥib hādha al-sha'n*). How could one set them aside while it is from him [i.e., the Prophet] and his rightly guided Companions that religion derives? God says, "We sent not ever any Messenger, but that he should be obeyed, by the leave of God" (Qur'ān 4.64), and, "Obey the Messenger" (Qur'ān 4.59). And the Prophet said, "My Companions are like stars. Whichever you follow, you will be rightly guided." This is a sound report (*al-ṣaḥīḥ*), lacking in defect. Following opinion that is not grounded in the sources (*al-ra'y*) in regard to duties was not commanded by the

[29] Al-ʿAynī could have strengthened his argument about abrogation by citing the variant of the Umm Waraqa tradition that indicates that she continued to lead the prayers of her household until her death in the reign of ʿUmar, as reported in Ibn Saʿd, *Ṭabaqāt* (Beirut: Dār Ṣādir, 1968), 8:457. This relevant detail was never noticed by any Ḥanafī jurist.

Prophet.[30] ... The first Muslims (*al-ṣadr al-awwal*) were not remiss in that regard, and went about it in the most perfect manner. The neglect was, rather, from most of the later Muslims (*al-khalaf*), who did not do justice to the matter (*qaṣṣarū fī al-tamhīd*). They failed in that they were uncritical, being content to emulate [past authorities] (*āfatuhum fīhi huwa al-tasāhul li-iktifā'ihim bi-al-taqlīd*). Do you see how they have filled their books with the words "because," "however," and "but"? One is justified to do so only after having laid a foundation of Tradition.

Thus, al-'Aynī takes his colleagues and predecessors to task for their uncritical allegiance to school precedent (*taqlīd*), a practice that for him amounts to preferring mere opinion (*ra'y*) to the traditions about the Prophet and his Companions. The reproach suggests that the prayer question may not be the only area in which he boldly goes against the current.

Al-'Aynī left a small, momentary dent in the trend. As I show next, Ibn al-Humām shows some receptivity to al-'Aynī's position, without actually endorsing it. However, not until the nineteenth century would a Ḥanafī author, namely the eminent Indian scholar al-Laknawī, wholly endorse al-'Aynī's position.

4.5. On the Fence: Ibn al-Humām

Ibn al-Humām does not refer to al-'Aynī, but goes over some of the same evidence, stating the strongest arguments that can be raised for the two sides in an even-handed, economical, and exact manner. Attestations of women's group prayers, he says, undermine the abrogation scenario, though he acknowledges that proponents of abrogation might assign the attestations to a period before abrogation. That leaves the saying of Ibn 'Abbās that "a woman leads women standing in their midst." This report, he says, may be countered by saying it is only a comment on where a woman must stand if she should lead (without implying that it is fine to lead), or else it can be countered by saying that Ibn 'Abbās had not become aware of the abrogating event. Still, neutralizing the traditions does not make for a positive argument for abrogation.

He affirms that one may not claim abrogation without offering a statement from the canon that functioned as the abrogator (*al-nāsikh*). He says that the only candidate abrogator anyone ever cited is the *mukhda'* tradition:[31] the *mukhda'*, as a storeroom, lacks enough space

[30] *Wa-al-dhahāb ilā-al-ra'y 'amal laysa 'alayh amr al-rasūl.*

[31] For the tradition, see Section 4.3.

to accommodate group prayers. He immediately reveals his skepticism of this argument by the way he begins his next sentence: "This is questionable, but supposing that one concedes it, then.... "[32]

In interpreting the *mukhda'* tradition, he takes into consideration something roughly similar to a point I made earlier, to wit, that the tradition can be taken to establish that avoiding group prayer is better, without implying that performing it is undesirable. He makes a more conservative version of that point, indicating that if the tradition abrogates anything, it is desirability; it cannot abrogate permissibility: "Supposing that one concedes (the relevance of the *mukhda'* tradition), it only indicates the abrogation of desirability (*al-sunniyya*). It does not entail undesirability *qua* prohibition (*karāhat al-taḥrīm*), but rather undesirability *qua* blamelessness (*karāhat al-tanzīh*), the latter being the assessment that applies to the omission of a preferred thing (*wa-marji'uhā ilā khilāf al-awlā*)." As described in Section 2.3, the category I have rendered as undesirability *qua* blamelessness covers perfectly permissible acts whose commission is not preferred. Here, Ibn al-Humām makes the point that the omission of a merely preferable act (as distinct from obligatory act) falls into that category.[33] In particular, the *mukhda'* tradition tells us of an act that is merely better. So, omitting it would not be unlawful.

Ibn al-Humām never actually states his own verdict. He refutes prohibition (and undesirability *qua* prohibition), but does not say whether he opts for desirability, neutrality, or for undesirability *qua* blamelessness. His tone ("This is questionable, but supposing that one concedes it," etc.) shows that he considers permissibility or desirability a better solution than undesirability *qua* blamelessness. That is suggested also by the sentence concluding his discussion: right after saying that the *mukhda'* tradition, *if assumed to be the abrogator*, would indicate undesirability *qua* blamelessness, he writes: "but we are not obliged to accept that; the aim is to go wherever the truth leads."[34] The phrase "the aim is to go wherever the truth leads" harks back to al-'Aynī's willingness to buck the legal inertia. Still, he is more inhibited than al-'Aynī. Content with showing the Ḥanafī stance to be arbitrary, he does not actually move to the pole diametrically opposed to it. His cautious revisionism contrasts with al-'Aynī's boldness.

32 *Wa-lā yakhfā mā fīh, wa-bi-taqdīr al-taslīm, ...*

33 Ibn Nujaym (*al-Baḥr al-rā'iq*, 2:56) and Ibn 'Ābidīn (*Ḥāshiya*, 1:704) say the same thing in an entirely different legal context.

34 By "that," I take it that he refers to the antecedent of the preceding conditional proposition, which I have italicized.

Later jurists would totally ignore Ibn al-Humām's (and al-'Aynī's) arguments against the standard position. Instead, many of them would cite Ibn al-Humām's explication of the standard view. Ibn al-Humām, as I mentioned earlier in this section, was not committed to that view. It is ironic that Ibn al-Humām's most visible legacy was to be his explanation of why al-Marghīnānī's "undesirable" meant "prohibited." His comment on the advancement of the imām was often cited: "The Prophet's persisting in it without fail entails obligation. Therefore, its omission entails undesirability *qua* prohibition."[35] Another feature of his elucidation that would remain very much a part of later Ḥanafī law was that while it was a sin for a woman to advance, the prayer would still be valid if she did so.

4.6. Later Ḥanafī Law

The last group of jurists showed more interest in concisely stating the standard law than in justifying it at length. They did display a certain clarity and consistency in the statement of the standard position that had been generally lacking before, and in doing so they effected an overall substantive change compared to early Ḥanafī law. To explain this development, it would be best to review certain apparent contradictions and ambiguities in al-Marghīnānī's statement of the law that later jurists had to grapple with. Al-Marghīnānī's treatment involved three propositions:

(1) Women's group prayer is "undesirable."
(2) Women's group prayer is "valid," meaning that the prayer need not be redone since the duty to pray has been fulfilled.
(3) Women's group prayer entails a prohibited thing (the imām's deviation).

It will be recalled that the first two propositions represent early Ḥanafī law. Al-Marghīnānī simply took them over from his predecessors. The second proposition (legal validity) was not usually stated explicitly, but it was implicit in the statement that the imām should pray in the row. If such a prayer were invalid, it would not make sense to say how it should be performed. The combination of the first two propositions was not

[35] Incidentally, it is actually not entirely clear that the Prophet always stood in the front when there was more than one worshipper "following" him. Al-Shaybānī relates through Abū Ḥanīfa—Ibrāhīm that Ibn Mas'ūd, when leading two men in prayer, had them stand to his left and right rather than standing in front of them. Al-Shaybānī then adds that he and Abū Ḥanīfa do not accept Ibn Mas'ūd's approach (*Āthār*, 179–80, no. 95).

problematic as long as "undesirable" was not understood to mean forbidden. In this regard, early Ḥanafī law was consistent.

Proposition (3) regarding the prohibited consequence was al-Marghīnānī's own lasting contribution. He introduced it as a proof for undesirability (first proposition), but it actually appears to contradict the first two propositions. The apparent contradiction with (1) arises from the fact that if something involves a forbidden thing, then it must be forbidden. In particular, if it is forbidden for an imām to stand in the row, and if that is the only way women can pray, then women's group prayer must also be forbidden, not merely undesirable. Clearly, women's group prayer and the imām's standing in the row should both have the same legal status: either undesirable (as women's prayer was hitherto said to be) or forbidden (as standing in the row was now asserted to be). Proposition (3) also appears to contradict (2), since one would expect an illicit prayer to lack legal validity. These conspicuous contradictions were untenable. After al-Marghīnānī, jurists sought to restore consistency in various ways, arriving at different equilibrium points.

The conflict of (1) and (3) can be eliminated if "undesirable" is understood to actually mean prohibited, as in undesirability *qua* prohibition, a category I explicated in Section 2.3. Such a reading would go against the views of the jurists who ruled for permissibility, such as al-Ṭaḥāwī, al-Kāsānī, and al-Bābirtī, while it would fit in better with the views of some others, such as al-Kākī and al-Zaylaʿī. At any rate, most later Ḥanafī jurists interpreted al-Marghīnānī in this manner, signaling a shift of the school doctrine toward prohibition.

But this shift still left the apparent contradiction with (2), raising the problem of the legal validity of an illicit deed. In other words, the consequence was that although a women-only prayer may be forbidden and hence sinful, once it is performed, it counts as "valid" in the sense that the prayer need not be redone. If, for example, women pray the noon prayer as a group, they have fulfilled the duty to pray the noon prayer and need not redo the noon prayer, but by doing it in a group they have sinned. Al-ʿAynī explicitly labeled this a "contradiction" on al-Marghīnānī's part, taking for granted that a forbidden act cannot be "valid." He helpfully observed that the contradiction would disappear if "prohibited" were understood in a nontechnical way to mean merely undesirable, since "that would allow for validity along with the undesirability." But Ḥanafīs finally settled for a different kind of resolution. They ruled that the prayer is prohibited, that is, sinful, yet legally valid if performed. Al-ʿAynī had not conceived that this could be the case, and he would probably not have approved of it.[36]

Al-Ḥalabī, especially in his *Ghunyat al-mutamallī*, considers women-only prayer "undesirable," but also says of it "*tajūz*," a word that can mean either "permissible" (not sinful) or "legally valid" (i.e., not in need of being redone as it fulfills the duty to pray). He could very well mean permissible, particularly since (1) in parallel with women-only prayer, he categorizes as "undesirable" the leadership of slaves,[37] which was generally acknowledged as undesirable *qua* permissible; (2) at one point he says of something that it "*lā yajūz*" but does not cause invalidation;[38] and (3) says nothing to imply prohibition. If so, he is unique among the last group of scholars in adopting a pre-Marghīnānī attitude.

Mullā Khusraw rules for undesirability. Although he does not say which kind of undesirability (*qua* permission or *qua* prohibition), he probably means prohibition. That is suggested by the way he tries to explain why it is consistent to say that the imām should pray in the row. "There are degrees of evil (*ba'ḍ al-sharr ahwan min ba'ḍ*)," he writes.[39] That is to say, it is more evil for the imām to advance than to stand in the row, but that does not make the latter blameless. It is less evil, but still evil nevertheless. Now, "evil" is a slightly unlikely way to describe something that is undesirable *qua* blameless. (Acts of the latter kind are discouraged primarily in the sense that their omission is praiseworthy and meritorious.) That suggests "undesirable *qua* forbidden" as the category in which the lesser evil properly fits.

In any case, most later scholars do not leave the matter ambiguous. Ibn Nujaym, too, mentions the degrees of evil, but he not only calls the greater evil (advancing) a sin, but also makes explicit the prohibition of the lesser evil (not advancing). His verdict is "undesirability *qua* prohibition."[40] He also makes explicit the legal validity of a woman's prayer with a female

[36] Incidentally, he wrote (in a context other than women's leadership): "prohibition entails the legal invalidity of that which is prohibited" (al-'Aynī, *Bināya*, 2:406). Admittedly, he may have been referring to cases where the canon itself uses the language of prohibition. Cf. Section 3.5.

[37] Al-Ḥalabī, *Multaqā al-abḥur*, 1:95.

[38] Al-Ḥalabī, *Ghunyat al-mutamallī*, 523.

[39] As far as my sources allow me to determine, in this context the "degrees of evil" argument was first raised in *al-Sirāj al-wahhāj*, as cited by Ibn Nujaym. The author of *al-Sirāj al-wahhāj* was Abū Bakr b. 'Alī al-Ḥaddād al-Zabīdī (d. 800/1398).

[40] Ibn Nujaym's rationale is the Prophet's persistence in advancing as the imām, following Ibn al-Humām's elucidation of al-Marghīnānī. Here, Ibn Nujaym forgets his own stated principles, which are actually different from those of Ibn al-Humām. I explain this point on page 103, footnote 57.

imām.[41] Al-Shurunbulālī's views are identical to those of Ibn Nujaym in all particulars. Harking back to Ibn al-Humām (and al-Sarakhsī), al-Shurunbulālī adds that even when the imām advances, the prayer is valid. Al-Ḥaṣkafī, Abū al-Su'ūd, Ibn 'Ābidīn, al-Ṭaḥṭāwī, and al-Afghānī rule explicitly for undesirability *qua* prohibition.[42]

The prohibitionists' retention of "legal validity" of women-only prayers (i.e., the position that such prayers fulfill the duty to pray) from pre-Marghīnānī days is of interest. In early Ḥanafī law, legal validity was acknowledged and could be backed up by 'Ā'isha's report. But once Ḥanafī law placed 'Ā'isha's prayers in the period before abrogation, legal validity ought to have become a question. It is telling that none of the prohibitionist jurists ever tried to explain the slightly peculiar fact of the illicit prayers being legally valid. Legal validity persisted due to legal inertia without much thought being given to its justification.[43]

4.7. The Counterexample from Funeral Prayers

I now come to the striking story of a serious contradiction. The Ḥanafīs agree that female group prayers are fine in the case of funeral prayers.

[41] *Iqtidā' al-mar'a bi-al-mar'a ṣaḥīḥ makrūh*, Ibn Nujaym writes.

[42] Al-Ḥalabī, al-Timurtāshī, and the Indian scholars who wrote *al-Fatāwā al-'Ālamgīrīya* state "undesirable" without saying which kind. Al-Nābulusī says "undesirable," too, but a comment he makes in another context (*Nihāyat al-murād*, 577) implies that he means prohibition: "undesirable" is used when the grounds for prohibition are probable, "forbidden" when they are certain.

Incidentally, Abū al-Su'ūd uses a phrase that is particularly revealing for my purposes. He writes: "if she advances, she has sinned ... **but** al-Ḥamawī quotes from *al-Khizāna* [by the fourth/tenth century jurist, Abū al-Layth al-Samarqandī] that it is *jā'iz* for their imām to advance (*taqaddum imāmihinna jā'iz*)." The word *jā'iz* can mean two different things: legally valid (i.e., counting as a valid prayer that fulfills the requirement to pray, so that it need not be redone) or permissible. (Permissibility entails legal validity, but it is conceivable that the reverse might not hold.) It is important for my argument in this chapter that the early Ḥanafīs considered women-only prayers permissible, not just legally valid (which is conceivably compatible with prohibition) when they used the verb *jāza*. I have already given two pieces of evidence for my interpretation (namely, al-Bābirtī's making permissibility explicit, and the quotation from al-'Aynī that cannot conceive of the simultaneity of prohibition and legal validity). This sentence is a weakly corroborating piece of evidence: the use of the word "but" suggests that Abū al-Su'ūd understood Abū al-Layth al-Samarqandī to mean lawful, not just legally valid.

[43] I would be skeptical of the conjecture that jurists did not question validity because they acknowledged the lack of definitive proof for prohibition. Such a conjecture might be inspired by a doctrine of Ḥanafī *uṣūl al-fiqh* that was abandoned by Ibn al-Humām, holding that an act of worship is invalid only if the proof for its prohibition is certain (*qaṭ'ī*), as discussed in Section 3.5. It is unlikely that the Ḥanafīs consistently applied this principle in practice. Section 3.5 showed that on the question of adjacency they failed

This brings up a question: if other female group prayers are unacceptable because of the illicitness of exposure or the illicitness of the leader standing in the middle of the row, should not group funeral prayers be forbidden for the same reasons? This apparent inconsistency requires resolution.[44]

Al-Zaylaʿī, al-Kākī, and al-Bābirtī rise to this challenge. They give similar arguments that are repeated by almost all later jurists down to the time of Ibn ʿĀbidīn.[45] I will quote al-Bābirtī. Before proceeding to refute it, al-Bābirtī formulates the objection as follows: "Women's leadership is not undesirable in the case of funeral prayers, where one of the two forbidden things [leader's exposure or positional deviation] takes place." He argues against the objection as follows:

> Women [are to] refrain from group prayers because it simultaneously involves a desirable thing [group prayers] and an undesirable thing [exposure or deviation from the proper place]. So, they refrain from the desirable thing in order to avoid the undesirable one. However, [women's leadership in] the funeral prayer simultaneously involves an obligatory thing (*al-farḍ*) [the prayers] and an undesirable thing [exposure or positional deviation]. So, they are forced to either forego an obligation to avoid committing an undesirable deed, or fulfill the obligation while also committing an undesirable deed. The latter choice is more suitable.

The key assumption in this passage is that it is obligatory for a female to perform the funeral prayer in a group rather than individually. He next explains why that is so:

> We say so because if they pray as a group with the *imām* in their midst, they have fulfilled an obligation, since the prayer is a collective obligation, and they have also committed an undesirable deed. But if they pray as individuals, they have refrained from an undesirable deed, but done so in a manner that exempts some of them from praying, since the obligation [to perform a funeral prayer for the deceased] vanishes as soon as one person performs it. So, it may happen that a woman finishes her prayer before the rest of the women, in which case the prayer of the rest of the women will be supererogatory. But it is not lawful to perform a supererogatory funeral prayer!

The crux of al-Bābirtī's point is that if women pray over the deceased individually, then the first woman to do so will have disposed of the

to apply the rule. There as here, their overriding concern was defending the received law rather than deriving the law using methodological rules.

[44] One might argue that what distinguishes funeral prayers is that they do not involve much movement (bending and prostration). However, what matters for my purposes is that jurists never utilize this distinction.

[45] Al-Ṭaḥṭāwī is the last scholar before Ibn ʿĀbidīn I have identified who repeats this argument. He was an older contemporary of Ibn ʿĀbidīn.

collective duty to pray upon the deceased, whereupon anyone praying after her will have committed a forbidden thing by praying a funeral prayer that is no longer obligatory. In order to ward off the possibility of worshippers committing that sin, they must all perform a single group prayer. The alternative to women praying in a group would be the commission of a forbidden thing; so, women must be allowed to pray as a group, choosing the lesser evil, the merely undesirable alternative as opposed to the forbidden one. This contrasts with other group prayers, where women avoid an inherently good thing (group prayers) that is not obligatory anyway in order to avoid undesirable consequences.

There is something artificial about this line of reasoning. By that I am not referring to the assumption of the unlawfulness of more than one prayer over the deceased. That is indeed what Ḥanafī law prescribed quite independently of the present question on women's prayers, and there is even a *ḥadīth* about it.[46] Rather, I mean that it would be far more natural to say that if a woman comes in and notices another woman praying, she should simply not pray.[47]

Its artificiality aside, al-Bābirtī's convoluted solution actually creates a bigger problem than it solves. The line of reasoning it employs should entail that where several men are available, a man may not pray individually over the deceased, since (just as in the case of women) it could lead some men to sinfully perform redundant prayers. Yet, this goes against Islamic law, which does allow the male to pray over the deceased individually. One would think that jurists would have noticed this problem right away, but it actually took five hundred years before anyone pointed it out. Ibn ʿĀbidīn refuted Ibn al-Humām's repetition of the rationalization in this way:[48]

> That means that when no one else is available to pray, it becomes obligatory for them [i.e., the women] to pray as a group.... That [line of reasoning] entails that a similar thing apply in the case of men praying individually. Thus, he [Ibn al-Humām] would be bound to consider it obligatory for them to pray as a group [rather than individually], even though it is stated expressly [in the canon] that it is not obligatory to perform funeral prayers in a group.

[46] ʿUmar wanted to pray over someone whom the Prophet had already prayed over, but the Prophet instructed him to supplicate (*duʿā'*) and ask God for the deceased's forgiveness rather than perform a formal funeral prayer. For the discussion of the point and the *ḥadīth*, see al-Kāsānī, *Badā'iʿ al-ṣanā'iʿ*, 1:311–12, where the Ḥanafī position is contrasted with the Shāfiʿī one.

[47] She could, instead, content herself with asking God for the deceased's forgiveness, just as the Prophet reportedly instructed ʿUmar to do.

[48] Ibn ʿĀbidīn, *Ḥāshiyat radd al-muḥtār*, 1:609.

Al-Laknawī cites Ibn ʿĀbidīn's refutation approvingly. He adds that it is a false dilemma to claim that without a female group prayer a *farḍ* will necessarily be omitted, for there is always the possibility of one woman doing the prayer by herself, thus disposing of the collective duty to pray for the deceased.

The far-fetched and artificial nature of the original argument leaves little doubt that it was simply concocted to justify the received law. Any remaining doubt is dispelled by the fact that al-Bābirtī, al-Zaylaʿī, and their numerous imitators never bothered to think through some of the rudimentary consequences of the purported rationale. The rationale served as a Band-Aid, as it were, exclusively designed to resolve the immediate problem at hand. Since that was all the rationale was meant for, jurists showed little interest in exploring its further ramifications. The phenomenon of ad hoc reasons, of course, is already familiar from the discussion in Chapter 3.

It is fascinating that scholars like Ibn Nujaym and al-Ḥaṣkafī repeated the same rationale even though they were prohibitionists. Al-Bābirtī was not a prohibitionist; he explicitly ruled for permissibility. And the rationale he gives in the passage I have quoted is crucially predicated on the permissibility of a female imāmʿs standing in the row! Without that premise, the rationalization would collapse. Therefore, prohibitionist jurists could not be consistent and cite the same rationale; yet, they did. This is yet another indication that legal reasons are often afterthoughts as compared to the legal effects they support.

Although Ibn ʿĀbidīn refuted the rationale, he did not offer an alternative resolution of the contradiction it was meant to resolve. This point remained a loose end in Ḥanafī thought.

4.8. Two More Issues

4.8.1. *Does Leadership Really Entail Improper Exposure?*

Recall that al-Bābirtī considers advancement undesirable since it increases exposure, which is undesirable. He raises and then answers a potential objection to that idea, namely that women, who are fully covered in prayers according to the law, cannot be said to be really exposing themselves, particularly if no man is present.[49] The question, thus,

[49] He writes:

> [Potential objection]: It is incorrect to identify increase in exposure as the underlying cause, since the rule endures in the absence of that cause. If a woman wears a garment that conceals her from head to toe, and leads women, and there is no man, then there is no exposure to begin with, let alone an increase in it. (Nonetheless, in

turns on exactly what constitutes excessive exposure. Al-Bābirtī answers that the discouragement of women advancing derives from the Prophet's *sunna*, not from the rationale of minimizing exposure; the latter is just an attempted explanation of the reason behind the Prophet's *sunna*.[50] Al-Bābirtī also appeals to the principle that the law shall be based on the ordinary rather than exceptional circumstances and labels the scenario envisaged by the objection as a rare one.[51] Al-ʿAynī and al-Laknawī would later refute this by pointing out that it is not a rare situation at all for women to be fully covered during prayers. Al-Laknawī also affirms that for a woman to stand in the front cannot be considered exposure if she is fully covered.[52]

4.8.2. *Did the Abrogation Remove Permissibility?*

I now come to an issue that speaks to the relationship between Ḥanafī legal philosophy (*uṣūl*) and positive law. According to a doctrine from Ḥanafī legal philosophy (*uṣūl*), once the obligatoriness of an act is abrogated, one cannot take that as an indication that the act remains desirable or even permissible. Of course, the act may in fact be permissible, but this can be established only through independent evidence; it cannot be inferred from the abrogated obligatoriness. To put the matter differently,

this case) it is (still) undesirable [according to the standard position] for her to step forward. But a rule cannot apply if its underlying cause is absent.

50 He does not say which *sunna* of the Prophet he is speaking of: the traditions about ʿĀʾisha or the traditions quoted by al-Zaylaʿī. Since the latter make no reference to the imām's position, it is probably the former that he has in mind. However, this raises the question of whether it is valid to argue from an abrogated practice, especially considering that in Ḥanafī legal theory the permissibility of an obligatory act does not necessarily survive the abrogation of the obligation.

51 He writes:

> [Answer to above objection]: That situation is rare and is unworthy of affecting the determination of the rule. For avoidance of stepping forward is established by the Prophetic norm (*sunna*), and the underlying cause [i.e., minimization of exposure] is mentioned [only] in order to explicate it [i.e., not to derive it].

52 Al-Laknawī adds:

> If by exposure is meant the exposure of that which should be covered [regardless of whether it be] during prayer or not, then stepping forward does not entail that [i.e., such exposure] (*lā yastalzamuhu*). If it refers to the exposure of that which need not be covered, then this [i.e., such exposure] is not incompatible with prayer [in general], let alone it being the cause of the undesirability of group prayers. If it refers to a woman standing out among the others and becoming conspicuous once she steps forward, this is something for which there is no indication (*dalīl*) of its being forbidden, and in addition, the same thing holds for a woman praying by herself.

Al-Laknawī also adds that standing in the middle cannot be forbidden *in general*, as the Ḥanafīs prefer that the imām stand in the middle when there are only two other worshippers.

obligatoriness entails permissibility, so when obligatoriness is abrogated, permissibility is no longer entailed. The Shāfi'īs disagreed, arguing that the inference to permissibility that exists prior to abrogation survives the abrogation (unless there is evidence to the contrary).[53]

Desirability entails permissibility just as obligatoriness does. So, the abrogation of the desirability of a thing gives rise to the same issue. Al-Bābirtī mentions, as a potential objection to the standard Ḥanafī position that he seeks to defend, that it may be argued that the permissibility of women's leadership ends once its desirability is abrogated, contradicting his view that the act remains permissible, if undesirable. He preempts this potential accusation of inconsistency by saying that the permissibility of the prayers is not deduced from the original desirability that was abrogated. Rather, it follows from independent considerations, namely the absence of anything that would invalidate the prayers.[54]

This discussion shows how, at a relatively late stage, scholars of positive law began paying some attention to whether their reasoning followed the theories developed in the *uṣūl* genre. (This burgeoning interest in interpretive norms within positive law may be compared to the case discussed in the previous chapter, Section 3.5, on the establishment of *farḍ* obligations.) However, such discussions did not change the legal decisions in points of positive law as one might imagine: they only affected the ways in which legal reasons were conceptualized, underscoring the primacy of the laws over the reasons given for them.

4.9. Concluding Remarks

With the exception of al-Laknawī, who agreed with al-'Aynī, later Ḥanafī law shifted from permitting women's group prayers to prohibiting them.

53 See al-Sarakhsī, *Uṣūl* (Beirut: Dār al-Kutub al-'Ilmiyya, 1414), 1:64–5.

54 The text in al-Bābirtī is as follows:

> [Potential objection:] Our doctrine is known to be that the termination of the attribute of obligatoriness entails the termination of the attribute of permissibility. In this respect, there is no difference between obligatoriness and desirability, as in both there is an occasioning indication (*mūjib*). ... So, if the desirability is abrogated, so is the permissibility, rendering the appeal to abrogation invalid.
>
> [The answer:] The permissibility that remains is permissibility that is included with undesirability. The permissibility that was included with (the desirability of) the desirable deed was abrogated along with it. The purpose of adducing 'Ā'isha's act was to explain that it was a desirable thing that was abrogated [i.e., it was not adduced to argue for permissibility]. It is permissible in our time [not on account of 'Ā'isha's tradition, but], rather, as a consequence of the permissibility that arises from the satisfaction of all the preconditions and the absence of the impediments for the permissibility of the prayer, despite its undesirability due to the commission of a prohibited thing.

To explain the shift to prohibition, one needs to understand why the law was prone to change. A readjustment was called for by the apparent incoherence of al-Marghīnānī's doctrine. Al-Bābirtī managed to say that a certain lawful act involves an unlawful act,[55] but most jurists did not. It was natural for thinking on this matter to move from such a precarious position toward a stable equilibrium.

The question is why the law moved in the particular direction it did. To answer that question, one must first consider what options were available. One was to rule for the neutrality or the desirability of the law, as did al-'Aynī. This would have provided the simplest explanation for the textual data. In a single stroke, it would have removed the need to reconcile the law with the apparent purport of the traditions and eliminated the discrepancy with the funeral prayers. But the gains in the simplicity of justification would have been outweighed by losses in another area. This approach would have marked the most radical break possible with the statements of the founders of the school. From the standpoint of legal continuity, it would have been a disaster. That the law did not move in this direction represents the triumph of inertia and continuity.[56]

The other possible destinations were undesirability *qua* blamelessness and prohibition (actually, undesirability *qua* prohibition). From the standpoint of legal continuity, these two options were more acceptable, as they could be related to the early Ḥanafīs' use of the term "undesirable." They were both inferior from the standpoint of conforming to the apparent meaning of the canon as embodied in the reports about the Prophet's Companions. This did not mean that the reports could not be tamed, but doing so required a relatively complex explanation, thus incurring a cost in terms of explanatory simplicity and adherence to the apparent meaning of the texts. Explanatory complexity resulted from an iterative

[55] To wit, exposure. See the quotation on page 85, footnote 19. Al-Bābirtī's statements verge dangerously on a genuine contradiction (i.e., a statement of the form "A and not-A"). One may ask if al-Bābirtī was really cognizant of this or whether it escaped his attention. I believe it was the latter on the principle that jurists tend to abhor genuine logical contradictions.

[56] This is not to say that legal inertia always triumphs. New social conditions may help tip the balance the other way. In the case at hand, social change was not a compelling factor. This is indicated, for example, by the fact that the Shāfi'īs and the Ḥanbalīs had no problem with desirability and showed no pressure to move toward restriction. The relative absence of compelling social factors in this case allows one to judge the relative strengths of the other two factors, legal inertia versus bias for the apparent meaning of the canon (which goes hand in hand with justificatory simplicity in this case), as they are left alone in the field to contend with each other.

process: an adjustment would be made to save the canon-blind law, leading to inconsistencies elsewhere in the system, prompting yet further adjustments to restore consistency. Moreover, this process made it easy for loose ends to appear and persist. All of this was the cost that jurists were prepared to pay for the sake of continuity.

The question is, why, of these two options, prohibition was preferred. This may have had to do with the justification al-Marghīnānī managed to devise for prohibition, which became a ready-made solution later jurists could have recourse to. The problem with such prayers was that the imām had to stand in the row. The status of the prayer was thus equated with the status of the abnormal position of the imām, which was thought to be forbidden, thus precluding mere undesirability *qua* blamelessness. The prohibition was consolidated by the influential commentary of Ibn al-Humām, where he highlighted the obligatory character of any act the Prophet persisted upon uniformly.[57] In the absence of social pressure for greater laxity or new pressing circumstances, jurists took the first way opened to them out of the quandary presented by al-Marghīnānī's formulation. In short, the prohibition outcome was the consequence of a historical accident (i.e., the form al-Marghīnānī's justification took) combined with legal inertia and the absence of countervailing social pressures. The evolution of law is path-dependent, like biological evolution, in that the prior trajectory does matter for the final outcome.

It is worth remembering what precipitated the dynamic that finally led to prohibition: it was al-Marghīnānī's attempt to interpret the early traditions about the Companions in a way that would accommodate the law. This endeavor was motivated by the fact that the traditions were binding. Yet, seemingly paradoxically, it resulted in the law moving away from the apparent import of the reports. "Traditionalism," in the sense of considering the *ḥadīth*s as binding, need not entail following their apparent meaning. It means, rather, acknowledging their authority and, therefore, accounting for them by showing that they do not contradict the school's law. That is done by building a bridge of exegetic rationales from the

[57] There are two indications that here, in stating this principle, Ibn al-Humām was not just working back from the law to its rationale. First, and most importantly, as I have shown, he was not committed to the law in this case. Second, he held the methodological principle quite independently of this particular law. (See Ibn al-Humām's view as discussed by Ibn Nujaym in his commentary at the first occurrence of the word *sunna*, in *al-Baḥr*, 1:35–36). Ibn Nujaym, however, disagreed with Ibn al-Humām, ruling for *sunna mu'akkada* rather than *wājib* in such cases. But he forgot this general principle of his when it came to the group-prayer issue (see page 95, footnote 40).

law to the traditions. The exegetic rationales against women-only prayers involved, among other things, abrogation. The fact that they were used to argue for a position that went against the apparent meaning of the canon relates to the fact that the standards governing the use of abrogation and other techniques were loose. It signifies nearly maximal hermeneutic flexibility.

5

Women Praying with Men: Communal Prayers

5.1. Introduction

At the time of the Prophet, women attended communal prayers, that is, group prayers that were performed publicly.[1] Sometime in the first century, in Medina and Kūfa, opposition arose to women attending communal prayers, while Baṣra and Mecca tended to stay with the status quo.

[1] This chapter is based on the following Ḥanafī texts – and the quotations in the chapter are from these sources unless specified otherwise: Abū Yūsuf, *Āthār*, 56, no. 277 (on daily prayers); 59–60, no. 293 (on *ʿĪds*); 80, nos. 396, and 82, no. 411 (on funeral prayers); al-Shaybānī, *Āthār*, published as Abū Ḥanīfa, *Āthār* (al-Shaybānī's recension), 205, no. 204; al-Ṭaḥāwī, *Mukhtaṣar ikhtilāf al-ʿulamāʾ*, in al-Jaṣṣāṣ, *Mukhtaṣar ikhtilāf al-ʿulamāʾ*, 1:231–2, no. 171; Abū al-Layth al-Samarqandī, *ʿUyūn al-masāʾil*, 2:35, no. 171; al-Qudūrī, *Mukhtaṣar*, 29–30; al-Sarakhsī, *Mabsūṭ*, 2:41; al-Kāsānī, *Badāʾiʿ al-ṣanāʾiʿ*, 1:157; Qāḍī Khān, *Fatāwā Qāḍī Khān*, printed in the margin of al-Shaykh Niẓām et al., *al-Fatāwā al-ʿĀlamgīrīya*, 1:183; al-Marghīnānī, *Hidāya*, 1:148–9; al-Mawṣilī, *Ikhtiyār*, 1:59; al-Manbijī, *Lubāb*, 1:278; al-Nasafī, *Kanz al-daqāʾiq*, see the inset text included with al-Zaylaʿī, *Tabyīn al-ḥaqāʾiq;* ʿUthmān b. ʿAlī al-Zaylaʿī, *Tabyīn al-ḥaqāʾiq*, 1:357; al-Bābirtī, *ʿInāya*, printed with Ibn al-Humām, *Fatḥ al-qadīr*, 1:365–6; al-ʿAynī, *Bināya*, 2:420–2; Ibn al-Humām, *Fatḥ al-qadīr*, 1:365–6; Mullā Khusraw, *Durar al-ḥukkām*, 1:107; al-Ḥalabī, *Multaqā al-abḥur*, 1:95; Zayn al-Dīn Ibn Nujaym, *al-Baḥr al-rāʾiq*, 1:581–2, 627–8; al-Timurtāshī, *Tanwīr al-abṣār*, 15; Sirāj al-Dīn Ibn Nujaym, *al-Nahr al-fāʾiq*, 1:250–1; al-Shurunbulālī, *Nūr al-īḍāḥ*, printed with al-Shurunbulālī, *Marāqī al-falāḥ*, 303, 306; al-Shurunbulālī, *Marāqī al-falāḥ*, 303, 306; al-Shurunbulālī, *Ḥāshiya* [on Mullā Khusraw's *Durar al-ḥukkām*], printed with Mullā Khusraw, *Durar al-ḥukkām*, 1:107; al-Ḥaṣkafī, *al-Durr al-mukhtār*, 1:99–100; al-Shaykh Niẓām et al., *al-Fatāwā al-ʿĀlamgīrīya*, 1:85, 89; Abū al-Suʿūd, *Fatḥ al-muʿīn*, 1:215; al-Ṭaḥṭāwī, *Ḥāshiyat al-Ṭaḥṭāwī ʿalā al-Durr al-mukhtār*, 1:245–6; al-Ṭaḥṭāwī, *Ḥāshiyat al-Ṭaḥṭāwī ʿalā Marāqī al-falāḥ*, 168; Ibn ʿĀbidīn, *[Ḥāshiyat] Radd al-muḥtār*, 1:567, 610; Ibn ʿĀbidīn, *Minḥat al-Khāliq*, printed with Ibn Nujaym, *al-Baḥr al-rāʾiq*, 1:380; al-Afghānī, *Kashf al-ḥaqāʾiq*, 1:55.

That the tendency opposed to attendance in the first century of Islam belonged to a secondary layer is betrayed by, among other indications, the fact that most of the traditions it generated acknowledge, implicitly or explicitly, that women had formerly been allowed to attend communal prayers. Opposition to women's attendance grew significantly in the first two centuries and left its mark on early Ḥanafī law.[2] In subsequent centuries, Ḥanafī law would become still stricter, eventually banning all women from all communal prayers.[3]

In mature Ḥanafī law, as formulated by Ibn Nujaym, a man must forbid his wife from leaving his house except in circumstances prescribed by the law. The list of these exceptional circumstances was a subject of wide disagreement. The cases that were discussed include communal prayers, religious gatherings, visiting parents and other relatives, funerals of relatives, the *Ḥajj*, public baths, the court of law, exacting a debt, and working as midwives or corpse-washers.[4] I now examine the trajectory of Ḥanafī positions on the daily prayers in the mosques, the *'Īd* prayers, and the Friday prayers. I investigate the degree of hermeneutic flexibility, the degree of bias for the apparent meaning of the canon, the priority of laws as compared to the reasons given for them, and the way exegetic rationales are used to reconcile the laws with the canon.

5.2. Early Ḥanafī Law: Abū Ḥanīfa to al-Qudūrī

5.2.1. *The Two 'Īd Prayers*

Abū Yūsuf quotes the following tradition through Abū Ḥanīfa—'Abd al-Karīm b. Abī al-Mukhāriq (d. 126/744, Baṣran, settled in Mecca)—Umm 'Aṭīya: "Women were granted a concession (*kāna yurakhkhaṣ li-al-nisā'*) in regard to going out during the two *'Īds*, so much so that two virgins would go out sharing the same garment [covering them, when one lacked a cover], and even the menstruating women would come out, sitting in the midst of the women, performing supplication but not the ritual prayer."[5] Al-Shaybānī quotes this tradition from Abū Ḥanīfa with the

[2] Research supporting the contents of this paragraph up to this point will be published separately.

[3] As Marion Katz has noted, Shāfi'ī jurists also limited women's attendance at communal prayers. They gave arguments that were similar to Ḥanafī justifications, including the appeal to the "corruption of the current age." See Marion Katz, "The 'Corruption of the Times' and the Mutability of the *Shari'a*," *Cardozo Law Review* 28.1 (2006): 171–85.

[4] See Ibn Nujaym, *al-Baḥr*, 4:331, within *Bāb al-nafaqa* (the chapter on the maintenance the husband provides the wife).

[5] Abū Yūsuf, *Āthār*, 59–60, no. 293.

same *isnād*, but truncates the *ḥadīth* beginning with "so much so that" through the end.[6] In addition, six other people reportedly relate this tradition from Abū Ḥanīfa with the same *isnād*.[7] This shows that the earliest Ḥanafīs understood that at the time of the Prophet women could attend the *ʿĪd* prayers regardless of age.

The use of the verb *rakhkhaṣa*, "grant a concession," might hint that women would not have "normally" been expected to leave the house to attend communal prayers, and that an exception was made for them. So the tradition may have arisen in a context where women's seclusion was considered normal. The word concession is absent in all the other variants of this relatively well-attested Baṣran *ḥadīth*. It is a uniquely Kūfan way of formulating the issue, as the only other references to concession in connection with the *ʿĪd* prayers go back to Kūfan authorities and Kūfan Imāmī *ḥadīths*. It seems that the reference to concession in Abū Ḥanīfa's tradition is a contribution of Abū Ḥanīfa himself: as the *ḥadīth* moved from Baṣra to Kūfa in the first half of the second century, it was recast to better fit the prevailing Kūfan legal language and outlook.[8] The Baṣran *ḥadīth*, on the face of it, required (in some versions) or at least recommended the participation of women, young and old. Abū Ḥanīfa changed this to a mere permission, in fact an exceptional one.

But the permission implied in the Prophetic report did not in fact reflect Abū Ḥanīfa's own position. Immediately after quoting the concession tradition, al-Shaybānī writes: "I would not like (*lā yuʿjibunā*) for [women] to come out, except for old women (*al-ʿajūz al-kabīra*). And that

[6] This Baṣran tradition is elsewhere related through Abū Ḥanīfa—Ḥammād—Ibrāhīm—someone who heard Umm ʿAṭīya—Umm ʿAṭīya; see al-Mullā ʿAlī al-Qāriʾī, *Sharḥ Musnad Abī Ḥanīfa* (Beirut: Dār al-Kutub al-ʿIlmiyya), 134. The common link of this tradition, which seems to have been confined to Baṣra in the first century, was Ibn Sīrīn (d. 110, Baṣra). It would be worth examining whether any of Ibn Sīrīn's traditions had found their way to Ibrāhīm. Another reason to be suspicious of this *isnād* is that its wording reflects the Abū Ḥanīfa *ḥadīth* I have quoted, refers like it to a "concession," and diverges in this respect from every other variant of this well attested tradition. In short, it is possible that the *matn* was based on the genuine tradition of Abū Ḥanīfa from his Baṣran authority and was then incorrectly supplied with the standard *isnād* of the Ḥanafī school back to Ibrāhīm.

[7] Al-Khwārazmī, *Jāmiʿ al-masānīd*, 1:371. The version quoted by al-Ḥasan b. Ziyād in his *Musnad* has the part that al-Shaybānī omits.

[8] This is not to question Abū Ḥanīfa's integrity. He was simply paraphrasing the tradition rather than relating it verbatim, a practice that was common and acceptable in the first two centuries of Islam, especially through the mid-second century. Paraphrasing, however, could introduce unintended substantive distortions by letting the presuppositions of the transmitter creep into a tradition. In this case, it turned an obligatory or recommended thing into an exceptionally permissible thing.

is the position of Abū Ḥanīfa."[9] He apparently imposes no restriction on the time of day old women may come out. Similarly, al-Ṭaḥāwī relates through Muḥammad [b. Samā'a] (d. 233/848, judge, companion and successor to Abū Yūsuf)—Abū Yūsuf that Abū Ḥanīfa said, "women were granted a concession in regard to going out on the two *'Īds*. However, as for today, I dislike it (*akrahuhu*)." This is consistent with the first report, despite the silence on the exceptional case of old women. Similarly, Abū al-Layth al-Samarqandī reports that in al-Ḥasan b. Ziyād's (d. 204/819) transmission, Abū Ḥanīfa said there was no problem with old women going out in the *'Īd* to pray with people.[10] Ibrāhīm al-Nakha'ī, the forefather of Ḥanafī law, had held the exact same view: disapproval for young women, permission for old ones. Abū Ḥanīfa does not quote him, but two independent early sources with two different *isnāds* down to Manṣūr b. al-Mu'tamir (d. 132/749, Kūfa) have preserved Ibrāhīm's view.[11]

Some later sources report an alternative opinion from Abū Ḥanīfa: disapproval even for old women.[12] These reports disagree with the early evidence, and are probably spurious, representing later figures' attempts to ground their own views in the authority of Abū Ḥanīfa.

Al-Ṭaḥāwī was not prepared to sacrifice existing law for the *Ḥadīth*; but neither was he going to simply discard the Prophetic report as Abū Ḥanīfa and al-Shaybānī had done. After quoting the *ḥadīth* of Umm 'Aṭīya that the Prophet commanded that women attend the *'Īd* prayer, al-Ṭaḥāwī expounds the vexatious report: "it may have been so when the Muslims were small in number and he (the Prophet) sought by their attendance to make them (appear) more numerous in order to intimidate the enemy. But today there is no need for that." Al-Ṭaḥāwī is here suggesting that women's attendance was permitted due to a rationale that would have ceased to be operative beyond the early days of Islam. He might also be hinting at abrogation, although this is not clear. This approach places him in a different class than Abū Ḥanīfa and al-Shaybānī, who appeared, on the surface at least, to go against Prophetic precedent, and who made no effort to dispel this appearance. Al-Ṭaḥāwī does not deny the perpetually binding quality of the Prophet's edicts. He denies only that this particular *ḥadīth* was meant to apply to all circumstances, or that it was the Prophet's last word on the subject.

[9] Al-Shaybānī, *Āthār*, 205, no. 204.

[10] Abū al-Layth al-Samarqandī, *'Uyūn al-masā'il*, 2:35, no. 171.

[11] The details will be published in a separate study.

[12] Abū al-Layth al-Samarqandī, *'Uyūn al-masā'il*, 2:35, no. 171, reports this as an alternative report without a source.

Al-Ṭaḥāwī does not substantiate his explanation. His wording ("it may have been so") makes its speculative nature clear. This leaves one with the puzzle of a jurist who knows what the law is but is not sure of the reason for it. This would appear paradoxical if one assumed that a law derives from the reason given for it, and that, therefore, if the law is known, then so must any premise be that led to that law. The paradox vanishes once it is realized that for al-Ṭaḥāwī the law is the starting point, and the reason offered for the law is secondary. The law he knows; the reason he has to devise. The outcome and result of his interpretive endeavor is a justification for the canon-blind law. The justification may vary greatly from Abū Ḥanīfa to al-Ṭaḥāwī, but the law remains stable by comparison.

5.2.2. *The Daily and Friday Prayers*

All agreed that women do not have to attend any communal daily or Friday prayers;[13] but if they do, their prayers are valid.[14] However, that leaves open the question of whether they should be allowed to attend such prayers in the first place. Given Ibrāhīm al-Nakhaʿī and Abū Ḥanīfa's apparent reluctance to countenance their attendance at the *ʿĪd*s, which are held just twice a year, one would expect no less sensitivity and antipathy in the case of the daily or Friday prayers. At the very least, one would expect disapproval regarding the younger women. The only question should be about the attendance of old women (who were allowed at the *ʿĪd*s).

Indeed, Abū Ḥanīfa, al-Shaybānī, and Abū Yūsuf are said by the sources, beginning with al-Ṭaḥāwī, to have "disliked" it in the case of young women. How about old women? Does the exception made for them at the *ʿĪd*s extend to other prayers too? According to al-Ṭaḥāwī, both al-Shaybānī and Abū Yūsuf held that old women could attend all prayers. Therefore, for them, age is the determining factor, not the type of prayer or time of day. Later sources consistently attribute to them the same view.

While Abū Yūsuf does not report Abū Ḥanīfa's view, he does report a relevant tradition from him: Abū Ḥanīfa—Ibn ʿUmar: "The Prophet granted women a concession (*rukhṣa*) to go out for the morning prayer

[13] For example, a *ḥadīth* runs: Muḥammad al-Shaybānī (*Āthār*, 204, no. 199)—Abū Ḥanīfa—Ghaylān and Ayyūb b. ʿĀ'idh al-Ṭā'ī—Muḥammad b. Kaʿb al-Quraẓī—Prophet: "Four (groups) do not have to attend the Friday prayer: women, slaves, travelers, and the sick."

[14] See, e.g., both Abū Ḥanīfa and al-Shaybānī in al-Shaybānī, *Āthār*, 204, no. 199.

and the latter evening prayer (*al-ghadā' wa-al-'ishā' al-ākhira*). A man said to Ibn 'Umar, 'But women will abuse it!' Ibn 'Umar said, 'I report from the Prophet and this is what you say?'"[15] However, this does not say what Abū Ḥanīfa's own position was.

I am unable to reconstruct Abū Ḥanīfa's position, since the earliest sources available to me do not mention it, while later sources are contradictory, mentioning three separate positions. The earliest report is from al-Ṭaḥāwī, who relates through Bishr b. al-Walīd (d. 238/852, Baghdad)—Abū Yūsuf—Abū Ḥanīfa: "women going out for the *'Īd*s is fine (*ḥasan*), but he [Abū Ḥanīfa] did not accept their going out for any prayer beyond the two *'Īd* prayers."[16] The language is unequivocal regarding disapproval for all other prayers. Later reports say that his approval extended to all prayers,[17] or alternatively to nighttime prayers only. The latter view is the most cited one, probably because it represents the closest fit to the subsequent Ḥanafī positions; yet, in a way it is the least likely one: for even though it perfectly fits al-Ṭaḥāwī's view, al-Ṭaḥāwī does not ascribe it to Abū Ḥanīfa.

Let us now examine al-Ṭaḥāwī's position. He says, "I dislike (*akrah*) their [old women's] attending Friday prayers and the required daily prayers (*al-maktūba*) in congregation. I permit the old women to attend the evening (*al-'ishā'*) and dawn prayers and nothing beyond that." Thus, the exception for the old women in the case of the *'Īd*s extends to other prayers as well, albeit this extension is restricted to the evening and dawn prayers. Why single out those prayers? Al-Ṭaḥāwī might have preferred to keep elderly women out of all communal prayers, but in deference to *ḥadīth*s that say plainly that women may go to the mosque, he had to

[15] Abū Yūsuf, *Āthār*, 56, no. 277. According to al-Khwārazmī (*Jāmi' al-masānīd*, 1:438), the tradition is reported with the same wording by Abū Muḥammad al-Bukhārī through Muḥammad b. Ibrāhīm b. Ziyād—Abū Bilāl—Abū Yūsuf—Abū Ḥanīfa—Ḥammād—Ibrāhīm—al-Sha'bī—Ibn 'Umar—Prophet. So, three links have been inserted between Abū Ḥanīfa and the Companion Ibn 'Umar to yield a perfectly connected Kūfan *isnād* with the standard Ḥanafī links down to Ibrāhīm.

[16] The attributions in the Arabic text are not straightforward. The text reads: *'an Abī Yūsuf* ***wa****-Abī Ḥanīfa annahu qāla khurūj al-nisā' fī al-'īdayn ḥasan* ***wa-lam yakun yarā*** *khurūjahunna fī shay'in min al-ṣalawāt mā khalā al-'īdayn*. My translation is based on reading *'an* for *wa*. Another possibility (that Hossein Modarressi brought to my attention) is reading *aw* for *wa*. In this reading, the narrator expresses uncertainty about whom the saying belongs to: Abū Yūsuf or Abū Ḥanīfa.

[17] The editor of Abū al-Layth al-Samarqandī's *'Uyūn al-masā'il* gives a quotation to this effect from Abū Ḥanīfa (*'Uyūn al-masā'il*, 2:28, footnote 1), citing *Mukhtalif al-riwāya*. This book is by 'Alā' al-Dīn al-Samarqandī. (Schacht mistakenly lists it as a book of Abū al-Layth al-Samarqandī in his *EI*[2] article on the latter.)

find some circumstance in which women might do so. That would enable him to say that he interprets the *ḥadīth* to refer to those specific circumstances. He is careful to quote a variant of the tradition of Ibn ʿUmar that mentions nighttime specifically, although most variants of the tradition make no reference to nighttime: Ibn ʿUmar—Prophet: "'Allow women at night,' meaning (allow them to go) to the mosque."[18] Then he adds, "this shows that in the daytime it is the opposite," meaning that women should not be given permission in daytime.

If one asked al-Ṭaḥāwī if his position did not contravene the Prophet's edict, "Do not bar God's handmaidens from God's places of worship," he would say no and offer the following analysis: The language of the tradition is general (*ʿāmm*). So, going by its surface meaning (*ẓāhir*), the *ḥadīth* sets no limits, implying that women of all ages should be allowed to attend all the prayers. However, external considerations allow one to swerve from its apparent sense to admit two qualifications. First, the seemingly general designation of women in the *ḥadīth* must have been intended to refer to the elderly among them only. Second, the edict was meant to refer only to the two nighttime prayers, ruling out, for example, the Friday prayers. He would justify the second restriction by citing the *ḥadīth* mentioning nighttime prayers. It is less clear, though, how he would justify the age limitation, something that he takes from his predecessors, going back ultimately to the Kūfan Ibrāhīm. Perhaps he would argue using a Companion tradition he quotes: Sufyān al-Thawrī—ʿAbd Allāh b. ʿUmar: "Woman is nakedness (*ʿawra*). She is closest to God in the depths of her house (*bayt*). If she goes out, Satan hovers above her (*istashrafahā*)." The problem, of course, is that whereas normally it takes a relatively specific statement to qualify a general one, this tradition is general itself and may plausibly be assumed to be qualified by traditions permitting women to go out to prayers. Besides, the age distinction is absent in the tradition; it crops up only in views ascribed to Successors and later authorities. However, one could link the tradition to age if one noted that Satan finds younger women more useful for his purposes. As is often the case, al-Ṭaḥāwī does not detail his argument in an explicit way. But, as is equally often the case, one can plausibly reconstruct his argument using the proof texts he quotes. In this case, one could probably best sum up his approach by saying that he uses qualification, in a flexible way and based on carefully selected variants of traditions, to

[18] The mention of "night" was a late addition to the tradition from the second or third century, as I will demonstrate in a separate publication.

fritter away the apparent contents of vexatious *ḥadīth*s to the maximum extent possible.

Al-Ṭaḥāwī's treatments respectively of the *'Īd* and non-*'Īd* prayers have some things in common. In both cases, he confronts a fundamental discordance between the apparently permissive *ḥadīth*s and the Ḥanafī laws. In both cases, he tries to tame the *ḥadīth*s rather than reject them, underscoring how conclusively the Prophet's *sunna* was vested with unexceptionable authority for him. The two cases differ, however, in the manner in which he neutralizes a norm apparently found in a *ḥadīth*: in one case, he posits a rationale for it that applies to very limited circumstances; in the other, he uses qualification to narrow its scope to relative insignificance.

5.2.3. *After al-Ṭaḥāwī*

Al-Qudūrī lays out this position concisely and precisely:

It is undesirable (*yukrah*) for women to attend the communal prayers (*al-jamā'a*). But there is no objection to elderly women going out [to attend the *jamā'a*] for the dawn, sunset, and dusk prayers – this, according to Abū Ḥanīfa. Abū Yūsuf and Muḥammad [al-Shaybānī] held that elderly women may go out for any prayer.

Al-Qudūrī, like the other sources examined so far, provides characteristically terse rulings. By contrast, al-Sarakhsī seeks to provide the wisdom and broad rationales behind the laws.

In the eyes of al-Sarakhsī, and indeed all later Ḥanafīs, acts of lewdness or harassment perpetrated by men constitute the reason why women are discouraged from going out. Going out at night is better as the darkness provides an additional layer of protection from the gaze of men. Friday prayers are unsuitable since in the congestion of the crowd, lewd men try to molest women. But *'Īd* prayers, less congested since held in the plain outside the city, are more suitable:

He [al-Ḥākim al-Shahīd Muḥammad b. Muḥammad (d. 334/945)] said[19]: "Women do not have a duty to go out in the two *'Īds*. They used to be allowed to do so (*wa-qad kāna yurakhkhaṣ lahunna fī dhālik*). But as for today, I dislike that," that is, for the young ones. They have been commanded to stay in houses and forbidden (*nuhīna*) to go out because of the temptation (or misdeeds, *fitna*) that would entail. As for old women, according to Abū Ḥanīfa they are allowed to go out to

[19] It is not clear to me where al-Ḥākim al-Shahīd's words end and those of al-Sarakhsī begin. It is possible that al-Shaybānī is quoted in the text without being identified, as his writing was the basis of al-Ḥākim al-Shahīd's work. I wonder about the authenticity of some of the material ascribed to Abū Ḥanīfa and his students in this text.

the communal prayers of the sunset, evening, morning, and the two *ʿĪds*, but they are not allowed to go out for the prayers of the midday, afternoon, and Friday. But Abū Yūsuf and Muḥammad (al-Shaybānī) gave old women permission in the case of all prayers, including those of the eclipse and rain-supplication because the going out of old women does not lead to misdeeds, because people are rarely desirous of them (*wa-al-nās qalla-mā yarghabūna fīhinna*), and because they used to go out to the *jihād* with the Messenger of God, tending to the sick, (bringing) water, and cooking. Abū Ḥanīfa said: in the case of the nighttime prayers the old woman goes out concealed, the darkness of the night interposing between her and the gaze of men, unlike in the case of the daytime prayers. But the Friday prayers are performed in the city, where because of the largeness of the crowds often she gets jostled (*tuṣraʿ*) and bumped into, which involves a misdeed (or temptation; *fī dhālik fitna*). As for the old woman, if a young man does not desire her, then an old man like herself will; and often excessive lust makes (even) a young man desire her and try to bump into her. As for the *ʿĪd* prayer, it is performed in the plain (outside the city), where she would be able to withdraw to a spot away from the men where she would not be bumped into.

Next, [the text reads] "when they go out to the *ʿĪd* prayer": it is related in the tradition of al-Ḥasan [b. Ziyād al-Lu'lu'ī, d. 204/820, Kūfa and Baghdad] about (*ʿan*) Abū Ḥanīfa (that he said): [that means that] the women pray, since what is meant by "going out" is (performing) the prayer. [The Prophet] said, "Do not bar God's handmaidens from God's places of worship. When they go out, they should go out unperfumed." Muʿallā [b. Manṣūr, d. 211/827, Baghdad] related about (*ʿan*) Abū Yūsuf, (that he said) about Abū Ḥanīfa (that he said): women do not pray the *ʿĪd* with the imām. The purpose of their going out is to make Muslims appear more numerous. It is mentioned in the *ḥadīth* of Umm ʿAṭīya that women used to go out for the two *ʿĪds* with the Messenger of God, even the secluded ones (*dhawāt khudūr*)[20] and the menstruating ones. Obviously, menstruating women do not pray, so it appears that their going out was intended to make Muslims appear more numerous.[21] So it is in our time.

A noteworthy feature of this passage is a possible allusion, by its choice of words (*fa-qad umirna bi-al-qarār fī al-buyūt*), to the Qur'ānic passage that asks the Prophet's wives to conduct themselves at home with dignity,[22] making him the first Ḥanafī jurist to connect the Prophet-specific verse to the issue of women's prayers. But the greater interest of the passage perhaps lies in its appeal to matters of a factual (as distinct from normative) nature, such as how lewd men typically behaved and where *ʿĪd* prayers

[20] This is probably a reference to young women and girls. The use of the word "even" implies that not all women were secluded.

[21] A version of the tradition indicates that menstruating women went out and listened to the sermons. So, the presence of menstruating women is not strong evidence for al-Sarakhsī's (and al-Ṭaḥāwī's) theory that the point was to make Muslims appear more numerous.

[22] Qur'ān 33.33. See Chapter 4, page 83, footnote 14.

were normally held. Here is another passage in al-Sarakhsī bearing on women that describes cultural and social realities and even has social custom trump a tradition of ʿĀʾisha as a source of law:

> There are those who say: "The public bath is the house of the devil. The Messenger of God called it an evil house, where nakedness is revealed, and where dirty wash water and impurities pour forth." Then there are those who distinguish between men's baths and women's baths. They say, "Having (*ittikhādh*) women's baths is reprehensible (*yukrah*) since they are forbidden to go out and have been commanded to stay indoors, and since their gatherings are hardly ever free of misdeeds (or temptation, *fitna*). It is related that some women came to ʿĀʾisha, and she said, 'You are among those who enter baths,' and ordered that they be made to leave." But the correct position according to us is that there is no problem with having baths for either men or women because of the need for it, especially in our country. The need for it in the case of women is more obvious, since women need to cleanse themselves of menstruation, childbirth, and major impurity, but they cannot do so in rivers and ponds the way men can; and also since it counts as adornment by virtue of the removal of filth, and women have a greater need for things that amount to adornment.[23]

It must have been practical considerations of this type combined with personal and cultural norms of propriety that led to the genesis of many laws in the first place. However, one cannot assume that the considerations on the minds of the founders, Ibrāhīm, Abū Ḥanīfa, and the latter's students, were necessarily those that al-Sarakhsī and later scholars imagined centuries later. Indeed, in some cases, one can be sure that they were not. An interesting example is provided by the distinction between the nighttime and Friday prayers. Al-Sarakhsī explains that nighttime is fine for old women because they are less conspicuous then, while Friday prayers are unacceptable because they are too crowded. But al-Marghīnānī, who just like al-Sarakhsī points out the contrast between Abū Ḥanīfa and his students and gives the former the last word, contrives an entirely different and colorful explanation in terms of (the presumably regular and synchronized) sleeping and eating schedules of those who harassed women: "Wrongdoers (*fussāq*) spread out at noon [prayers] and afternoon [prayers] and on Fridays [when Friday prayers are held]. But during dawn [prayers] and evening [prayers, shortly after sunset] they sleep. And at sunset [prayers] they are preoccupied with eating." One sees again that

23 Al-Sarakhsī, *Mabsūṭ*, 15:156. Elsewhere, he adds: "The manifest custom in all countries to construct public baths for women and to let them enter the baths indicates the correctness of our position" (*Mabsūṭ*, 10:147). This sentence is valuable for the light it might shed on actual practice. See Section 7.4.

jurists are much more consistent about the laws than about the reasons for them, a sign that the laws are the starting point, not the legal reasons. In this case, neither al-Sarakhsī's nor al-Marghīnānī's reason is what had generated the law. As I suggested previously, the evening exception was probably a last resort concession to the *Ḥadīth*.

Al-Kāsānī is the first jurist to speak of prohibition rather than undesirability for younger women; and he leaves older women alone:

> It is not permissible for younger women to go out to communal prayers because of the report from 'Umar – that he forbade the young ones from going out – and because their going out to prayer is the cause of temptation (or misdeeds, *fitna*). Temptation (*fitna*) is forbidden, and what leads to a forbidden thing is forbidden as well.

Qāḍī Khān writes that younger women "do not go out" to any communal prayers. For old women, he cites two opposite views: Abū Ḥanīfa's (*'Īds* and *'ishā'* are fine, but not any others, that is, not Friday, dawn, noon, afternoon, or sunset) and that of his two disciples (all fine). Al-Marghīnānī considers attendance undesirable for young women. His treatment, quoted here, was cited by numerous jurists after him:

> "It is undesirable for [women] to attend communal prayers": referring to the younger ones among them, because of the misdeeds [or temptations] that may ensue. "And there is no problem with old women going out to the dawn, sunset, evening, and *'Īd* prayers" – this is according to Abū Ḥanīfa. "But the two [Abū Yūsuf and al-Shaybānī] maintained that they could go out for all prayers," as that would be no misdeed since there would be little desire for her; so, it is not undesirable, just as in the case of the *'Īd*. But in favor of his [Abū Ḥanīfa's] position [is the argument]: excessive lust compels [some to sin against the elderly], so misdeeds occur. Except, wrongdoers (*fussāq*) spread out at noon [prayers] and afternoon [prayers] and on Fridays [when Friday prayers are held]. But during dawn [prayers] and evening [prayers, shortly after sunset] they sleep. And at sunset [prayers] they are preoccupied with eating."

Al-Manbijī says it is undesirable for young women to attend any prayer, night or day, on grounds similar to al-Kāsānī's rationale: 'Ā'isha had said, "if the Messenger of God had seen the things women have started doing, he would have barred women from mosques."

By a century after al-Marghīnānī, an important shift had taken place in Ḥanafī doctrine: the elderly were now treated like younger women. That rendered unnecessary the distinctions about which prayers they could or could not attend: they could attend none. Al-Mawṣilī writes that "the preferred view (*al-mukhtār*)" is thoroughgoing prohibition due to the "decadence of this age and (the rise of) open indecency (*fasād al-zamān wa-al-taẓāhur bi-al-fawāḥish*)." Similarly, in his *Kanz al-Daqā'iq*, al-Nasafī writes, "[women] do not attend communal prayers."[24] In his *al-Kāfī*, he writes, "The view in this age is undesirability in the case of all prayers due to the prevalence of misdeeds (*al-fatwā al-yawm 'alā-al-karāha fī al-ṣalāt kullihā li-ẓuhūr al-fasād*)." Al-Nasafī then adds, "And if attending prayers in the mosque is deemed undesirable, it is all the more undesirable for them to attend preachings (*wa'ẓ*), especially with these ignorant ones (as preachers) who put on the garb of scholars."[25] Whoever the "ignorant ones" may be, the intensity of the sentiment and the digressive character of the comment indicate a genuine reflection on reality rather than a fictional legal construction.

Al-Zayla'ī also quotes al-Nasafī, "[women] do not attend communal prayers," and then goes on to explain: "That is, in the cases of all prayers. The same holds with regard to the young ones and the elderly. That is the position of the later scholars (*al-muta'akhkhirūn*) due to the corruption in our time." After quoting al-Marghīnānī without attribution, al-Zayla'ī adds:

> But the generally preferred position (*al-mukhtār*) in our time consists of barring in all cases (*al-man' fī al-jamī'*) because of the change of the time. Thus, 'Ā'isha said, "Had the Messenger of God seen what we have seen, he would have barred women from the mosque as the Children of Israel had barred their women." Women had begun to adorn themselves and wear perfume and jewelry. For this reason, 'Umar barred them. There is no problem with changing laws (*al-aḥkām*) because of changes of the time, as, for example, in the case of the locking up of mosques, which is lawful in our time, as will be explained later, God willing.

It is not clear if al-Zayla'ī viewed the barring as indicating prohibition or undesirability. A century later, al-Bābirtī expresses a similar position. On young women he writes:

> It used to be lawful (or neutral, *mubāḥ*) for women to go out to prayers. Then they were barred (*muni'a*) from it on account of conditions leading to misdeeds (or temptation, *fitna*). It is mentioned in Qur'ānic exegesis on God's statement, "We

[24] Quoted in Ibn Nujaym, *al-Baḥr*, 2:380.

[25] Ibn Nujaym, *al-Baḥr*, 2:380. Ibn Nujaym systematically quotes the book *al-Kāfī*, without ever naming its author. The title *al-Kāfī* could refer either to the book of that title of al-Ḥākim al-Shahīd Muḥammad b. Muḥammad (d. 334/945), which was the main source for al-Sarakhsī's *al-Mabsūṭ*, or to *al-Kāfī sharḥ al-Wāfī* of al-Nasafī. The absence of the *fatwā* in al-Sarakhsī and its apparently later character support the latter choice. Furthermore, it would make sense for Ibn Nujaym to systematically use another work of al-Nasafī to fill in the details in the latter's more succinct *Kanz*.

know the ones of you who press forward, and We know the laggards,"[26] that it was revealed with reference to the Hypocrites who keep to the rear (rows) in order to get to see the women's nakedness.[27] 'Umar forbade (*nahā*) women from going out to the mosque. So, women complained to 'Ā'isha about it. She answered, "if the Prophet had come to know what 'Umar has come to know, he would not have allowed women to go out." Our scholars have used this tradition as evidence and comprehensively barred (*mana'ū*) younger women from going out.

In other words, the Ḥanafīs acknowledged that younger women had not been barred from going out at the time of the Prophet. Harking back to al-Kāsānī, they argued on the basis of the 'Ā'isha tradition that the Prophet would have barred women had he lived to observe the conditions of 'Umar's time. This was enough to bar younger women even though the Prophet had not done so. As for the elderly, 'Umar may not have banned them, but he had set the precedent of changing the rules with changing times. Thus, al-Bābirtī then goes on to say, "But the view in our age (*al-fatwa al-yawm*) is the undesirability (*karāha*) of [even old women's] attendance at all prayers because of the occurrence of misdeeds (or temptation, *al-fitna*)." At this point, the Ḥanafīs had not yet laid down a formal argument for the legitimacy of departure from the Prophetic precedent due to the changing times. They must rather have had an intuitive understanding that a legal effect may be reversed to satisfy the underlying purpose of the law. A formal explication of the matter would have to wait until the ninth/fifteenth century, when Ibn al-Humām wrote.

[26] Qur'ān 15.24, Arberry's translation.

[27] The words *mustaqdimīn* ("those who press forward") and *musta'khirīn* ("those who lag behind") in Qur'ān 15.24 are from the same roots as the words used in the *Ḥadīth* for the front and rear rows of the worshippers. That explains why some reports ineptly connected the verse to communal worship despite the inhospitable Qur'ānic context. The connection shows up in one of several possible interpretations cited by al-Ṭabarī. He writes, "It is possible that this verse was revealed with regard to those (men) who moved forward in the rows (of worshippers) because of women [occupying the rear rows] and to those who kept to the rear rows (of men) for the same reason. ... It would be a threat and warning to those who stay in the rear rows because of the women ... and a promise to those who advance forward in the rows because of the women." Al-Ṭabarī quotes a number of traditions in support of this view. Displaying an aptitude for invocation of vivid detail, one of them has Ibn 'Abbās say that a very beautiful woman used to pray with the Prophet. Those wishing to avoid seeing her went to the front rows, while certain others prayed in the men's back row, and during the prostrations viewed her from under their arms, leading to the revelation of the verse (al-Ṭabarī, *Jāmi' al-Bayān*, 14:34–6). I have nowhere come across the interpretation quite as al-Bābirtī has put it. At any rate, his citation of the verse is irrelevant to the points he is making, as the misdeed of men viewing women did not lead the Prophet to ban women.

5.3. Al-ʿAynī

Al-Bābirtī upgraded lawfulness for the elderly to undesirability and undesirability for younger women to prohibition. Al-ʿAynī, writing in the ninth/fifteenth century, takes the same positions. Commenting on the passage from al-Marghīnānī quoted in the previous section (on Abū Ḥanīfa's views on young women), he writes: "What is meant by undesirability is prohibition, especially in this age because of the corruption of the people living in it."[28]

Al-ʿAynī endorses al-Marghīnānī's colorful reasons for the acceptability of nighttime prayers: "[Scholars] say that all of that was in their time, but in our time it is undesirable for women to go out to communal prayers because of the prevalence of wickedness (*fisq*)." Wrongdoers, it appears, must have changed their sleeping habits. Then al-ʿAynī gives the last word to al-Nasafī's commentary in *al-Kāfī*, quoted above, on the barring of women of all ages.

It is quite remarkable that so far no jurist had given a methodologically conscious treatment of the contrary traditions. Al-ʿAynī is the first one to make explicit the qualification that I wrote may have taken place in the back of al-Ṭaḥāwī's mind. Al-ʿAynī sets out to neutralize the following widely-quoted tradition that could be described as favorable to women's attendance: (F1) ʿUmar—Prophet: "When at night your women ask you for permission to go to the mosque, let them." To deal with it, he says that this tradition "is interpreted to refer to the elderly." That is to say, it must be understood in a highly qualified sense. In corroboration, he cites three unfavorable Companion traditions and a Prophetic one: (U1) al-Bayhaqī relates through Ibn Masʿūd: "He [the Prophet] prevented (*nahā*) women from going out, except the old ones (*al-ʿajūz fī manqalayhā*[29])." Al-ʿAynī adds that it is sounder to regard this as a statement of the Companion Ibn Masʿūd's conduct rather than the Prophet's (*wa-al-aṣaḥḥ annahu mawqūf*

[28] His claim that Abū Ḥanīfa and al-Marghīnānī originally used "undesirability" to refer to prohibition is open to question. It might reflect a jurist's instinct to ground novel ideas in the authority of legal precedent, in this case in that of the eponym of the school. That al-ʿAynī may not have been sure that Abū Ḥanīfa had intended prohibition is suggested by his phrase, "especially in this age." Obviously Abū Ḥanīfa or al-Marghīnānī could not have known of the conditions of al-ʿAynī's time.

[29] The term *fī manqalayhā* ("in her *manqals*") is an archaic and slightly obscure expression in the *Ḥadīth*, where it is glossed by transmitters as "in her shoes" or "a woman who takes only small steps (*qad taqāraba khaṭwuhā*)," presumably due to old age (see al-Ṭabarānī, *al-Muʿjam al-kabīr*, 9:293–4). The former definition (shoes) is the right one, as it enjoys independent support from poetry (see Ibn Manẓūr, *Lisān al-ʿArab*, 11:675).

'alayh). In other words, he thinks that the attribution to the Prophet is erroneous. (U2) "Ibn 'Umar used to detain (his) womenfolk (at home) (*yaḥbisu al-nisā'*) except on Fridays, and they would leave (*yakhrujna*) the mosque." This awkward report is not attested anywhere. It must be a corruption of the following tradition: "I saw Ibn Mas'ūd throw pebbles at women (*yaḥṣibu al-nisā'*), removing them (*yukhrijuhunna*) from the mosque on Friday."[30] (U3) Abū 'Amr al-Shaybānī: Ibn Mas'ūd took an oath, swearing emphatically that a woman does not pray any prayer more pleasing to God than the one in her house, except in the case of the *Ḥajj*, the *'Umra*, or a woman who has despaired of marriage (due to old age). (U4) Aḥmad: Umm Salama—Prophet: "the best place of worship for women is the depths of their houses."

How strong are al-'Aynī's reasons? I lay aside the important question of the authenticity of these traditions, since al-'Aynī and other jurists normally treated the traditions as part of the canon without fussing too much over their *isnāds*. It will be noted right away that the relevance of U3 and U4 is open to doubt. To say that A is better than B does not mean that B is bad in itself. That point aside, none of the traditions for or against women's attendance makes an issue of women's age except U1, a Companion tradition. Thus, al-'Aynī is using the Companion tradition U1 to qualify the rule embodied in the Prophetic tradition. For a statement to qualify another statement presupposes not only that both are authentic, but also that they represent the same point of view. Put simply, it presupposes that the Prophet and the Companion had exactly the same views, so that the apparent contradiction between them is not a real contradiction. But, on the assumption of the authenticity of both F1 and U1, how plausible is it to assert that if the Prophet said "your women," he meant only a minority of them, namely the elderly? It is more natural to see F1 and U1 not as consistent, but rather as genuinely contradictory, representing different points of view. Some Ḥanafīs indeed took this view.[31]

Another feature of al-'Aynī's discussion is that it ignores other relevant traditions. What about 'Ā'isha's tradition? What of Umm 'Aṭīya's tradition? No doubt, al-'Aynī would have been able to explain these traditions away using the highly flexible techniques of qualification, abrogation, and so forth. But he did not. It is significant that seven hundred years after Abū Ḥanīfa, no Ḥanafī scholar had yet troubled himself to

[30] Ibn Abī Shayba, *Muṣannaf* (Beirut: Dār al-Fikr, 1409), 2:227.

[31] This standpoint (genuine contradiction) had been that of al-Bābirtī and al-Nasafī, who ascribed the barring to 'Umar, not to the Prophet. And it would also be the stance of later scholars such as Ibn al-Humām.

undertake a comprehensive analysis of the relevant traditions. Again, one would not expect this if jurists sought to derive the law from the *Ḥadīth*. Thus, with al-ʿAynī, one sees again a jurist endeavoring not to derive the law from the canon, but to justify the canon-blind law, which in this case is the received law. As it happens, al-ʿAynī's attempt was not only too little in terms of substance and range, but also too late. The recent Ḥanafī appeal to the "corruption of the time" had made the whole discussion moot. Thus, he would be the last jurist to ascribe the Ḥanafī decision directly to the Prophet. Later jurists would ascribe to the Prophet at most the rationale behind the ruling.

5.4. Ibn al-Humām's Recipe for Legal Change

Ibn al-Humām, after discussing the differences of earlier Ḥanafīs on whether the borderline cases of Friday and sunset prayers are acceptable for old women, brushes those distinctions aside: "The accepted position (*al-muʿtamad*) as I see it (*fī mā yaẓhar lī*) is the barring of all (women regardless of age) in (the case of) all (prayers), except for old women with a foot in the grave, not including old women who adorn themselves or those who still have a breath of life left in them."

The main interest of Ibn al-Humām's discussion is his sophisticated and elegant treatment of the methodological problems. He provides a theoretical justification for departing from the letter of the Prophetic edict due to "corruption of the time." He quotes and acknowledges the soundness of the *ḥadīth*: "Do not bar God's handmaidens from God's places of worship." But he argues that such statements of a general appearance must be understood in a restricted sense. He explains, "Scholars have qualified [the permission] by things that are either explicitly mentioned in the canon (*manṣūṣ ʿalayh*) or accepted by analogy." The first class of qualifications includes two *ḥadīth*-based ones: (1) the barring, according to the *Ḥadīth*, of women who have used incense or perfume.[32] (2) The *ḥadīth* quoted by Muslim, "Do not prevent women from going out to the mosques by night," which he understands to implicitly require barring at other times. In the second category, there are qualifications based on an analogy to the perfume restriction. The point is that if perfume causes barring, then so do other things that share its rationale. Perfume is relevant

[32] He quotes the *ḥadīth*: "Any woman perfumed with incense (*aṣābat bakhūran*) shall not attend the evening prayer (*al-ʿishāʾ*) with us." For the *ḥadīth* see Ibn Ḥanbal, *Musnad*, 2:304; etc.).

because it stimulates men. Therefore, other stimulants may be treated in the same manner as perfume, stimulants such as beautiful clothing on women or overcrowding that can lead to jostling. The presence of any of these factors is a cause for preventing women's attendance.

But is Ibn al-Humām not reversing a Prophetic injunction? He explains why he is not:

> It cannot be objected that this is a case of annulment of the law of the Prophet by virtue of the appeal to the reason behind it (*al-naskh bi-al-ta'līl*). For we shall reply: in this case prohibition follows from general principles that forbid tempting (*al-taftīn*). Alternatively, it is like when a thing applies on a certain condition, so that it is inoperative in the absence of the condition; as when a rule ceases to apply once its effective cause (*'illa*) ceases to exist.

In other words, Ibn al-Humām would argue that the law he advocates is identical to the Prophet's own law. The Prophet himself would have stipulated certain preconditions for the permission. Permission is granted if, and only if, these conditions are met, be it at the Prophet's time or later. So, the Prophet himself would have barred women if those conditions had been violated, for example, if there had been large crowds of men who would seek to jostle women. And, by the same token, if at some time in the future all the conditions are satisfied again, then permission will be granted again. The law, when understood integrally to include the preconditions for its application, has undergone no change since its inception at the time of the Prophet. Thus, there is no reversal to speak of.

Some of these conditions for permission are known from transmitted information: namely, abstention from perfume and fineries.[33] Others are inferred by analogy to the transmitted preconditions: for example, the absence of large crowds of men who would seek to jostle women, or an abundance of the wrongdoers:

> Considering the abovementioned identification of the cause (of the conditions leading to barring) (*al-ta'līl al-madhkūr*), unadorned women are also barred due to the overabundance of wrongdoers *(al-fussāq)*, and (they are barred) at night, too, even though the letter of the canon (*al-naṣṣ*) declares it lawful then, since at the present time wrongdoers spread out and are active (*ta'arruḍ*) mostly at night.

[33] Ibn al-Humām quotes two traditions: (1) A *ṣaḥīḥ ḥadīth* of 'Ā'isha: "Had the Messenger of God seen the things women began doing after him, he would have forbidden women [from going to the prayers], as the women of the Children of Israel had been forbidden." (2) "A report in Ibn 'Abd al-Barr's *al-Tamhīd*," through 'Ā'isha—Prophet: "O, people! Prevent your women from wearing adornments and perfume in places of worship. The Children of Israel were not cursed until their women wore adornments and perfume in places of worship."

Accordingly, it would follow from Abū Ḥanīfa's position that old women must be barred also at night, as opposed to the morning when wrongdoers are typically asleep. Nay, indeed the later scholars (*al-muta'akhkhirūn*) have generalized the prohibition to the old women and young ones in all prayers due to the overabundance of corruption at all times (of the day and the year).

Ibn al-Humām's insistence that a condition stipulated by the Prophet be observed in perpetuity is an incontrovertible part of Islamic legal thought. The more interesting and notable part of his argument is his expansion of the preconditions for prohibition by the use of analogy. Whatever the theory behind analogical reasoning may be, in practice it ensures hermeneutic flexibility by leaving the legal decision indeterminate. Depending on how it is applied, it can be used to justify drastically different solutions to a problem. In the hands of a jurist with a restrictive disposition, it can be utilized to expand the preconditions so drastically as to reduce to practical insignificance the situations in which the original assessment of permission applies. On the other hand, a more liberally inclined jurist, content with the plain sense of the available *ḥadīth*s, may choose to not resort to analogy in this case. Alternatively, he may posit a different effective cause (*'illa*) and hence different conditions under which the assessment applies. It is even conceivable that the jurist could think of an *'illa* that would imply permission where the Prophet had ruled for prohibition. Moreover, another jurist may still draw an analogy, but do so to something entirely different from the first jurist's choice. The indeterminacy introduced at several levels by analogy provides ample opportunity for jurists to justify the laws in terms of the practice of the Prophet.

These general remarks on the indeterminacy involved in analogy can be made clearer through the concrete example of the use Ibn al-Humām makes of it, and by imagining how other hypothetical jurists sharing Ibn al-Humām's methodological framework but not his values or his regard for legal precedent might approach the same question. It will be recalled that Ibn al-Humām identified temptation as the cause (*'illa*) behind the exclusion of perfumed and adorned women from mosques. The same factor, he argued, is present when there are large crowds of men, or when there are lewd men around. Another (hypothetical) jurist may point out that one of the things distinguishing perfume and fineries from the other factors is that in the former cases, it is the woman herself who enhances her desirability, taking an action that is gratuitous in a way that merely leaving one's house is not. The abundance of wicked men, he might argue, is not the handiwork of women themselves. He may then posit that the relevant factor behind the prohibition in the case of perfume and fineries is an act of gratuitous self-enhancement or seduction, or, put differently, a form of allurement that the woman can do something about short of staying home. If that is understood to be the relevant factor, then a woman's amorous singing and seductive dancing may be an impediment to her participation, as she can clearly do something about it – namely, stop singing and dancing – but the excessive libidos of some men, as alluded to by some earlier jurists, or their lack of morals will not be an impediment. The consequence of this approach would be the general acceptability of the participation of women, both young and old, in all prayers. Yet another hypothetical jurist might posit as a relevant factor the absence of a police force at the time of the Prophet to curb the activities of wrongdoers. Thus, he may "identify the cause" (*taʿlīl*) of the impediment to be self-enhancement in the absence of a police force when it is likely to lead to an assault on the woman. The consequence of this approach would be to allow even adorned women's attendance at all prayers in a society where wrongdoers are under control, even though self-adornment could still be considered a sin. This third approach uses Ibn al-Humām's method, and departs like it from the letter of the canon to apply a putative underlying principle, but it arrives at the opposite conclusion.

Here, my point is not that one or the other approach is better. I seek only to illustrate that the same methodology can accommodate a variety of incompatible conclusions, including opposite decisions and positions in between. In fact, one can imagine other variations in the application of analogy – including the choice to not apply analogy – allowing for a colorful array of solutions. Some solutions may be a stretch. But, for one thing, there will be a variety of plausible solutions, and for another thing, in practice jurists are not strangers to strained interpretations. In sum, to ground the law in the canon is not to derive the law from it, but to show its consistency with the canon. Hermeneutic flexibility allows jurists to reconcile the canon-blind law with the canon.

The effort to infer the preconditions behind an instance of Prophetic legislation that were not made explicit by the Prophet or the Qur'ān constitutes an attempt to understand the Prophetic and divine intent behind the original law. I do not subscribe to the view that it does not make sense to speak of the intent behind the law, or that finding out that intent is in principle an impossible task. But the determination of the intention involves a leap from what is known (relatively speaking, that is) to a hypothesis, that is, to a conjecture inviting confirmation or refutation. In this way, it is akin to moving from observation to theory/law in natural sciences, or from a sentence to the meaning behind it. The conjectures may be capable of corroboration or disconfirmation, sometimes to a striking degree, while at other times they are not much strengthened or weakened by the evidence. To be sure, the evidence, before it becomes evidence, is selected and perceived through the lens of the jurist's worldview, which does not necessarily mirror the world that generated the evidence. But leaving aside the complication created by that potential discrepancy, one must recognize that the evidence, through whatever perceptual and interpretive filters it may have passed, still may leave varying degrees of indeterminacy of interpretation. This provides leeway for the legal heritage or present conditions and values to help tip the balance one way or the other. The force of such factors should not be underestimated. Not only do they play the decisive role in cases of indeterminacy, but also they may overcome evidentiary resistance even when the evidence is not so malleable.

With the exception of Ibn Nujaym, the scholars who came after Ibn al-Humām questioned neither his methodology nor his conclusions. Nor did they show much interest in detailed discussions of the methodological principles involved, at least not in their handbooks of positive law. However, the Ottoman jurist Muḥammad al-Āydīnī, writing in 1104/1692, does offer a variation on the "recipe" for legal change in his "Note on the Persistence of Legal Effects."[34] He quotes Ibn al-Humām to the effect that if the inferred effective cause (*'illa*) that occasions a legal effect (*ḥukm*) ceases to exist, that does not necessarily mean that the legal effect must be abandoned. For Ibn al-Humām, in the absence of an effective cause behind an original legal effect, the original legal effect may or may not continue to apply. Al-Āydīnī gives a criterion for when it does. He espouses the enduring validity of a legal effect unless maintaining it causes considerable harm (*mafsada*). In fact, for him, even when the effective cause behind the law still exists, the presence of harm may overturn the ruling. He thus endorses a form of inertia reminiscent of the default status of received law in the formation of canon-blind law, and he seemingly considers no law immune to change.

5.5. After Ibn al-Humām

Mullā Khusraw quotes al-Marghīnānī, but then gives the last word to al-Nasafī's verdict of comprehensive undesirability in his *al-Kāfī*. In his

[34] Muḥammad al-Āydīnī, "*Risāla fī dawām al-ḥukm,*" edited and translated with a commentary in Kevin Reinhart, "When Women Went to Mosques," in *Islamic Legal Interpretation: Muftis and their Fatwas*, ed. Muhammad Khalid Masud, Brinkley Messick, and David Powers (Cambridge: Harvard University Press, 1996), 116–27. In his introduction, Reinhart points out the indeterminacy of the procedure outlined by al-Āydīnī (121–2).

Multaqā, al-Ḥalabī rules: "Women will not attend communal prayers except for the elderly in the case of the dawn, sunset, and evening prayers." (He also mentions that al-Shaybānī and Abū Yūsuf permitted old women's attendance at all prayers). Al-Timurtāshī considers all women's attendance undesirable at all communal prayers "according to the position of the school," except for funeral prayers.[35]

The tenth/sixteenth-century scholar Zayn al-Dīn Ibn Nujaym contrasts the restrictive views of "the later scholars" such as al-Nasafī and Ibn al-Humām on older women with the more permissive views of Abū Ḥanīfa and his disciples. Alluding by his choice of words to Ibn al-Humām, and taking a swing at him, he writes, "To rule for the barring of the elderly ones in (the case of) all (prayers) goes against all [of the authorities of the school] (*wa-al-iftā' bi-man' al-'ajūz fī al-kull mukhālif li-al-kull*). Thus, the position to follow is that of Abū Ḥanīfa." In support of the restriction on young women, he cites Qur'ān 33.33, the *ḥadīth* on the superiority of a woman's prayer in her home,[36] and the prospect of *fitna*. Therefore, Ibn Nujaym advocates a return to the letter of the original doctrine of the school. It would be worth investigating whether he consistently rejects new developments in the school, thus representing a tendency resistant to changes in legal effects, as opposed to the others, like Ibn al-Humām, for whom obeying legal precedents (*taqlīd*) did not preclude change in legal effects.

Those who departed from the legal effect as laid down by Abū Ḥanīfa and his students were not against the emulation of the founders (*taqlīd*). They accorded the founders of the school as much authority as any of their colleagues did. They just viewed the change as the natural application of the original law when the intent behind the law is taken into consideration, treating the original school doctrines in the same manner that Ibn al-Humām treated the scriptural norms of the Qur'ān and the *Ḥadīth*.[37] Exactly such an approach is exemplified by Sirāj al-Dīn Ibn

[35] He also comments on group prayers held in the privacy of homes. It is undesirable for a man to lead women in a house if there is no other man there beside him and no woman there who is either his wife, a close relative (*maḥram*), or a handmaiden. But there is no problem as long as any man or woman belonging to one of these categories is present (al-Timurtāshī, *Tanwīr*, 15). Abū al-Su'ūd, al-Ṭaḥṭāwī, and the Indian scholars who wrote *al-Fatāwā al-'Ālamgīrīya* agree.

[36] "Her praying in the depths of her house (*bayt*) is better than her praying in the courtyard of her house (*dār*), which is better than her praying in her mosque. Their houses are best for them."

[37] This observation is inspired by Sherman Jackson. See Jackson, "Kramer versus Kramer," *Islamic Law and Society* 8.1 (2001): 27–51; Jackson, *Islamic Law and the State*, chapters

Nujaym, the younger brother of the above Ibn Nujaym. In his *al-Nahr*, he criticizes his brother's liberal view on old women. He avers that Abū Ḥanīfa had been permissive only because the highly libidinous men who had to be avoided ate at sunset and slept through the night and dawn. On the assumption that they were on the prowl at other times, "as is the case at our time," general barring would be the plain consequence of Abū Ḥanīfa's approach: thus, prohibitionist scholars did follow Abū Ḥanīfa's position after all. Sirāj al-Dīn's interpretation of Abū Ḥanīfa did not elicit the criticism of later scholars.[38]

Comprehensive barring remained the Ḥanafī view. Al-Shurunbulālī simply writes in one place (*Marāqī al-falāḥ*) that women do not attend communal prayers and makes explicit elsewhere (*Ḥāshiya*) the barring of the elderly from all prayers. Al-Ḥaṣkafī considers as undesirable elderly women's participation in all prayers (*'Īd*, Friday, daytime, and nighttime). The Indian scholars who wrote *al-Fatāwā al-'Ālamgīrīya* and Ibn 'Ābidīn agree. Abū al-Su'ūd makes explicit that the undesirability is *qua* prohibition and al-Afghānī replicates Ibn al-Humām's argument for comprehensive barring. In his *Ḥāshiya 'alā al-Durr al-mukhtār*, al-Ṭaḥṭāwī confirms comprehensive barring as the view of the later scholars, and he apparently endorses that view in his *Ḥāshiya 'alā Marāqī al-falāḥ*.

This is the last of the case studies. The conclusions are consistent with those obtained in the previous chapters for mainstream jurisprudence. While there was a fair amount of legal inertia, and while the laws remained more stable than legal reasons, the laws were not static: in the case of women's public prayer, the Ḥanafī position changed over time, becoming more restrictive. This change was in a direction away from the apparent meaning of the *ḥadīths*, revealing minimal bias for the apparent import of the canon. Thus, the cause of this shift can be found neither in the binding texts nor in the methods of interpretation. By a process of elimination, it can be ascribed only to new social conditions, to a change in the canon-blind, precedent-blind law. But exactly what constituted this change? Was it a pious backlash against an increase in ostentation? Did it represent sociological transformations in the class of jurists, say, demographic or economic change? Or did jurists become more puritanical over time for reasons unrelated to what was going on in society, in a form of

3 and 4; Jackson, "Islam, Muslims, and Socio-Political Reality in the United States," *American Journal of Islamic Social Sciences* 17.3 (2000): 1–25.

[38] This was not for lack of attention to his comments. More than one commentator would express delight in a clever pun Sirāj al-Dīn indulged in on the word *ẓuhr*. With regard to prayers other than the noon prayer, he wrote: *kāna al-man' fīhā aẓhar min al-ẓuhr*.

cultural development analogous to genetic drift? These are questions of great interest for historians to pursue. In any case, despite the changes in the law, the bridge of exegetic rationales that connected the laws with the canon remained intact. What made it possible to maintain the harmony of the shifting law with the binding texts was the nearly maximal degree of hermeneutic flexibility that characterized textual interpretation. The next three chapters contain further reflections on the case studies and the logic of law-making.

6

The Historical Development of Ḥanafī Reasoning

6.1. The Forming Canon: Ḥanafī Beginnings

Had Ḥanafī law been named after Ibrāhīm al-Nakhaʿī, that would not have been a misnomer. The bulk of Abū Ḥanīfa's doctrine is identical to that of Ibrāhīm. Nine out of ten traditions reporting Ibrāhīm's rulings received Abū Ḥanīfa's unqualified endorsement. But "Ḥanafī" is not a misleading label either. Besides the obvious fact that Abū Ḥanīfa's word carried much more weight for the Ḥanafīs than that of Ibrāhīm, there is at least one other important respect in which "Ḥanafī" is more appropriate: Ḥanafī law is closer to Abū Ḥanīfa's teaching than to that of Ibrāhīm. Thus, al-Shaybānī disagreed with Abū Ḥanīfa only about one-third as often as Abū Ḥanīfa did with Ibrāhīm. (And these departures of al-Shaybānī from Abū Ḥanīfa were usually not in the direction of Ibrāhīm.) It was thus with Abū Ḥanīfa that the most salient features of the law reached something of a steady state.[1]

Much work remains to be done on the bearers of authority for these early jurists; yet some preliminary findings may be presented. Ibrāhīm for Abū Ḥanīfa and Abū Ḥanīfa for al-Shaybānī are sources of authority. This is not indicated by the fact that each accepts the decisions of his predecessor, for one may choose to accept something that is not authoritative but happens to be right in one's view. Rather, it is indicated by the manner in which they reject their predecessors. Where al-Shaybānī agrees with both Abū Ḥanīfa and Ibrāhīm, he on occasion cites additional authorities

[1] For the statistics in this paragraph, see the Appendix. The analysis in this and the next several paragraphs is based on al-Shaybānī, *Āthār*. The authenticity of this book is established in the Appendix.

in support of his position,[2] but he does so only about four percent of the time. By contrast, when he disagrees with Abū Ḥanīfa, he is significantly more likely to recruit the aid of other authorities; he does so about eighteen percent of the time (in six out of thirty-three disagreements). It is a sign of Abū Ḥanīfa's authority that if al-Shaybānī goes against him, he is more likely to ground his departure in other precedents. It follows also that these other precedents, too, enjoy some authority. They, by the way, may stem from anyone from the Prophet down to al-Shaybānī's contemporaries, Abū Yūsuf and Zufar, but mostly they are Companions and first/seventh-century Kūfan figures.

Which of these authoritative sources form part of the canon (i.e., are absolutely binding)? It is clear which ones do not: the Companions and all later figures down to Abū Ḥanīfa. Their views may be discarded even without the invocation of authorities of equal or greater rank.[3] Moreover, their doctrine is normally disposed of by frank disagreement, not by harmonization.[4]

The question of whether in this early period the canon included Prophetic precedent requires examination. One tradition from Ibrāhīm conveys the idea that the Prophet's precedent is binding,[5] and another two indicate that it is at least very special.[6] So, certainly, there was an awareness of the Ḥadīth Folk's thesis. In one case, al-Shaybānī tries to neutralize a Prophetic tradition that contradicts his position, a procedure that could signify canonicity. Yet, in a few instances, Abū Ḥanīfa and al-Shaybānī quote a Prophetic tradition and then go against it without attempting harmonization. In these cases, they ostensibly treat the Prophet just as they might treat any other authority. This makes one ask if the Prophet's practice was fully part of the canon for them. Before

[2] Disproportionately, he does so to counterbalance some other authority's contrary view.

[3] Examples of disagreeing with a Companion without invoking another Companion, the Prophet, or the Qur'ān: al-Shaybānī, *Āthār*, 163, no. 24 (Sa'd b. Abī Waqqāṣ); 179–80, no. 95 (Ibn Mas'ūd); 189, no. 132 (Ibn Mas'ūd); 194–5, no. 158 (Abū Hurayra); 198–9, no. 174 (slight difference with Ibn Mas'ūd); 208, no. 217 ('Ā'isha); 256–7, nos. 409–10 ('Alī); 262, no. 430 ('Alī, citing against him "the generally accepted position"); 309–10, no. 618 (Ibn Mas'ūd); 313–14, nos. 633–4 (Abū al-Dardā' and Abū Mas'ūd al-Anṣārī); 359, no. 818 (Ibn 'Abbās, citing against him "many traditions" without being specific); 363–4, no. 838 (Anas b. Mālik).

[4] There is an exceptional case in which al-Shaybānī explains away a report about 'Umar's manner of prayer (al-Shaybānī, *Āthār*, 174, no. 72). However, none of the examples in the last footnote involve any explaining away or harmonization. That is also true of the cases in which a Companion's view is countered by an authority of equal or greater rank.

[5] Al-Shaybānī, *Āthār*, 255, no. 406.

[6] Al-Shaybānī, *Āthār*, 213, no. 238; 357, nos. 809–10.

reaching any conclusion in this regard, more research needs to be undertaken, with attention to the possibility of distinctions between Prophetic acts and Prophetic commands, between commands addressed to specific individuals and generally worded ones,[7] and between ritual matters and other areas of the law.

In sum, traditions serve a dual purpose for Abū Ḥanīfa and al-Shaybānī. They are a convenient means of introducing legal questions before describing one's own judgments. They also furnish precedents for the judgments of Abū Ḥanīfa and al-Shaybānī. Such precedents are not necessary, but it is nice when they are available. In al-Shaybānī's *Kitāb al-Āthār*, the doctrines of past authorities are generally not considered binding, and, therefore, no attempt is made to systematically collect all relevant opinions and harmonize them. Nor do the two jurists assail traditions running contrary to their own doctrine by questioning their authenticity. Except in a couple of instances, they do not interpret away such traditions either. This nonchalant attitude reflects the noncanonical status of these authorities.[8]

These considerations raise a question as to the degree to which the *Ḥadīth* were binding for Abū Ḥanīfa and al-Shaybānī. That they were to be treated as binding, in any case, would soon become perfectly clear under the pressure of the Ḥadīth Folk. The beginning of the vociferous objections of the Ḥadīth Folk to the Iraqi practitioners of personal discretion, *ra'y*, including Abū Ḥanīfa, Abū Yūsuf, and al-Shaybānī, has been dated to the 180s/796–805.[9] This is in agreement with the style of al-Shaybānī, who died in 189/805. Had he already been severely attacked by the Ḥadīth Folk, he might have dealt with *ḥadīth*s in a more delicate manner so as to avoid giving the impression of going against Prophetic precedent.[10]

[7] See Schacht, *Origins*, 48.

[8] The contents of this paragraph address traditions in general, not specifically Prophetic ones. For the small number of similarly rejected Prophetic traditions, as I mentioned, more research is needed. Moreover, exceptions to these ways of handling contrary Prophetic traditions do crop up, particularly in a few cases in al-Shaybānī's *Muwaṭṭa'*, a work directed against the Medinese and composed probably after al-Shaybānī's *Āthār* (on the dates of these two books, see the Appendix); cf. Schacht, *Origins*, 28.

[9] Melchert, *Formation*, 6–7.

[10] Incidentally, the fact that al-Shaybānī does not behave like the Ḥadīth Folk in his *Kitāb al-Āthār* and does not take precautionary measures against the Ḥadīth Folk's objections is consistent with the book being authentic. Moreover, some of the traditions in the *Kitāb al-Āthār* can be confirmed independently as having existed in the first half of the second/eighth century or even earlier. It is possible to reconstruct the wording of these traditions in the first half of the second century and track changes in wording through time, that is, determine which transmitter made what change at what time. There is no evidence for

The assimilation of the Ḥanafīs into the Ḥadīth Folk's ideology has been dated to the third/ninth century.[11] At this time, the *Ḥadīth* were clearly binding. Al-Ṭaḥāwī's work represents an early illustration of the impact of this approach to the *ḥadīths*. Rather than simply turn away from some Prophetic reports as Abū Ḥanīfa and al-Shaybānī had seemingly done, he fully acknowledged their authority and, instead, tamed them, for example, by qualifying them with the aid of carefully chosen reports or by making ad hoc appeals to abrogation.[12]

The opponents of the Ḥanafīs criticized Abū Ḥanīfa and his students for having let their personal discretion (*ra'y*) override *ḥadīth*s. However, the Ḥanafīs, now assimilated into Ḥadīth-Folk ideology, were not about to concede that they had parted company with Abū Ḥanīfa's method; instead, they projected their new ideology back onto Abū Ḥanīfa and his students. They used at least three methods to portray Abū Ḥanīfa as a devotee of *ḥadīths*.

First, they related apocryphal anecdotes that portrayed Abū Ḥanīfa as a dyed-in-the-wool Ḥadīth-Folk ideologue. For example, Abū Ḥanīfa was quoted as having said, "Reports from the Messenger of God – why, I swear by my father and my mother, I treasure and revere them (*fa-'alā al-ra's wa-al-'ayn*); there is no opposition [to them] on my part!" The defensive tone betrays something of the insecurity of the Ḥanafīs. Another report uses the time-honored technique of putting praise in the mouths of the icons revered by the opponents. This anecdote has a group of well-known traditionists of Iraq reproach Abū Ḥanīfa for overindulgence in analogical reasoning and remind him that Iblīs, the devil, was the first to use analogy. Abū Ḥanīfa debates with them in public, proving that he first applies the Qur'ān, then the precedent of the Prophet, and then

E. Chaumont's view (in *EI*[2], art. "al-Shaybānī") that "al-Shaybānī cannot really be considered in anything other than a remote sense the real author of the corpus attributed to him." See also the Appendix, where I argue at length for the authenticity of two books of al-Shaybānī, the *Āthār* and the *Muwaṭṭa'*, based primarily on analysis of style.

[11] Melchert, *Formation*, 48–60.

[12] Al-Ṭaḥāwī's work is an important early source for the study of justification in Ḥanafī law. He often does not spell out the reasoning/justification involved, but this should not mislead one into supposing that none underlies his positions. There is more to him than at first meets the eye. Upon close examination, it appears that he chooses his *ḥadīths* (and particular variants of given *ḥadīths*) extremely carefully: there is a fit between such evidence and his formulation of the laws, in the sense that the inferential gap between them can be filled with an (often straightforward) application of qualification and other techniques. Having received his early legal training as a student of the Shāfi'ī scholar al-Muzanī, he must have been adept at the use of such techniques. Incidentally, his role as a great harmonizer of the laws with the traditions was noted in Schacht, *Origins*, 30, 48.

the judgment of the Companions. Only then, if the Companions disagreed among themselves, does he analogize. The traditionists are deeply impressed. One by one, they kiss his hands. They call him "the lord of the scholars" (*sayyid al-ʿulamāʾ*) and apologize. Abū Ḥanīfa graciously forgives them.[13]

Second, Abū Ḥanīfa's affinity for the *Ḥadīth* was underscored by compiling the *ḥadīth*s transmitted by him.[14] I would not claim that all such compilations served this apologetic purpose, but some of them did, such as the *ʿUqūd al-jawāhir al-munīfa* of Murtaḍā al-Zabīdī (d. 1205/1790). In this book, al-Zabīdī gathers those *ḥadīth*s of Abū Ḥanīfa that also appear in the Six Books. In the introduction to the book, he explains his motivation: "With this book I aim to refute certain zealots who ... claim that our Imām [Abū Ḥanīfa] gives precedence to analogy over texts from the [Divine] Legislator."[15] A different yet related purpose was served by al-Khwārazmī's impressive collation of Abū Ḥanīfa's *ḥadīth*s. His motivation, the author explains in his introduction, was to counter ignorant folk in Syria who claimed that unlike al-Shāfiʿī or Mālik, Abū Ḥanīfa had not transmitted Prophetic reports.[16]

Third, the genre of comparative law – associated with the words *al-ikhtilāf*, *al-khilāf*, or *al-khilāfiyyāt*, meaning "disagreements" – became an arena where the roots of Ḥanafī law in the *Ḥadīth* could be demonstrated.[17] The format of some such books was to list differences over positive law with other schools and to furnish the Ḥanafī justifications.

[13] For these reports and others in a similar vein, see Muḥammad b. Muḥammad Murtaḍā al-Zabīdī (d. 1205/1842), *[Kitāb] ʿUqūd al-jawāhir al-munīfa* (Beirut: Mu'assasat al-Risāla, 1406), 1:20–22. For a discussion of another report that puts praise for Abū Ḥanīfa in the mouths of famous members of the Ḥadīth Folk, see Melchert, *Formation*, 53. For biographical accounts of Abū Ḥanīfa and their role in the rehabilitation of his image, see especially Eerik Dickinson, "Aḥmad b. al-Ṣalt and his biography of Abū Ḥanīfa," *Journal of the American Oriental Society* 116.3 (1996): 406–17.

[14] This has been pointed out before in Eerik Dickinson, "Aḥmad b. al-Ṣalt," 407–9; cf. Melchert, *Formation*, 66–7, 49, 51.

[15] However, he fails to accomplish the goal he sets for himself, since he does not properly compare the *ḥadīth*s he lists with Abū Ḥanīfa's legal rulings. A case in point: he quotes the *ḥadīth* of Umm ʿAṭīya under the heading, "The report *permitting* virgins and menstruating women to go out to the place of worship"; but that is precisely what Abū Ḥanīfa forbade. See al-Zabīdī, *ʿUqūd al-jawāhir al-munīfa*, 1:125–6.

[16] Al-Khwārazmī, *Jāmiʿ al-masānīd*, 4; this has been cited also by Dickinson, "Aḥmad b. al-Ṣalt," 406–17.

[17] For a very useful listing and description of some Ḥanafī works in this genre see al-Naqīb, *al-Madhhab al-Ḥanafī*, 2:588–602. Al-Naqīb's work is a valuable reference work on many aspects of the Ḥanafī tradition.

Again, not all comparative books served an apologetic purpose, but some did, such as *al-Lubāb* of al-Manbijī (seventh/thirteenth century).[18] In the brief introduction to the book, he explains his motivation:

> When I saw those who study with us (*ya'khudhūna minnā*) and take the science of *ḥadīth* from us for plunder, and who [then] use it to besmirch and malign [us] (*yaj'alūna dhālik 'ayban wa-ṭa'nan*) ... and who ascribe to us in particular the exercise of analogy, going about this openly among people ... I set out on a path that would expose their envy and iniquity and make naught of their aspiration and exertion. I shall mention the *ḥadīth*s that our colleagues [Abū Ḥanīfa, Abū Yūsuf, and al-Shaybānī][19] appeal to in the disputed legal questions ... so that it may become manifest to anyone who contemplates it impartially that we obey the book of God more than anyone else and follow the *Ḥadīth* of the Messenger of God most firmly.[20]

The posthumous metamorphosis of Abū Ḥanīfa and al-Shaybānī into members of the Ḥadīth Folk is to a great extent what defined their image in the eyes of posterity. Modern writers, too, are sometimes persuaded by this constructed image. In his recent article on al-Shaybānī for the second edition of the *Encyclopaedia of Islam*, E. Chaumont, approvingly quoting al-Bazdawī, endorses the usual Ḥanafī apology for al-Shaybānī that portrays him as a genuine devotee of the *Ḥadīth*. Chaumont then proceeds to argue that al-Shaybānī appears to have been "the initiator of Shāfi'ī-like theses" about the primacy of Prophetic traditions. He bases this conclusion on the fact that al-Shaybānī quotes many *ḥadīth*s. Leaving aside the puzzle of how Chaumont knows these things about al-Shaybānī given that he does not consider him the true author of the corpus bearing his name, it can be pointed out that these views do not appear as obvious once al-Shaybānī's actual treatment of the *ḥadīth*s he quotes is examined. The late Muḥammad Abū Zahra is another modern scholar whose views may be similarly criticized. He writes that if Abū Ḥanīfa rejected a Prophetic *ḥadīth*, it was because he may not have known a particular transmitter well enough to trust his report. In other words, Abū Ḥanīfa did not have adequate reason to accept the authenticity of the report. Abū Zahra supports this interpretation by pointing out that the Ḥanafīs have unusually strict criteria for establishing the

[18] For more on the *ḥadīth*-oriented scholar al-Manbijī, see Chapter 3, pages 69–70, and Chapter 4, pages 81–2.

[19] On this meaning of "our colleagues" (*aṣḥābunā*), see al-Naqīb, *al-Madhhab al-Ḥanafī*, 1:313–4.

[20] Al-Manbijī, *al-Lubāb*, 1:65–6.

reliability of narrators, as indicated by a passage from al-Bazdawī's work on legal philosophy (*uṣūl*).[21] Four objections must be raised here. First, Abū Ḥanīfa and al-Shaybānī do not reveal doubts about authenticity. On the contrary, their language indicates that they take historical veracity for granted. For example, al-Shaybānī says that if a woman leads women, she should stand in their midst "as 'Ā'isha did." So, he does not betray any doubt about the authenticity of the report about 'Ā'isha, even though he does not recommend that women lead women. As another example, Abū Ḥanīfa acknowledges plainly that the Prophet allowed women to attend the *'Īd* prayers, and then adds "as for today, I dislike it." Secondly, it is probably anachronistic to portray Abū Ḥanīfa as an *isnād*-critic. For, notwithstanding an exceptional case such as al-Ṭaḥāwī, it would be several centuries before Ḥanafī jurists began concerning themselves with the qualities of the transmitters in the *isnād*s in a systematic manner.[22] Besides, Abū Ḥanīfa himself was not above giving *isnād*s that were incomplete or had "weak" links; and there is no evidence that he disapproved of anyone named in any of his own *isnād*s. Thirdly, after Ḥanafī jurists began paying attention to *isnād*s, some of them justified the school positions by openly endorsing the use of "weak" traditions, including those with unknown transmitters or missing links in the *isnād*s.[23] It is, therefore, misleading to point to the high standards of *ḥadīth* evaluation expounded in works of legal philosophy (*uṣūl*), such as that of al-Bazdawī, since these norms have little to do with jurists' actual use of *ḥadīth*s. Fourthly, some of the traditions that Abū Ḥanīfa and al-Shaybānī disregard are "sound" by the standards of the traditionists – thus, the Umm 'Aṭīya tradition made its way into the prestigious collections of al-Bukhārī and Muslim. No one really made an issue of their authenticity.[24]

[21] Muḥammad Abū Zahra, *Abū Ḥanīfa* (Cairo: Dār al-Fikr al-'Arabī, 1366), 291–2, 277.

[22] Al-Kīrawānī has, conveniently for my purposes, collected reports in support of his view that Abū Ḥanīfa was a *ḥadīth* critic. Most of these are anecdotes generated to prove that Abū Ḥanīfa's theology was sound; to show, for example, that he was not a *murji'ī*, which he was. See al-Kīrawānī, *Abū Ḥanīfa wa-aṣḥābuh* (Beirut: Dār al-Fikr al-'Arabī, 1989), 57–62. For how such reports were generated in order to counter accusations against Abū Ḥanīfa, see, for example, Melchert, *Formation*, 54–9. Only a few of the reports are *prima facie* legitimate evidence of Abū Ḥanīfa's *ḥadīth* criticism.

[23] See, e.g., the views cited by the nonjurist Ḥanafī al-Zabīdī, *'Uqūd al-jawāhir al-munīfa*, 1:22. Al-Zabīdī himself, though, expresses doubt that the Ḥanafīs have such a liberal attitude, but does not rule it out. *If* it is true that the Ḥanafīs use weak traditions, he offers, that only demonstrates their eagerness to use every last scrap of evidence that is potentially of Prophetic origin.

[24] Another modern portrayal of Abū Ḥanīfa that is similarly anachronistic is given in U. F. Abd-Allah, "Abū Ḥanīfa," *Encyclopaedia Iranica*.

6.2. The Shifting Canon: The Rise of Ḥadīth-Folk Ideology

Given that Ḥanafī law did not originate in the *Ḥadīth*, it is important to ask what became of the gap between the law and the *Ḥadīth* once the *Ḥadīth* were firmly incorporated in the canon. One has to explain how and to what degree the new emphasis on *ḥadīth*s affected the laws on the one hand and legal reasoning on the other hand. In particular, did Ḥanafī law yield to the laws apparently embodied in the *Ḥadīth*? To put it more precisely, did the triumph of the Ḥadīth Folk's ideology mean a hermeneutic-methodological approach with a greater bias for the apparent meaning of the canon?

The answer is negative. As my case studies confirm, one repeatedly encounters examples of the law proving impervious to the apparent import of the *Ḥadīth* and other contrary evidence. (The only possible exception encountered in this book was the permission for old women to attend nighttime prayers, a limited concession that was later abandoned.) As a matter of course, jurists interpreted the canon in light of canon-blind law rather than derive the law from the canon. They did this in good faith. It is not clear to what degree various jurists were conscious of this, but at least al-Karkhī (d. 340/952), who was the head of the Ḥanafīs in his time, seems quite aware of it. He wrote:[25]

> Any Qur'ānic verse that contradicts the position of our colleagues [Abū Ḥanīfa, Abū Yūsuf, and al-Shaybānī] is treated by means of abrogation or preponderance, and it is best that it be treated by means of harmonizing interpretation (*tuḥmal 'alā al-naskh aw 'alā al-tarjīḥ wa-al-awlā an tuḥmal 'alā al-ta'wīl min jihat al-tawfīq*) ... Any tradition contradicting the position of our colleagues is treated by means of abrogation, or it is treated by [saying that] it contradicts another [report] like itself, so that [the two cancel each other out and] it comes down to some other evidence, or [by means of] preponderance ... or by means of harmonizing interpretation. This is done only on the basis of evidence.

As an additional case of how the *Ḥadīth* affected, or did not affect, the law it may be worthwhile to consider the reversal of the Ḥanafī acceptance of *nabīdh*, the potentially intoxicating beverages made from substances other than grapes. Ibrāhīm al-Nakha'ī and Abū Ḥanīfa had

[25] 'Ubayd Allāh b. al-Ḥusayn b. Dallāl al-Karkhī, *Risāla fī al-uṣūl allatī 'alayhā madār furū' al-Ḥanafiyya*, printed with 'Ubayd Allāh b. 'Umar b. 'Īsā al-Dabūsī, *Kitāb Ta'sīs al-naẓar* (Egypt: al-Maṭba'a al-Adabiyya, n.d.), 84. The term "preponderance" might refer to qualification or to declaring a report spurious if it contradicts another report. "Harmonizing interpretation" may take different forms, and qualification is one of them.

permitted *nabīdh*,[26] a view that was eventually abandoned. Was it the pressure of the Prophetic and Companion reports that caused the reversal? I would rather suggest that the change was meant to gain the acceptance of other Muslims, being motivated by a form of peer pressure.[27] Objections can be raised to the view that the shift resulted from the pressure of the anti-*nabīdh ḥadīths*. First, there is some evidence for powerful social pressures.[28] Second, tolerating *nabīdh* was not inherently any more inimical to the *Ḥadīth* than forbidding it. Ibn Abī Shayba quotes eight traditions from the Prophet in favor of *nabīdh*, in addition to some from the Prophet's Companions.[29] Had Ḥanafī jurists desired to keep *nabīdh* permissible, they could have considered the anti-*nabīdh* traditions as either abrogated or qualified by these pro-*nabīdh* traditions; after all, they readily used such techniques in other areas of the law when dealing with perplexing reports. In sum, the legal status of *nabīdh* changed because the canon-blind law changed.

6.3. The Canon and Interpretation in Mature Ḥanafī Thought

The triumph of the Ḥadīth Folk's ideology did not mean that the Ḥanafī jurists now turned into assiduous students of the *Ḥadīth*. The jurists

[26] Abū Yūsuf, *Āthār*, 223–8, nos. 991–1012; al-Shaybānī, *Āthār*, 219, no. 629; 362–5, nos. 829–43; Melchert, *Formation*, 48–51.

[27] There is some early evidence for *nabīdh* being stigmatized in some circles. For example, there is the anecdote about the Kūfan *ḥadīth* transmitter Layth b. Abī Sulaym: someone caught him with *nabīdh*, whereupon Layth asked him not to relate what he had seen to the *ahl al-ḥadīth*. See Ibn 'Adī, *al-Kāmil*, 3rd ed. (Beirut: Dār al-Fikr, 1409), 6:87.

[28] The controversy over *nabīdh* was not a typical case of legal disagreement. Its special significance explains why in biographical dictionaries it was sometimes noted which traditionists drank it. Drinking *nabīdh* was deemed relevant to one's moral character. It had the potential of turning into the Ḥanafīs' *mut'a* (temporary marriage), a practice that was sometimes held up as an example of the depravity of the Shī'īs. Indeed, a tradition from al-Awzā'ī condemns the two practices together in a list of scandalous doctrines: "Pay no heed to Meccan doctrine when it comes to *mut'a* and money changing (*al-ṣarf*), nor to Medinese doctrine on music and anal intercourse with women, nor to Syrian doctrine on predestination and obedience (*al-jabr wa-al-ṭā'a*), nor to Kūfan doctrine on *nabīdh* and sorcery." See Ibn 'Asākir, *Ta'rīkh madīnat al-Dimashq* (Beirūt: Dār al-Fikr, 1415), 1:361. That these troublesome doctrines had the potential to haunt a legal school centuries later is illustrated by the way al-Ṭarsūsī (d. 758/1357), the head of the Ḥanafīs in Damascus, played on the permissive views of some Mālikīs on sodomy and *mut'a* in a work geared to currying favor with the Mamluks on behalf of the Ḥanafīs. See Najm al-Dīn al-Ṭarsūsī, *Kitāb Tuḥfat al-turk* (Damascus: Institut français de Damas, 1997), 19 (Arabic text).

[29] Ibn Abī Shayba, *Muṣannaf*, 5:485–90.

formed a separate and distinct class from the traditionists, working in a discipline that was removed from the concerns and standards prevailing in *ḥadīth* studies. It was an exceptional jurist who was also a competent traditionist, as al-Ṭaḥāwī was. Thus, for centuries jurists did not attempt a thorough analysis of the traditions, and, in the meantime, they kept handing down certain Prophetic reports among themselves that no accomplished traditionist would have found acceptable – and I do not mean only "weak" *ḥadīth*s, but also ones unworthy of the label *ḥadīth*, including sayings that apparently no one in the first two or three centuries of Islam had ascribed to the Prophet.[30]

The relative insularity of the two disciplines would not endure. In the seventh/thirteenth and eighth/fourteenth centuries, some jurists began displaying a significantly greater interest in the *Ḥadīth*. Thus, the seventh/thirteenth century ushered in an interest in integrating distinct religious sciences. It is in keeping with this spirit of integration that in this period one also sees a greater interest among jurists in whether Ḥanafī law was true to the principles of Ḥanafī legal theory as developed in the genre of *uṣūl al-fiqh*.[31] Jurists began discussing whether their reasoning met the theoretical standards for justifications. A consequence of such attempts at synthesis was greater complexity and sophistication in legal argumentation. However, in keeping with the primacy of laws over legal reasons, these discussions did not affect the decisions in points of positive law. This is not to say that the laws did not change. The point is that when they did, it was because of social conditions and attitudes, not textual or methodological considerations.

As a result of the new encounter with the *Ḥadīth* in the seventh/thirteenth and eighth/fourteenth centuries, jurists began to make two types of discoveries: *ḥadīth*s they had not known previously, and *ḥadīth*s they had known and used all along that they now realized were non-*ḥadīth*s. They undertook readjusting their deliberations to account for both the "new" and the "now lost" *ḥadīth*s. It is a tribute to the hermeneutic flexibility of their methodology that these expansions and contractions in the known body of the canon left the laws intact.

The ninth/fifteenth-century jurists al-ʿAynī and Ibn al-Humām epitomize the new interest in justification and the *Ḥadīth*. Al-ʿAynī stood out for quoting the largest number of *ḥadīth*s. (However, no Ḥanafī jurist

[30] For more details on the contents of this paragraph and the next two, see especially Section 3.5.

[31] See, e.g., Sections 4.8.2 and 3.5.

ever would discuss all of the relevant reports; there remained relevant *ḥadīth*s that no jurist mentioned.) Ibn al-Humām, standing on the shoulders of his predecessors, provided the most cogent and coherent Ḥanafī interpretation of the canon and was often and deservedly quoted by later scholars.

These two scholars are also distinguished by a deviation from the mainstream of the school with regard to hermeneutic flexibility, leading to a degree of tension with the received law. Al-ʿAynī criticized fellow Ḥanafīs for supporting laws that went against *ḥadīth*s, a stance that apparently made a difference in his rulings. In the case of women-only prayers, he jettisoned the standard Ḥanafī law in favor of the apparent import of the traditions, a position that would be embraced only by al-Laknawī in the nineteenth century; but al-ʿAynī toed the Ḥanafī party line in the somewhat more malleable case of communal prayers. Displaying a degree of bias for the apparent meaning of the canon, he shows up as somewhat less hermeneutically flexible than the Ḥanafī mainstream.[32] With regard to women-only prayers, Ibn al-Humām, too, expressed serious reservations about the received law, although he did not say outright that he opposed it.

While such deviations are noteworthy, it must not be forgotten that the *raison d'être* of law is its communal dimension. One or two jurists, no matter how prestigious they may be, do not make a school of law. The rest of the Ḥanafīs, except al-Laknawī, quite comfortable with the law on women-only prayers, never so much as mentioned al-ʿAynī and Ibn al-Humām's dissent, let alone addressed their arguments. However, should social conditions someday militate against the received law, one can be sure that the Ḥanafī scholars will begin noticing the hitherto ignored views of al-ʿAynī and attempt to make the law conform to the new canon-blind law. The recent publication of the thirteenth/nineteenth-century scholar al-Laknawī's defense of al-ʿAynī might be a sign that this process is already under way.[33]

In some respects, Ibn al-Humām may appear to have been less hermeneutically flexible than the Ḥanafī mainstream, for example, in his insistence that a norm enjoy the support of an early report before it can be said to have abrogated another norm.[34] But, ultimately, he too is highly

[32] See Section 4.4.3.

[33] I do not know whether al-Laknawī's view was motivated by methodological concerns. One ought to investigate the extent to which it may have been influenced by a canon-blind law reflecting possible changes of values brought about by the social environment.

[34] See Section 4.5.

hermeneutically flexible, as indicated by his sophisticated demonstration of how, in order to do justice to the divine intention behind the law, the application of the law may change depending on the circumstances. Whereas Ḥanafī arguments appealing to "the corruption of the current age" (*fasād al-zamān*) depended on a specific type of social change, namely moral decline, and could be used only for making the law stricter, the method applied by Ibn al-Humām is more general in that it can take into account any relevant social change, and it could be used for making laws laxer as well as stricter. The nature of this method, because of its dependence on analogical reasoning, is such that it leaves great latitude in the determination of the intended principle behind a law.[35] This mechanism is thus flexible enough to allow the law to closely approximate canon-blind law. In particular, it permits the evolution of the law in line with perceived social needs (should such realities, embodied in precedent-blind, canon-blind law, become pressing enough to override received law).

The idea that a legal effect may change in response to changing circumstances is a very old one, at least as old as the 'Ā'isha tradition, "If the Prophet had come to know.... "[36] Among the Ḥanafīs, it often took the form of an appeal to the "corruption of the current age" (*fasād al-zamān*). For example, as the Ḥanafīs were turning against the *nabīdh* beverage, an early Ḥanafī jurist attributed the change to newly developed decadence: in the second century people had not been liable to abuse *nabīdh*, but in the third century they were.[37] Thus, jurists' acceptance of this mode of legal reasoning opened the door to using claims about social reality – claims that were not always historically accurate – as a way of arguing for a legal position. One sees an example of far-fetched reflections on society in the case of the discussions about the sleeping and eating patterns of wrongdoers.[38]

The most important element of Ibn al-Humām's treatment is his explanation of the way in which the legal effects stated in the canon could be changed depending on the social context without in any way detracting from the authority of the canon (Section 5.4). The procedure he uses to

[35] On analogical reasoning as employed by Ibn al-Humām, see especially Chapter 3, pages 70–1; Chapter 5, pages 120–4.

[36] For one variant of this tradition and the way it is used, see Chapter 5, page 117.

[37] Melchert, *Formation*, 50.

[38] See Sections 5.2.3 and 5.3. For the "corruption of the current age," see also Katz, "Corruption," 171–85; Basim Musallam, *Sex and Society in Islam* (Cambridge: Cambridge University Press, 1983), 118.

justify legal change is so flexible that it can be used by different jurists to argue for very different legal outcomes. Its inherent indeterminacy is a source of considerable hermeneutic flexibility.

He formulated the argument while taking the Qur'ān and the *Ḥadīth* to represent the canon; but it is equally applicable to the interpretation of the established school doctrine – and, indeed, Sirāj al-Dīn applied Ibn al-Humām's method precisely in this way. Thus, Ibn al-Humām's approach makes possible significant legal change within the framework of *taqlīd*, belying the commonly held notions that commitment to a school's doctrine stifles dynamism and that only by passing through the gate of *ijtihād* may the law be adapted to new circumstances.[39] It does not appear, however, that Ibn al-Humām's methodological approach was accepted by all, as Ibn Nujaym criticized it.[40]

[39] See Chapter 5, pages 125–6. The point about *taqlīd* has been made by Sherman Jackson, on whom see Chapter 5, page 125, footnote 37.

[40] See Chapter 5, page 125.

7

From Laws to Values

7.1. Introduction

One sometimes encounters the idea that Islamic law captures the spirit of Muslim civilization.[1] It is thus not entirely unexpected to find a scholar extracting sentences from the Qur'ān, *Ḥadīth*, or legal handbooks and thence deducing the Muslim perspective and character across time and space, without reference to the myriad interpretations and applications of these statements in specific, localized contexts.[2] Still more prevalent is the assumption that doctrines, interpretations, and ideologies – in a word, ideas – shape external reality to a far greater extent and in a more enduring

[1] For example, Joseph Schacht wrote, "Islamic law is the epitome of the Islamic spirit, the most typical manifestation of the Islamic way of life, the kernel of Islam itself" (Joseph Schacht, "Pre-Islamic Background and Early Development of Jurisprudence," in *Law in the Middle East*, ed. Majid Khadduri and Herbert J. Liebesny (Washington, D.C.: The Middle East Institute, 1955), 28. For a critical discussion of the idea of a kernel, essence, or spirit animating Muslim civilization, see, for example, Chase Robinson, "Reconstructing Early Islam: Truth and Consequences," in *Method and Theory in the Study of Islamic Origins*, ed. Herbert Berg (Leiden: Brill, 2003), 104–8.

[2] It is, for example, in accordance with such an approach that a competent scholar provided a description of gender roles in "medieval Islamic societies" in just two pages in an account that presumably covers societies both urban and rural, settled and nomadic, from Spain to India. See Paula Sanders, "Gendering the Ungendered Body: Hermaphrodites in Medieval Islamic Law," in *Women in Middle Eastern History: Shifting Boundaries in Sex and Gender*, ed. Nikki Keddie and Beth Baron (New Haven: Yale University Press, 1991), 74–95. By a coincidence, the article that comes immediately after this one in this collection of essays focuses on Cairo at a particular place and time and hints at a more complex picture of male-female interaction: Huda Lutfi, "Manners and Customs of Fourteenth-Century Cairene Women," 99–121.

fashion than social reality shapes or constrains ideas.[3] When seen in this light, Islamic law, as a set of ideas, functions not only as a mirror of society, but also as its genetic blueprint.

Clearly, there is much that can be debated here. Leaving aside the question of whether Islam (or any civilization or community) has an essence, there is the question of why legal literature should be said to reveal that essence rather than, say, historiography, a genre that is often equally imbued with a religious spirit but that sometimes exhibits views and attitudes that are different from those found in juristic discourse. Moreover, the causal relationship between social reality and ideas is a particularly difficult question that demands a complex explanation, and the view that ideas determine long-term social reality in predictable ways is unlikely to be a valid first approximation to such an explanation.

With such reservations in mind, prudent students of the legal handbooks (*fiqh* genre) may decide to settle for goals humbler than capturing the essence of Muslim societies. They may acknowledge that Islamic law has not been static. They may recognize that the norms laid down may not necessarily represent the practice, or may not have been applied always and everywhere. They may also concede that the values displayed by jurists would not have been necessarily shared by others in society. In other words, they may conservatively infer from the legal handbooks little beyond the values of jurists. But would one be finally safe if one narrowed the scope in this way? Can one infer from the laws at least the values of the jurists who wrote and defended them?

[3] Thus, for some authors, the Asha'arite doctrine of occasionalism explains why Muslims fell behind Europe in science. In my mind, any valid theory of the ultimate causes of this phenomenon will be framed primarily in terms of facts of economics, geography, and social organization, not of theology or philosophy, which can constitute at most *proximate* causes or correlates. (This is not to mention that occasionalism is not even relevant: since the time of David Hume, we have known that the notion of causes is not necessary for science.) The same methodological objection may be raised against authors who argue that the injunctions in the Qur'ān to think and reflect on nature are what brought about the impressive flowering of Islamic sciences and learning in the Middle Ages.

Similar approaches crop up in discussions about women. For example, in her early work, Leila Ahmed considered the injunctions of the Prophet Muḥammad and the Qur'ān as the direct cause of the low status of Muslim women throughout the centuries (Leila Ahmed, "Women and the Advent of Islam," *Signs* 2.4 (1986): 665–91). She distanced herself from that position in her later work. In contrast, some authors claim that Muslim women have had a relatively high status throughout history, attributing this again to the injunctions of the Prophet Muḥammad and the Qur'ān. Thus, these two opposite sides are united in their underlying assumptions regarding the causal relationship between the ideas promulgated by the Prophet Muḥammad and the long-term unfolding of Muslim history.

The thesis of this chapter is that, even within such a cautiously narrowed and modest purview, the inferential road from juristic literature to jurists' values and other aspects of social reality is littered with hazards. This is so because (1) jurists may valiantly defend a law even though they find the values underlying it alien or even abhorrent; (2) the reasons they give in favor of a law are often not the same as their motives for advocating it; (3) their claims about social reality may be factually incorrect pieces of speculation designed in good faith to achieve needed legal outcomes; and (4) they speak for the legal traditions to which they belong, which at times makes it difficult to determine their views as individuals. All of this is not to say that jurisprudence teaches nothing about social reality, and some of what can be learned is explored in Section 7.6.

These observations raise questions about the ways in which the legal handbooks are sometimes used. For example, the secondary literature on gender in Islam tends to approach this vast and sometimes difficult literature with a view to finding statements about women. Once such a statement is spotted, it is taken as representative of jurists' values and motives. In this process, usually no attempt is made to reconstruct the function of the statement within its legal-historical context. Yet failure to do so can be fatal to inferring values, since legal manuals reflect not just the values of jurists but also the constraints imposed by jurisprudence as a field with specific disciplinary norms and by law as a social phenomenon with dynamics of its own.

7.2. The Acceptability of Laws Birthed by Unacceptable Values

When jurists find a law intolerable, they tend to change it. So, it might appear at first sight that if they do not change a law, then they must find the values underlying that law acceptable – which should tell us something about their values. Such an inference, however, is not valid since it neglects the role of legal inertia. As a result, it misconstrues law as being necessarily the realization of an underlying set of ideas and values.

If jurists retain a law, the correct inference is that they find the law itself tolerable, but not necessarily the values that underpin it nor necessarily the values that generated it in the first place. That is so because finding a law tolerable is not always the same as finding the values underlying it tolerable. Those values people may reject while they live contentedly with the law itself. They may do so, for example, by reading new meanings and values into a law. Alternatively, they may maintain the law thanks to legal inertia without attaching a specific meaning to it. So, the fact that jurists support a law does not necessarily mean that they uphold its underlying values; all it tells us is that they can live with the law itself.

To illustrate this point, one may consider the striking history of the adjacency law, a distinctly Ḥanafī law according to which if a man and woman prayed in congregation standing side by side, his prayer would be invalidated but not hers. Delving into the prehistory of the adjacency law in the first/seventh century reveals it as a vestige of an Iraqi minority notion with origins in Baṣra that treated women as perpetual transmitters of ritual impurity. Furthermore, the features of the law are objectively a better fit to the early Baṣran values than to the various explanations of later jurists that had nothing to do with ritual impurity – and, in this sense, the values that had given birth to the law could be said to also underpin the law, that is, to be implicit in the law. Yet, those values (i.e., women as perpetual transmitters of impurity) were profoundly incompatible with the attitudes, concepts, and legal assumptions of jurists in the centuries that followed. The key point is this: while jurists would not have countenanced those values, they were perfectly able to live with the law itself. And, naturally, the explanations jurists gave for the law were altogether different from the original, long-forgotten values that led to the law's creation.

The adjacency law is not exceptional: a "great deal, if not most, of law operates in a territory for which it was not originally designed, or in a society which is radically different from that which created the law."[4] The relative irrelevance of the original values to the survival and continuation of a law receives support from another phenomenon: the pervasiveness of legal implants in the world's legal traditions shows how commonly and readily laws move from one legal system to another unhampered by ties to specific cultural or legal contexts.[5] These facts together with other evidence cited by Alan Watson support his contention that laws do not, in general, mirror the spirit or character of a people, and that the legal differences among legal traditions cannot, for the most part, be explained by differences in cultural values or attitudes.[6] Islamic history further corroborates

[4] Alan Watson, *Legal Origins and Legal Change* (London: Hambledon Press, 1991), 73.

[5] Watson, *The Evolution of Law*, 66–97; Watson, *The Nature of Law*, 99–113; Watson, *Society and Legal Change*, 98–114; Watson, *Ancient Law and Modern Understanding* (Athens, Georgia: University of Georgia Press, 1998), 3–4; Watson, "Legal Change: Sources of Law and Legal Culture," *University of Pennsylvania Law Review* (1983): 1121–57; reprinted in Watson, *Legal Origins and Legal Change*, 69–105.

[6] See the sources in the last footnote.

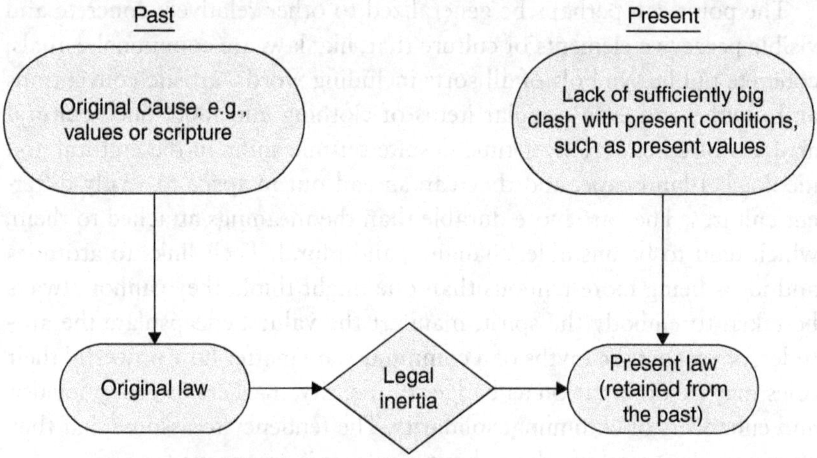

FIGURE 15. The causes that generated a law originally are not those that contribute to its perpetuation through time. There is no arrow directly from the original cause to a present law that is retained from the past.

the latter point in a straightforward manner: different *madhhab*s (legal traditions) could exist in the same locale and culture, while vastly different cultures located far apart could subscribe to the same *madhhab*. The distribution of a *madhhab* in the postformative period was determined not by any intrinsic cultural affinity to a specific set of laws, but rather by patterns of social association, patronage, institutional factors, and historical accidents.

At its moment of inception a law may originate from an underlying worldview or text and it may mirror the values of a community – for example, those of jurists – a tribe, or a city. However, once it has come into being, a law no longer requires this basis or any other. Thanks to legal inertia, it can endure through time independently as long as it does not clash too sharply with the new social needs and values of the law-making class (Figure 15). It can also be borrowed without mirroring the values of the borrowing legal tradition. It now has a life of its own, propagating through time and space by dint of its own status as law. For the historian, no explanation is needed for why an inherited law is retained: it is retained simply because it was the law previously. The legal tradition itself may explain the law on the basis of binding texts or social values, but these are generally justifications, not causal explanations. At most, they might truly represent the historical genesis of the law, but they are not true descriptions of why the law was retained.

The point can perhaps be generalized to other relatively concrete and visible pervasive elements of culture that, like law, are communal: rituals, concrete public symbols of all sorts including words, artistic conventions and motifs, and even popular items of clothing and food. Such cultural artifacts often endure over time despite seismic shifts in the cultural and ideological landscape, and they can spread out in space to vastly different cultures. They are more durable than the meanings attached to them, which tend to be unstable, changing, and plural. Their links to attitudes and ideas being more tenuous than one might think, they cannot always be taken to embody the spirit, manifest the values, encapsulate the attitudes, or reenact the myths of a community, no matter how powerful their roles may be on occasion as badges of identity, markers of group loyalty, and enhancers of communal solidarity. The tendency to assume that they must encode something deep about a culture is erroneous.[7]

However, clearly this argument can be taken only so far. The disjunction between laws and social values is not complete, and values do put certain limits on the trajectory of a law in time and space. Many a law would be rejected out of hand in a different era or culture. The early modern European and American punishment of nasal cutting for fornication or polygamy would be inconceivable in today's Europe or Americas. Nor could one imagine contemporary traditional societies borrowing certain permissive European laws in the near future. When a law is such a poor fit to a society that it passes a certain threshold and becomes unacceptable or impractical, it will be rejected. If it is part of the community's cultural heritage, the unfit law will be jettisoned. If it belongs to another culture, it will not be borrowed and enforced (except perhaps by ideologically driven ruling cliques whose power does not depend on a wide social base). The point is that if a law is retained or borrowed, it does not necessarily mirror the values of the law-making class, since it need not be desirable in and of itself: all one can conclude is that it is not very undesirable or impractical. Such a law need not be a good fit to society: all one can infer is that the law-making class can live with it. Legal inertia suffices to explain why the law is retained.[8]

[7] Scholars have conceptualized ritual in a variety of ways, including ways similar to mine. See Marion Katz, *Body of Text*, 1–27; Marion Katz, "The Study of Islamic Ritual and the Meaning of *Wuḍū'*," *Der Islam* 82 (2005): 106–45; and Catherine Bell, *Ritual Theory, Ritual Practice* (New York: Oxford University Press, 1992), 30–46 and 182–96.

[8] My comments throughout are about laws that jurists consider to be binding. Laws that are dead letters are inconsequential.

7.3. Justifications Need Not Reflect Motives

A jurist's justification for a law often has little to do with the reason why he or she advocates it. This observation must appear familiar from our own contemporary experience. Consider jurists who argue in an American courtroom about abortion, stem cell research, or euthanasia. If they are religious, they may aim at a certain legal outcome simply because they follow their parents, their Church, or their personal reading of the Bible. Yet, when arguing for those positions, they do not treat the statements of their parents, the pope, or the Bible as proof text. In the courtroom, they will not say, "This is the right position because the Bible says such-and-such." In contrast, a competent nonreligious, secular activist attorney in Iran's judicial system might not hesitate to cite religious texts and precedents. These two legal systems, despite their differences, have one thing in common with many others: in each, legal arguments conform to certain patterns. An argument is not considered to be legitimate unless it follows the expected pattern. The choice of the argument used in support of a position may reflect these expectations rather than the jurist's motives.

Jurists, in other words, are required to argue in terms of what one may call *public reason*. By this term, I mean the shared standards of argumentation that help to create a framework within which different actors and interests in a community could pursue conflict or cooperation. In the Ḥanafī context, public reason allows such interactions to proceed on a footing of equality *ceteris paribus*. That is so because it does not commit the community, in advance, to a specific answer to each and every question, and therefore it allows for arguments to be made for contrary positions on a wide array of issues. The hermeneutic flexibility of Ḥanafī standards made it possible to give valid arguments for opposing views. Thus, for example, jurists with contrary views on women's status could, in principle, both produce arguments for their positions that meet the requirements of public reasoning. As a matter of historical fact, arguments were offered for contrary positions, and the schools of law offer examples of legal consensus undergoing changes that were justified by new legal arguments.[9]

In premodern Islam, as in modern jurisprudence, juristic arguments were crafted in the first instance to conform to the requirements of public reason in the field of law, not necessarily to describe the ultimate motives

[9] See the excursus entitled, "A Historian's 'Public Reason.'"

of their authors. A jurist may have been motivated to uphold the law by, say, the desire for legal continuity, but his reasons could have been formulated on entirely different grounds. Certainly in the Ḥanafī tradition the given legal reasons were usually not the motives that made jurists support a law.

That one cannot equate given reasons with the motives or causes is shown by the fact that, once a reason given for a law proved to be weak or defective, jurists created another reason for the same law; yet if the given reason truly had been the cause or motive, the law would have fallen along with the reason. In addition, it is often not plausible to consider a reason as the cause or motive for a law unless it predates the law; yet frequently reasons come into being after the laws they support.

Furthermore, the fact that different jurists gave different and sometimes incompatible reasons for a law is best explained not by positing different motives for the same law, but by supposing that the need to uphold the law motivated attempts at justification and elicited a variety of solutions. In other words, if legal reasons were motives and causes, one would expect them to be more stable than the laws they inspire, since the same end typically could be achieved by a variety of laws or variations on a law. On the other hand, if legal reasons were after-the-fact justifications, one would expect them to be less stable than the laws since more than one justification can be devised for a law. Of these two patterns, the second one – relative instability – characterizes legal reasons in the Ḥanafī tradition, pointing to their justificatory function and secondary status.

7.4. Jurists' Reflections on Social Reality

The manifest custom in all countries to construct public baths for women and to let them enter the baths indicates the correctness of our position.

– al-Sarakhsī[10]

Legal arguments have both factual and normative components. A typical law says that if certain facts obtain, then certain legal consequences follow. The said facts often have to do with what goes on in society. Consequently, jurists sometimes predicate certain legal consequences on facts about their societies. For the historian, such statements about facts are potential troves of valuable information about social history. Yet, it is worth asking whether the facts could be manipulated (in good

[10] Al-Sarakhsī, *Mabsūṭ*, 10:147.

conscience) to yield desired legal conclusions. If normative statements are to be approached with caution, can we at least let down our guard with propositions about facts?

At times, statements about facts yield reliable evidence about society. Al-Sarakhsī's observation that women's attendance at public baths was widespread at his time must have been accurate, even though one may doubt whether the practice was common in absolutely "all countries." This matter did not depend on conjecture, and it is hard to see how he could have deluded himself into believing it unless it were largely true. And if he had been in error, he would not have gotten away with it for the availability or lack of bathhouses for women would have been well known.

At other times, statements about facts could be dubious. Take Ḥanafī views about the alcoholic beverage *nabīdh*. The Ḥanafīs originally considered *nabīdh* lawful. Arguing for its unlawfulness, a Ḥanafī jurist posited a general decline in morals that by the third century had made it more likely for people to abuse the beverage.[11] This claim is highly speculative and difficult to ascertain, resting as it does on a comparison of people's largely private habits in two different centuries. It is a piece of speculation that was intended to justify a new ruling on the beverage, one that had an altogether different cause than moral decline, to wit, the trenchant disapprobation of other religious scholars.

As another example one may consider one of the arguments the Ḥanafīs gave to forbid non-elderly women from leaving home to pray certain prayers in mosques. Explaining why women were forbidden from noon and afternoon prayers in the mosque, but not the other prayers (morning, sunset, night), al-Marghīnānī (d. 593/1197) cited the habits of lustful men on the prowl who roamed the streets, harassing women. At sunset they were preoccupied with dinner, he claimed, and they slept soon after, making it safe for women to venture out for the prayers at these times (sunset and night). But it seems implausible that the harassers behaved in the synchronized fashion he described or that they behaved similarly in various localities. In addition, this rationale is two or three centuries younger than the law, which had been hitherto supported by other arguments. It is unlikely that over the centuries sexual harassers had followed the same pattern; and if they had, that it would be discovered as the reason for the law only in the sixth/twelfth century. How these justifications evolved as the law changed is also telling. Over time the Ḥanafī prohibitions were

[11] Melchert, *Formation*, 50.

extended to all prayers, including those at night, and all women, including the elderly. The extension was justified, in part, in terms of the changing habits of harassers. Now, we are told, harassers roamed the streets at all hours of the day and night, and they no longer spared the elderly. It is more reasonable to take these statements of fact as speculation designed to justify a law that was motivated by different concerns.

Historians recognize that actual practice did not necessarily follow the normative statements of Islamic law.[12] However, there is understandably greater readiness to give credence to factual (as distinct from normative) elements in legal discourse, that is, to statements about how the world is, as opposed to how it ought to be. While doing so may often be sound, one should not always take such information at face value. Judicious use of such information requires taking into account the nature of legal argumentation and the function of such passages in that process. Clearly, it would be unwise to conclude that lewd men in premodern Islamic societies had dinner at sunset without fail and did not wake up before the sun was up, or that lascivious men targeted seventy-year-old ladies at Friday prayers. While these statements are suspect at face value, they suggest that there may be other assertions about facts that seem innocuous and yet function similarly: they may serve as justifications of the laws in the same way as arguments based on the Qur'ān and *Ḥadīth*. When a justification is needed, a jurist may speculate about facts freely. In conjuring up these facts, the jurist may imagine that these states of affairs obtain (e.g., that wrongdoers behave in a certain way) in just the same way that he posits, without any firm evidence, that a norm embodied in a *ḥadīth* was abrogated during the Prophet's lifetime. In sum, the advocated law is taken as the true standard by which everything else is judged. The text of the canon and the "text of the world" are equally interpreted to let that truth shine forth.

7.5. The Jurist as Part of a Corporate Entity

Immanuel Kant (d. AD 1804) remarked that a cleric may, in good conscience, conduct his duties as a cleric in accordance with teachings that he may not personally subscribe to:

> Similarly a clergyman is obligated to make his sermon to his pupils in catechism and his congregation conform to the symbol of the church which he serves; for

[12] For example, Joseph Schacht, *Introduction to Islamic Law*, 56, 76–85.

> he has been accepted on this condition. But as a scholar he has complete freedom, even the calling, to communicate to the public all his carefully tested and well-meaning thoughts on that which is erroneous in the symbol and to make suggestions for the better organization of the religious body and church. In doing so, there is nothing that could be laid as a burden on his conscience. For what he teaches as a consequence of his office as a representative of the church, this he considers something about which he has no freedom to teach according to his own lights; it is something which he is appointed to propound at the dictation of and in the name of another. He will say, 'Our church teaches this or that; those are the proofs which it adduces.' He thus extracts all practical uses for his congregation from statutes to which he himself would not subscribe with full conviction but to the enunciation of which he can very well pledge himself because it is not impossible that truth lies hidden in them, and, in any case, there is at least nothing in them contradictory to inner religion. For if he believed he had found such in them, he could not conscientiously discharge the duties of his office; he would have to give it up.[13]

Some aspects of this passage can best be understood in light of its historical context. But, here, Kant speaks also to a kind of inner tension that can arise universally. A jurist represents something larger than himself, namely, the legal tradition of which he or she is a part. Like states or churches, legal schools were corporate entities. Just as a foreign minister or a priest functions as a representative, so may a jurist. A Muslim jurist may readily state the established opinion of his school without examining its grounds afresh, especially when the position does not appear wrong on the face of it – and very few laws do. Alternatively, even if he does disagree with a position of his school, he may choose to omit his own view and state only the school's position.

Studying Muslim legal handbooks, one can often ascertain that a jurist does accept his school's position; but on occasion the matter is not clear-cut. Where a jurist states his school's position, one may be left wondering whether the position was also his.

Complicating the matter further, the established school position was nothing more than the majority view of jurists in the school. Therefore, jurists were not merely mouthpieces; they also participated in forming the school's position. They performed the seemingly paradoxical twin functions of representing and shaping the legal school, a duality that could generate a certain amount of tension when a jurist dissented from his school's position on a legal question. At times the tension could be mitigated by grounding the dissenting view as much as possible in the legal principles

[13] Immanuel Kant, "What is Enlightenment?" in *The Enlightenment: A Sourcebook and Reader*, ed. Paul Hyland et al. (London: Routledge, 2003), 56.

and precedents of the school and by amending existing laws rather than eliminating or replacing them, a topic that is explored in the next chapter.

In short, because juristic works reveal, above all, the majority positions and arguments, inferring the views of the individual authors is on occasion challenging – indeed sometimes impossible. The work of the Spanish philosopher and Mālikī jurist and judge, Averroes (Ibn Rushd), provides a fascinating concrete example of how a premodern jurist may have consciously curbed the influence of his personal predilections on his jurisprudence.

The philosophical writings of Averroes, including his commentaries on Aristotle and Plato, offer insights about his worldview that can be checked against his legal output. Unlike Aristotle, whom he admired deeply, Averroes did not consider women almost a different species than men.[14] In addition, he lamented the condition of women in his society: he complained that because women were limited to the tasks of procreation and the rearing of children, they did not have the opportunity to develop "the human virtues."[15] Commenting on Plato's *Republic*, he wrote that women were fit to fight, become philosophers and rulers, and be admitted to the priesthood. In contrast, Plato had little to say about women as priests; clearly, Averroes's suggestion that some women had the qualities needed for religious leadership reflects his own view rather than Plato's.[16]

One may now ask whether Averroes's relatively egalitarian attitudes were reflected in his legal opinions. There are tantalizing hints of that possibility: for example, he dissents from the view of his own school of law in holding that a woman does not need a guardian's permission to marry.[17]

[14] For Averroes's views as expressed in his philosophical works, I rely on two sources: Prudence Allen, *The Concept of Woman: The Aristotelian Revolution, 750 B.C. – A.D. 1250* (Grand Rapids, MI: William B. Eerdmans, 1985), 339–50; and Catarina Belo, "Some Considerations on Averroes' Views regarding Women and Their Role in Society," *Journal of Islamic Studies* 20.1 (2009): 1–20. Averroes's commentaries on Plato and Aristotle seem discordant, reflecting the conflicting views of the Greek philosophers. Allen raises two possibilities (349–50): (1) Averroes initially accepted Plato's views and later changed his mind; (2) he presented Aristotle's views without assenting to them. See also Nelly Lahoud, *Political Thought in Islam: A Study of Intellectual Boundaries* (London: Routledge Curzon, 2005), 119–22. Allen ultimately prefers the second option and conjectures that the Platonic views were more characteristic of Averroes's thought while Lahoud takes the opposite view.

[15] Belo, "Some Considerations," 9.

[16] Belo, "Some Considerations," 9.

[17] Ibn Rushd, *Bidāyat al-mujtahid* (Beirut: Dār al-Fikr, 1415), 2:10. This is also cited by Belo, "Some Considerations," 14.

On the whole, however, Averroes does not argue against the patriarchal elements of classical Islamic law. For example, he does not give a personal opinion on the issue of whether a woman may lead men in prayer. On this point, he reports the different opinions of his predecessors without expressing a view of his own.[18] One may surmise that while he believed that some women had the natural qualities needed for religious or political leadership, the legitimacy of their playing such roles depended entirely on the specifics of each society. In some societies (such as in the ideal *Republic*) it would be right for them to take such positions. But in the time and place in which he lived, that would not have been right given the social and legal context. As a jurist, his first duty was to secure the interests of the community, both the juristic community and the larger society, not to create laws for a society other than his own. Had he constructed from the bottom up a fully egalitarian version of Islamic law, he would have only revealed himself as an incompetent jurist and made it impossible for any community to adopt his rulings. The social and economic circumstances and pressures in our time that have allowed the popularity of egalitarian values in many places and moved egalitarian laws into the realm of plausibility were absent in the time of Averroes.

7.6. From Laws to Society: What We *Can* Learn

Rules that would be destructive of, or otherwise intolerable to, society or its ruling elite, will be replaced, but it is a *non sequitur* to argue from that to the conclusion that law reflects the needs and desires of society or its ruling elite.[19]

– Alan Watson

If it is imprudent to take every statement in legal texts at face value, it is equally naïve to dismiss law entirely as a source of information about society. If I identified pitfalls, it is only to suggest that the inference to values be done in a more savvy way than is customary. Let us consider one of the ways in which one can infer social conditions or values.

As stressed previously, a law is often maintained due to legal inertia; it endures because it used to be the law, regardless of whether the original underlying values and concerns have endured. So, continuity is of limited use for inferring social values and conditions: it only indicates that a

[18] Ibn Rushd, *Bidāyat al-mujtahid*, 1:118. My viewpoint here is distinct from those found in Belo, "Some Considerations," 13–7, and Lahoud, *Political Thought in Islam*, 119–22.

[19] Watson, *Legal Origins and Legal Change*, 84.

retained law is not intolerable; it does not tell us whether the law is actually valued. But what about the opposite of continuity: change?

Given the paramountcy of legal inertia, the historian should take note when inertia is overcome and a law is replaced. With the usual cause for a law – inertia – out of the picture, an explanatory gap opens up. The correct explanation for the new law often includes new social and political circumstances, possibly including new values. Therefore, new laws that replace old ones can potentially reveal more about a community than preexisting laws.

As an example, one may consider the increasing legal restrictions in the Ḥanafī tradition on women's attendance at public prayers. By the seventh/thirteenth century, the trend culminated in a total prohibition. As shown in Chapter 5, neither Ḥanafī doctrines and decision history nor concern for textual evidence played a role in bringing about this change. The cause, therefore, must be sought in extralegal and extratextual factors such as a shift in social circumstances or values. The precise nature of the social changes that transformed the law warrants research in nonlegal historical sources.

Legal change may be an important clue to social reality, but it is certainly not the only one. If jurists uphold an inherited law, that does reveal something about their worldview: it means that they probably did not find the law unbearable. If they give a justification for a law, that means they did not find the justification offensive or absurd on the face of it. In addition, even though many inherited laws do not mirror a community's values, some do, particularly in cases where values have not changed since the corresponding law came into being.

7.7. Conclusion: Seeing Law as Law

Oliver Leaman has lamented that art historians frequently see Islamic art as something other than art. They often explain works of art exclusively in nonaesthetic terms, taking them to represent something else: religion, society, a set of essential ideas or artistic principles, or the symbolic meanings some Muslims have attached to them.[20] These approaches are born of a scholarly mindset that is replicated in different fields with similar results. Thus, much of what Leaman says about the field of art history can be repeated verbatim with the word "art" replaced with "law" or "ritual."

[20] Oliver Leaman, *Islamic Aesthetics: An Introduction* (Notre Dame, IN: University of Notre Dame Press, 2004), 1–8, 11–17, 47–9.

This common mindset can, for example, lead to the notion that laws are coextensive with underlying religious tenets or social values.

Echoing Leaman, I argue that Islamic law should be understood in the first instance as law.[21] This appeal presupposes that law is an independent variable, in that many laws cannot be explained in terms of social values, underlying religious tenets, class interests, the meanings that jurists or believers attach to laws, the interpretive standards of legal theory, or the ideologies of ruling elites. This applies, in particular, to the laws bearing upon gender.

Laws cannot be explained adequately by jurists' legal theories. This is illustrated by the fact that legal dynamics can be similar in communities that espouse incompatible legal theories. For example, it is well known that Sunnīs held that jurists must rely on the authority of past jurists while Shī'īs believed that they should not. (Such reliance is often called *taqlīd*, and abstention from it *ijtihād*.) This might lead one to conjecture that Shī'ī law has been historically more dynamic than its Sunnī counterpart. But that is not the case. In reality, Sunnī and Shī'ī legal traditions were all characterized by legal inertia, yet they often accommodated change when necessary. Sunnī and Shī'ī jurists took very seriously the rulings and arguments of earlier jurists within their schools of law, but this did not always prevent reinterpretation. Taking a narrower view, within Sunnism the legal differences among the schools of law are not reducible to disagreements on legal theory,[22] and in any case the canons of interpretation in the genre of legal theory (*uṣūl al-fiqh*) were often disregarded. Moreover, turning one's attention from that genre to the hermeneutic standards operative in positive law (in the *furū'* genre), this book has shown that those standards left the laws indeterminate. Nor is the underdetermination of laws by theory unique to Islam.[23] In its failure

[21] To my knowledge, in the academic field of Islamic studies, the only other significant attempt to theorize Islamic law as law has been undertaken by Sherman Jackson. See Jackson, *Islamic Law and the State*, 69–141; Jackson, "Kramer versus Kramer," 27–51; Jackson, "Fiction and Formalism," 177–201.

[22] Sherman Jackson, "Fiction and Formalism," 179–80.

[23] For hermeneutic indeterminacy in Jewish law, see Haim Cohn, "Legal Change in Unchangeable Law: The Talmudical Pattern," in *Legal Change: Essays in Honour of Julius Stone*, ed. A. R. Blackshield (Sidney: Butterworths, 1983), 16. In American jurisprudence, the theoretical controversy over originalism does not determine legal outcomes. (Originalism holds that interpretation should aim at discovering the original intention behind the text of the Constitution.) A jurist's position on originalism does not predispose him or her to take a particular position. See Steven Knapp and Walter Benn Michaels, "Intention, Identity, and the Constitution: A Response to David Hoy," in *Legal Hermeneutics: History, Theory, and Practice*, ed. Gregory Leyh (Berkeley: University

to conform to what one may predict from legal theory, law appears to have a life of its own.

Law also has a mind of its own in the face of state ideology, ideology being another variable that is inadequate for explaining law. As can be recognized also in our own time, legal dynamics may be similar in countries ruled by diametrically opposed ideologies – which is not to say that ideology cannot shape or influence law. Setting aside special cases, Muslim countries ruled by Islamist elites (like Iran) and secular ones (like Egypt before 2012) are broadly similar in the way they relate to the premodern heritage: none have held on to the institution of slavery, almost all retain a premodern version of family law that has been modified to increase women's rights, and almost all have borrowed banking and commercial laws wholesale from some European country. This pattern is noteworthy given that many academics consider the restoration of old laws as the raison d'être of Islamism. The resilience of legal dynamics in the face of state ideology is illustrated starkly in the case of Iran. In the Islamic Revolution of 1979, its American-installed, relatively secular dictator was supplanted by an Islamist theocracy at loggerheads with the United States. After an initial period in which the revolutionaries abolished some of the liberalizing family-law reforms as part of their campaign to erase the vestiges of the regime they demonized, the Islamist government came to resume and indeed expand such reforms. Thus, the normal pattern in the modern Muslim world has been one of radical change in the laws of commerce and slavery and incremental evolution in family law, no doubt reflecting the different degrees to which different areas of the law have come into conflict with the new economic and social realities.[24] This pattern suggests that legal inertia is operative everywhere: the laws remain as they were, but may change when they clash with the new environment. Cases in which a Muslim country has departed from this pattern by abolishing Islamic law altogether have arisen only in the aftermath of war or revolution and have involved coercion by authoritarian ruling cliques or occupation by the Soviets.[25]

of California Press, 1992), 187–99; cf. Stanley Fish, "Play of Surfaces: Theory and the Law," in *Legal Hermeneutics: History, Theory, and Practice*, ed. Gregory Leyh (Berkeley: University of California Press, 1992), 297–9.

24 By the word "evolution" I do not imply progress toward something better. Rather, I mean adapting to better fit the environment. I am drawing an analogy to biological evolution, in which clashes with environmental challenges favor the spread of fitness-enhancing adaptations. The evolutionary analogy is pursued further in Chapter 8, "The Logic of Law-Making."

25 Kecia Ali has argued that it is not possible to change Islamic family law in a piecemeal fashion. Her argument is based on the assumption that the premodern laws were based

If legal dynamics are not fully reducible to ideology and culture, there ought to be instances of the same mechanism operating in different cultures and time periods, thus legitimizing comparative investigations. It may therefore be useful to consider analogues in other legal traditions to some of the processes found in Islamic jurisprudence. I have done so already in the discussion of legal inertia, defined as the tendency of the laws to endure. Now I would like to focus on processes of textual interpretation by noting some similarities in the ways in which the U.S. Constitution on the one hand and the Qur'ān and the *Ḥadīth* on the other hand are interpreted. Despite the use of the present tense, my focus is on the premodern postformative schools of Islamic law. I offer only a brief and preliminary attempt, though such comparisons could form the subject of many monographs. Six parallelisms may be mentioned:

1. The U.S. Constitution and the Qur'ān and *Ḥadīth* are texts, not a completely trivial commonality since historically not all legal traditions rely on texts.
2. Statements from the U.S. Constitution and the Qur'ān and some *ḥadīth*s are absolutely binding, unless amended (in the American

on certain patriarchal models that Muslims today tend to find unacceptable, for example, models that analogized marriage to sale or slavery. It follows that Muslims cannot have it both ways: they cannot modify some of the laws while retaining others that were originally derived from those same now-objectionable values and models. Their only option is to give up the entire framework along with all of the laws that rest upon it. See Kecia Ali, "Money, Sex, and Power: The Contractual Nature of Marriage in Islamic Jurisprudence of the Formative Period" (PhD diss., Duke University, 2002), 477; Kecia Ali, *Sexual Ethics and Islam* (Oxford: Oneworld, 2006), 13; Kecia Ali, "Progressive Muslims and Islamic Jurisprudence: The Necessity for Critical Engagement with Marriage and Divorce Law," in *Progressive Muslims: On Justice, Gender and Pluralism*, ed. Omid Safi (Oxford: Oneworld, 2003), 180–3.

This argument is based on a misunderstanding of legal dynamics. Here I set aside Ali's problematic implicit assumption that the models premodern jurists cited in support of the laws had actually generated those laws. For the sake of argument, let us assume that they did. Equally problematically, she also assumes that the laws depend on the reasons given for them, so that if the legal reasons are delegitimized, then so are the laws. In reality, however, legal reasons have a secondary status compared to the laws: normally they adapt to accommodate the laws rather than the other way around. Case studies show that if a rationale is disqualified, the laws resting upon it do not necessarily fall. Jurists may tenaciously hold onto a law without accepting the rationales and values that were originally associated with it. In any case, the best proof for the proposition that Islamic family law can be modified in a piecemeal fashion is the fact that it has been modified in a piecemeal fashion in most Muslim countries. Piecemeal change has also been achieved in non-Muslim cultures that possess legal heritages that are no less patriarchal. Ali's paradigm thus fails to explain the empirical facts – facts that on the other hand fit well with the present book's conception of legal dynamics.

case) or abrogated (in the Islamic case).[26] Although nobody considers the American Constitution scripture or its authors infallible, for the American jurist the Constitution is just as binding as the Qur'ān is for the Muslim jurist: a jurist cannot declare any un-amended part of the Constitution as nonbinding. Here and in a number of other cases an essential difference between the two legal traditions – namely, one being religious and the other secular – turns out to be less consequential than it might first appear.

A well known consequence of having fixed, binding texts is that one normally cannot change the sources in order to effect legal change; instead one has to reinterpret the sources.[27] Thus, in both the American and classical Islamic cases there is the phenomenon of legal change through reinterpretation. But there is one mechanism of legal change in the constitutional case that is not available in the Islamic one, namely constitutional amendments.

Because one can amend a constitution but not the Qur'ān, it may be tempting to assume that legal change can happen more frequently in a secular legal tradition. However, that assumption is likely to prove false. On the one hand, on the American side, constitutional amendments are an unusual way of effecting legal change; in the majority of cases legal change is achieved through reinterpreting the relevant precedents and the existing text. On the other hand, on the Islamic side, while no text or law can be abrogated after the Prophet's death, the determination of exactly what was abrogated is often a matter of interpretation and is subject to frequent disagreement. This ambiguity thus introduces an extra measure of flexibility in the Islamic case. There is no comparable gray zone in the American tradition: jurists agree on what amended what. In sum, in both traditions interpretation is the primary mechanism for justifying legal change, and it is not to be taken for granted that the methods of interpretation make change easier in one tradition than the other.

[26] Cf. Jaroslav Pelikan, *Interpreting the Bible and the Constitution* (New Haven and London: Yale University Press, 2004), 8–11.

[27] However, prior to the closing of the canon, legal change can take place through changes in the canon, as can be observed, for example, in the *ḥadīth* literature or in the Hebrew Bible. On the latter, see, for example, Bernard Levinson, *Legal Revision and Religious Renewal in Ancient Israel*. Despite its title, Levinson's book is about theological change rather than legal revision.

3. In both traditions the interpretations of previous jurists carry a great deal of authority, though not the absolute authority of the canon (the Qur'ān and *ḥadīth*s or American Constitution).[28] This point is not trivial since one could imagine a world in which jurists normally paid no attention to precedent and worked directly with the foundational texts. (Such an unfettered approach is one of the senses in which the word *ijtihād* is used.) In reality, jurists work within traditions – within the schools of law (*madhhab*s) in the classical Islamic case.
4. Related to the last point is the counterintuitive fact that if one were limited to reading the canon, one would not be able to predict the law reliably without the benefit of hindsight. In a sense, the legal meaning of the text is fixed by later interpretation. In some cases this meaning differs from what a reader may gather by reading the canon without reference to the jurisprudence constructed upon it and without knowledge of the new social values and conditions that may have occasioned new interpretations. In the striking formulation of one author, "no one is sure what the law is today, but later, when the Supreme Court resolves the split, we will have known what the law was all along."[29]
5. Furthermore, legal change often tends to take place through adjusting previous laws when possible rather than through building new construals from the ground up. Legal reasoning thus tends to develop in a cumulative and incremental fashion. If jurists wish to change the inherited ruling in a particular case, rather than getting rid of the existing law that governs the case, they will tend merely to qualify it with a different *existing* law or legal principle or qualify it with a *new* law or principle of relatively limited scope. The jurist thus usually makes the minimum amount of change in the system needed to achieve the purpose. This phenomenon is illustrated and analyzed in Chapter 8, "The Logic of Law-Making."
6. Each tradition has its own public reason, including requirements for how a legal argument may be formulated. Public reason has features that are distinctive and unique to the tradition. But there

[28] Compare Pelikan, *Interpreting the Bible and the Constitution*, 115–22.

[29] David Carlson, "The Traumatic Dimension in Law," *Cardozo Law Review* 24.6 (2003): 2287.

are also remarkable commonalities in the patterns of argumentation. For example, in a legal dispute the opposing jurists often justify their positions by drawing analogies to different cases, appealing to the plain meaning of the text, or delimiting the scope of a law or legal principle in different ways.

In conclusion, once law is envisioned as an independent variable, its relationship with social reality ceases to be transparent, and legal literature is revealed as a treacherous guide to social reality. While some laws may mirror the values of a community, such as those of jurists, many do not. In attempting to learn about a society from its laws and legal literature, four caveats should be borne in mind:

First, inherited laws can be retained due to legal inertia even if their underlying values are rejected. The adjacency law in the Ḥanafī tradition provides a striking example. The values that generated its prototype in the first/seventh century soon became alien and unacceptable to Islamic thinkers; nevertheless, the law itself could be tolerated, and therefore it endured, and has endured until today. This is so because laws have greater staying power than the meanings or values attached to them.

Second, the justifications given for the laws should not be equated with jurists' motives for supporting the laws. The justifications are tailored to fit the recognized standards of legal argumentation, and in many cases one can show that jurists' actual motives were altogether different from the justifications they constructed.

Third, statements in legal literature about social conditions and values should not always be taken at face value. The endeavor to justify the laws provides the subtext for some such statements. The law to be justified was at times taken as the touchstone by which other evidence was judged. Just as the binding texts, such as the scripture, were interpreted to accommodate the law, so was the "text of the world" on occasion reimagined, refracted, and reshaped. In sum, statements of fact in the legal literature should be evaluated against the backdrop of jurists' efforts to justify the laws.

Fourth, one cannot always assume that everything a jurist wrote represented his personal conclusions and positions, since jurists effectively served as spokesmen for their legal schools.

All of this is not to argue for a complete disjunction between laws and other social realities, including values. When a law changes, it is normally a sign of social or political change of one sort or another. There are also other ways of inferring values, a few of which were mentioned in the previous section. While these methods are not enough to claim that law mirrors values in general, they do make it plausible to say that law has to reach a tenuous accommodation with values. Putting the matter this way presupposes that law possesses dynamics of its own that make it somewhat independent of other elements of social reality such as the values of a community.

Excursus: A Historian's "Public Reason"

In Section 7.3, I used the term "public reason" in the sense of "the shared standards of argumentation that help to create a framework within which different actors and interests in a community could pursue conflict or cooperation." This term has been used by a number of authors, most famously John Rawls, in different senses.[30] Rawls writes, "There is no settled meaning of this term. The one I use is not I think peculiar."[31] The sense in which I use the term is different from that of Rawls, and it is not peculiar either. The most important difference between Rawls's usage of "public reason" and mine concerns the community to which it is applied. Rawls dwelt on the concept in the context of the citizens of a liberal, democratic, constitutional state. By contrast, my usage is not limited to a democracy. It could apply to a community of male citizens before suffrage is extended to women or of free persons before slavery is abolished. Indeed, public reason as I define it is applicable to an arbitrary community, be it a country, a class of oligarchs, a group of jurists, or a professional guild. This difference with Rawls reflects the different interests of the historian who aims to describe real communities versus the moral philosopher who prescribes principles governing an idealized political order that may or may not exist in reality.

A comparison to Rawls might at first appear superficial on the assumption that his "public reason" cannot accommodate comprehensive doctrines such as Islamic religion or Ḥanafī law. This may appear so because for Rawls public reason involves "political" conceptions that "can be presented independently from comprehensive doctrines of any kind (although

[30] John Rawls, *Political Liberalism*, expanded ed. (New York: Columbia University Press, 2005), 212–54 and 440–90. The last part of this expanded edition of the book (440–90) reproduces a 1997 article that constitutes a significant revision of the rest of the book and a fairly clear statement of the ideas. It originally appeared as Rawls, "The Idea of Public Reason Revisited," *University of Chicago Law Review* 64.3 (1997): 765–807.

[31] Rawls, *Political Liberalism*, 443.

they may, of course, be supported by a reasonable overlapping consensus of such doctrines)."[32] (By "comprehensive doctrines" Rawls means religious or secular ideologies or worldviews that take stances on concrete questions of law and policy – the penal code, marriage laws, whether abortion should be legal, whether there should be a draft, the forms of taxation, and so on. "Public reason," by contrast, belongs primarily to the more restricted "political" realm, involving the means by which such concrete questions are determined, including but not limited to constitutional and procedural standards and such notions as the equality of citizens regardless of sex or race. Comprehensive doctrines may treat such properly "political" questions alongside "nonpolitical" ones.) Indeed, since Rawls and I use "public reason" in different senses, it is not necessary that my usage be isomorphic to his.

However, there is a fundamental affinity between our conceptions. The key to seeing this lies in the qualification that Rawls places within parentheses in the above quotation, namely, that the principles of public reason may "be supported by a reasonable overlapping consensus of [comprehensive] doctrines." For Rawls, principles from a comprehensive doctrine can form part of public reason if they are shared by other reasonable comprehensive doctrines in the community – in other words, if they are part of what he calls an "overlapping consensus." A country that is comprised of different religious and secular groups may or may not come to agree on political principles that are recognizably characteristic of one religion. However, public reason, as I use the term, is always defined relative to a community, and if the community in question is that of Ḥanafī jurists, the overlapping consensus will be characteristically Islamic and indeed Ḥanafī.

Ḥanafī jurists with different comprehensive doctrines – for example, those with a patriarchal agenda and those who are relatively egalitarian – can then argue for their respective positions on different points of law by use of the shared standards of reasoning. In this way, distinctively religious standards could indeed allow different comprehensive doctrines to compete on a level playing field. For both Rawls and me, public reason can thus have an equalizing effect *ceteris paribus* within the community to which the term is applied. And for both of us, public reason represents an overlapping consensus of comprehensive doctrines. Most of the inconsistencies in his concept and mine are consequences of a single difference: the fact that we apply the term to different communities.

[32] Rawls, *Political Liberalism*, 453; cf. 218, 223.

8

The Logic of Law Making

8.1. Introduction

The reasons jurists give for the laws ("legal reasons") adapt to accommodate the laws, and the laws adapt under the pressure of social conditions. The analogy to biological evolution invoked by the verb "adapt" is fitting for more than one reason. The arrow of causation points in the opposite direction to that of adaptation: from the environment to the species. Likewise, social reality affects laws, and laws affect legal reasons, as shown in Figure 16.

Yet, the sort of causation entailed by the word adaptation is not deterministic. Just as the precise manner in which a species adapts to an environmental challenge is unpredictable, so too different sets of legal reasons can equally ensure the needed legal outcome, and different legal outcomes may provide equally acceptable solutions to real-life problems. This is because the form of causation that is operative involves constraints: it is negative in the sense that it specifies what cannot be, rather than exactly what has to be. Just as the environment rules out unfit mutations without determining the survival-enhancing mutation that eventually spreads, so too life experience puts limits on legal outcomes by ruling out those that clash too sharply with it, without thereby dictating a unique solution. Another reason it cannot be said that present social conditions determine the laws involves legal inertia. Just as heredity in evolution means that some present features of an organism may reflect the bygone environmental challenges of a previous era, so too laws may endure due to legal inertia even if they do not mirror new social conditions and values

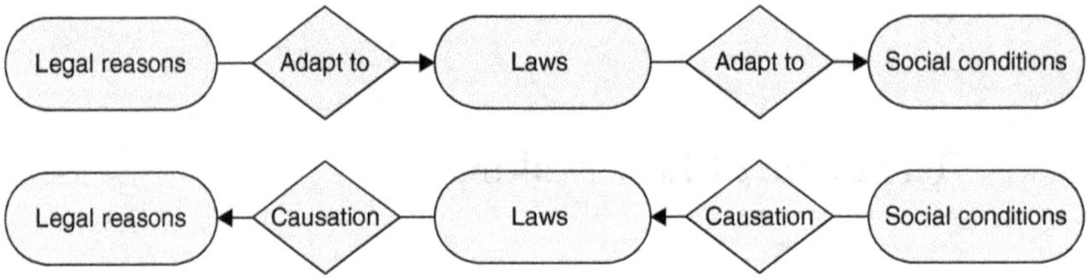

FIGURE 16. Causation is in the reverse direction of adaptation.

(Chapter 7). Though it may be overridden upon clashes with new conditions, legal continuity is the default state.

Any attempt to explain legal continuity and change requires an account of how laws come about. In trying to determine the factors that generated the laws in mainstream Ḥanafī jurisprudence, this book began by considering four candidates:

(i) The canon, namely the Qur'ān and binding *ḥadīth*s.
(ii) The techniques of interpreting the canon, such as abrogation, qualification, and analogy.
(iii) The previous legal decisions in the Ḥanafī tradition.
(iv) The present social conditions, needs, and values of the law-making class.

One who believes that societies reimagine themselves from the ground up in every generation will be attracted to the last factor, namely, present circumstances. So will a scholar who holds that laws mirror current social conditions. On this last view, a law that is inherited from an earlier generation and retained signifies its suitability to present needs. On the opposite pole would stand a scholar who holds that a society or religion has ideas that endure through the ages even if they clash with other aspects of social reality. A proponent of this view will pick one or more of the first three factors. Within this category, a common answer involves *i* and *ii*, texts and interpretation. Such an approach is rooted in the normative cast of the genre of legal theory (*uṣūl al-fiqh*), which requires that the laws be derived from the canon by means of specific interpretive techniques. The problem with this idea is that the norms in the *uṣūl* genre are not always applied in practice, and the norms that are applied in practice are deployed in such a loose manner that they do not determine the laws. Another answer in the same category, given by Joseph Schacht and rooted in the normative ideals of some premodern jurists such as Zayn al-Dīn Ibn Nujaym, highlights *iii*, the legal heritage. It holds that the laws of the school are unchanging, and that therefore for a premodern jurist "present" law is the same as previous law where precedent exists. This cannot be quite right either, since recent scholarship has shown and this book has confirmed that the laws occasionally changed.

The right answer is a modification of Schacht's position that combines *iii* with *iv*: the legal precedents normally determine the laws, but when they clash with present conditions, they can be overridden. The interpretation of the canon plays no causal role in this, which is not to deny its having shaped some of the legal decisions in the formative period that became a part of the Ḥanafī heritage, decisions such as the prohibition of wine. Accordingly, the legal reasons normally do not play a causal role in determining the laws in the postformative period in cases where there is a precedent: they serve to justify the laws, not to generate them. The arrow of causation points from laws to reasons. This applies, in particular, to reasons that are formulated as interpretations of the canon. The laws are thus canon-blind.

In this conception, legal reasons – that is, the reasons jurists give for the laws – are secondary in relation to the laws they justify. They adapt to the laws. They are dispensable and hence relatively unstable compared to the laws. Stated in terms of the concepts of Chapter 1, legal reasons are more revisable than laws. One of the ways in which this relative revisability is manifested historically is that legal reasons react to changes in the laws. When a law changes, the justifications given for it are adjusted.

But how do the legal reasons change? Revisiting the discussion of revisability in Chapter 1, one may ask whether changes in reasons historically follow certain patterns. In this chapter, I argue that they do. Indeed, it is possible to characterize change in reasons to a degree. The characterization can be obtained by breaking up a typical reason into its constituents and examining how each part is affected as the initial reason is replaced with a new one. The first step, then, is to identify the building blocks of a typical reason. It so happens, though, that there is not one type of reason – there are two: there is (*i*) reasoning with legal principles, where a particular legal effect is derived from general laws ("principles") and (*ii*) formal exegesis of the canon, where a law follows logically from an interpretation of the text. Although often both types of reasoning are present in an argument, for the sake of simplicity it helps to consider them separately. In this chapter, "law" and "legal effect" refer to decisions of positive law.

8.2. Reasoning with Legal Principles

Here is an example of reasoning with legal principles, cast as a deductive inference.

DEDUCTION 1. *Reasoning with legal principles (an eventually undesirable legal effect)*

A woman standing next to a man and sharing the same group prayer (that is, "adjacency") invalidates his prayer.	[legal principle 1]
The validity of a worshipper's prayer (in group prayers) depends on the validity of the imām's prayer.	[legal principle 2]
	[*ceteris paribus*]
A woman joining the prayer standing next to the imām invalidates the prayer of every worshipper joining in the group prayer.	[legal effect] (became undesirable)

This example illustrates Ḥanafī reasoning on adjacency as it stood in the second and third centuries (eighth and ninth centuries AD). The horizontal bar separates the premises from the conclusion. The premises include two principles. The first is the adjacency principle, and the second the proposition that the imām's prayer has to be valid for that of a worshipper to be valid. The *ceteris paribus* clause is the simplifying assumption that no factors are involved other than those listed. The conclusion is that a woman praying next to the imām invalidates everyone's prayers.

The inference being deductive, one should note two things. First, the premises are more general than the conclusion. This is why I call the premises principles and the conclusion an effect. To be sure, this terminology is relative; what is a principle in one deduction could be a legal effect in another if it can be derived from more general propositions. The second thing to note is that in a deduction, if the premises are true, then so is the conclusion. So, truth transmits from the premises to the conclusion. Falsity works the other way around, as it transmits from the conclusion to the premises: if the conclusion is false, then so is at least one of the premises. This fact is called *modus tollens* in logic.

It is a general feature of such deductions that among its different components it is the conclusion that most concretely impinges on real-life experience. By comparison, the premises are "higher-level" and relatively abstract, and the more general and higher-level a principle is, the more nebulous its bearing becomes on a particular and concrete question of positive law, since there are potentially a larger number of principles that may interact with it, for example, by qualifying it. Because it is palpable experience that most often motivates change, and because it is the deduction's conclusion that most concretely comes into contact with experience, it is at the level of the conclusion that one expects change to be initiated, whence it "trickles up" to the rest of the system of propositions.

The Ḥanafīs were increasingly unhappy with the burdensome conclusion concerning adjacency that allowed the easy invalidation of the prayers of entire congregations, and they tried to rid themselves of it. By *modus tollens*, to do away with the conclusion, one should readjust the premises. More precisely, one calls the existing conclusion false, which logically entails the falsity of one or more of the premises, thus prompting their revision. The Ḥanafīs thus came up with this new deduction:

DEDUCTION 2. *Reasoning with legal principles (an acceptable legal effect)*

A woman standing next to a man and sharing the same group prayer (that is, adjacency) invalidates his prayer.	[legal principle 1]
A two-foot gap does not count as adjacency.	[ad hoc principle]
The validity of a worshipper's prayer (in group prayers) depends on the validity of the imām's prayer.	[legal principle 2]
The imām may (mentally) exclude an adjacent female from sharing in the group prayer.	[ad hoc principle]
A woman joining the prayer next to the imām or another man does not necessarily invalidate the prayers of others.	[legal effect] (desired)

This development exemplifies a general pattern in the adaptation of laws to real-life social concerns, namely that the principles are adjusted to avoid unacceptable or intolerable legal effects. In this sense, legal effects enjoy a form of priority over legal principles. Aside from this broad observation, a more specific characterization of change can be obtained by a close examination of case studies, including the example at hand:

In the new deduction, the two principles from the original deduction are still present. But the adjacency principle is now amended by an ad hoc principle to the effect that a two-foot gap does not count as adjacency. The second legal principle is left intact. However, the old *ceteris paribus* clause is violated by the introduction of an ad hoc principle allowing the imām to mentally exclude adjacent females.

The result is an acceptable legal effect, one that, in principle, made the concrete experience of prayers in Ḥanafī law much more similar to those of, say, the Shāfiʿī school, which did not have the adjacency principle to begin with. The crucial observation here is that this outcome was achieved not by giving up the old principles, but rather by introducing ad hoc principles of lower generality that amend the old ones. The amendments, in turn, could be amended to fine tune the legal effects to desired specifications. For example, some jurists introduced the principle that the imām may not "will out" women in the case of the Friday prayers. This is a general principle, but it is less general than the original principle that it amends. The result is an iterative process of back-and-forth between principles and desired effects that generates a sequence of principles consisting of ad hoc amendments to higher level, more general, principles followed by ad hoc amendments to those amendments, and so on.

Other examples of this sort of iteration arose in the problems posed by funeral prayers for two areas of the law: (1) adjacency and (2) women-only prayers:

(Example 1) The rationale offered for the adjacency law (i.e., the "keep them behind" report) would entail that the same adjacency rules apply to funeral prayers, an undesirable consequence. So, al-Sarakhsī introduces three ad hoc principles to distinguish funeral prayers from other prayers. First, avoidance of sexual thoughts is viewed as the rationale behind the "keep them behind" report. Second, sexual thoughts invalidate only prayers that constitute communication with God. Third, funeral prayers do not constitute communication with God in the way other prayers do.

(Example 2) Since women-only prayers were deemed acceptable in the case of funeral prayers, it needed to be explained why the rationales against them in the case of other prayers were not applicable in this case. Al-Bābirtī and others responded with a convoluted and (as Ibn ʿĀbidīn showed) contradictory rationalization involving a number of general principles.

Once one recognizes that principles change to accommodate effects, the question becomes: in what way? That is to say, *modus tollens* means that the principles as a whole are not acceptable, but it does not tell us which has to be modified and how. In thinking about this question, it helps to note that in the adjacency example the legal principle was amended rather than eliminated or replaced. The use of amendments indicates a tendency to preserve as much of the contents of the existing legal principles as possible. Thus, a premium is placed on generality.

But generality alone is not sufficient to explain the specific form of change. After all, if the Ḥanafīs had simply given up the adjacency rule, then the resulting rules of group prayer would have been no less general (and no less desirable as far as lived experience was concerned). So, as a rule of thumb, there is a premium on generality, but only for propositions that are already part of the tradition. In sum, existing principles have inertia of their own.

What could explain the inertia of legal principles? In other words, what makes giving up a legal principle in its entirety disadvantageous compared to amending it in order to ensure the new legal effect? The following consideration provides an explanation: If one gave up a general principle, that would remove the justification for all the other legal effects explained by means of that principle, which would necessitate a costly effort to justify those effects afresh. Such effort can be minimized by amending the principle instead. In this way, one could remove the justification for an unacceptable legal effect without thereby removing the justification for all the other legal effects potentially supported by the principle. (To be sure, this benefit will not arise in all cases, as there may be situations in which no other legal effect is derived from a principle beside the one being modified. But it is far simpler to treat all cases in a similar fashion than to determine in each case whether there are other legal effects touched by the principle.) While it is natural to explain the inertia of legal principles in terms of loyalty to the precedents in one's legal tradition, these considerations show that it has practical benefits. These benefits constitute a rational basis for what may otherwise seem an emotional attachment.

Another noteworthy pattern in the case studies is the accumulation, over time, of principles. At times, such an increase in complexity is concomitant with a seeming disregard for what may appear to be a simpler solution. Alan Watson has pointed out that legal interpretation often leads to complexity that seems unnecessary.[1] The adjacency example

[1] Watson, *Society and Legal Change*, 87–96.

illustrates just such a phenomenon. Over time Ḥanafī legal effects drew considerably closer to those of, say, Shāfiʿī law, in which adjacency did not invalidate anyone's prayer. The simplest way for Ḥanafī legal effects to get close to this final destination would have been simply giving up the adjacency rule. Instead, new principles were piled up, thus increasing complexity. In the end, a legal effect similar to the Shāfiʿī effect was obtained, but in a somewhat roundabout way.

A rise in complexity often characterizes belief systems or organisms that undergo adaptation. When adaptation takes place under the constraint that *change has to be incremental*, such complexity sometimes takes a form that may superficially appear unnecessary, in the sense that a different type of adaptation, one involving a single leap rather than a series of incremental changes, would have achieved a simpler system. This type of complexity occurs in nature as a result of evolution (e.g., in the case of eye migration in flatfish[2]), but more pertinent to our purposes, it also occurs in certain belief systems. Examples are systems of legal principles within a legal tradition and scientific explanations within scientific research programs, where new empirical observations that contradict a core theory are accounted for by adding an ad hoc hypothesis that has lower generality than the core theory, not unlike the way new legal effects are accommodated by means of ad hoc amendments.[3]

2 As a bottom feeder, an adult flounder has both of its eyes on one side, while a newly hatched flounder has its eyes on opposite sides, just like other fish. Soon after hatching, the right eye migrates around the head to the other side, the shape of the fish becomes flat, and the fish moves to the bottom of the sea and tilts on its side, permanently assuming a new posture, with the eyed left side now its upside. The journey of the individual juvenile flounder to the sea bottom reenacts the evolutionary journey of the species to a new habitat. That is to say, originally the flounder was not a bottom feeder. The eye migration, flattening of the shape, and permanent tilting are adaptations to the new habitat at the bottom of the sea. To be sure, evolving a new eye in the needed spot would have appeared a simpler and less costly solution, but it would have involved an evolutionary leap. By contrast, eye migration could be achieved incrementally, with a small amount of additional survival-enhancing migration per generation. See Matt Friedman, "The Evolutionary Origin of Flatfish Asymmetry," *Nature* 454 (July 2008): 209–12.

3 In the scientific case, new observations drive theoretical adaptation. An observational fact appears as the conclusion of a deduction, like legal effects. New observations thus prompt theoretical revision thanks to *modus tollens*. The requirement that theoretical change be incremental is related to a commitment to the core theory of a research program (or what Thomas Kuhn called a paradigm). Thus, a research program may respond to an observational challenge by introducing ad hoc hypotheses, whereas revolutionary science gets rid of the core theory instead. See the discussion of ad hoc hypotheses in Imre Lakatos, "Falsification and the Methodology of Scientific Research Programmes," in *Criticism and the Growth of Knowledge*, eds. Imre Lakatos and Alan Musgrave (Cambridge: Cambridge University Press, 1970), 91–195; Gunnar Andersson., *Criticism and the History of Science: Kuhn's, Lakatos's and Feyerabend's Criticisms of Critical Rationalism* (Leiden: E. J. Brill, 1994).

These similarities of legal change with evolution in nature and the development of scientific thought are not superficial. They arise from two shared features, adaptation and incrementality, that will tend to generate seemingly unnecessary complexity almost as a matter of logical entailment: where adaptation has to be incremental, on occasion a simplifying nonincremental adaptation will be ruled out, making the actual outcome more complex than the excluded, simpler solution. Both conditions for the rise of such complexity, that is, adapting and being limited to incremental change, are present in legal reasoning: (1) There is adaptation in legal reasons, for laws should not be intolerable to the law-making class, and this leads to constraints on legal effects and the corresponding adaptation of legal reasons. (2) Furthermore, in reasoning with legal principles, such adaptations tend to be incremental, due to the premium placed on the contents of existing legal principles, in other words, due to the inertia of the principles.

In summary, the manner in which legal change "trickles up" to legal principles follows certain patterns. The process can be characterized as cumulative and incremental. It is cumulative because new principles are piled up to amend old ones, and incremental because of the tendency to preserve as much of the contents of existing principles as possible. This tendency to preserve the contents of principles serves to accommodate legal change with the least amount of overall effort, by avoiding the ripple effect occasioned by the loss of a principle and minimizing the consequences for the rest of the system of reasons. Legal change under these constraints can lead to the rise of seemingly unnecessary complexity.

8.3. Formal Exegesis of the Canon

Though one could hardly choose a simpler example, the following captures all the basic elements of formal exegesis:

DEDUCTION 3. *The elements of exegesis*

An abrogating statement is binding.	[Hermeneutic principle]
The canon's command to pray toward Mecca is an abrogating statement. (That is, the earlier command to pray toward Jerusalem is abrogated.)	[Exegetic Rationale]
Praying toward Mecca is binding.	[Legal effect]

Formal exegesis, as the example shows, has three main elements when cast as a deductive inference. First, there is the legal effect or consequence ("one must pray toward Mecca"), which appears in the conclusion. The second element consists of exegetic rationales that assign roles to specific statements in the canon. For example, an exegetic rationale may call a particular verse of the Qur'ān an abrogating verse, saying that it abrogates prayer toward Jerusalem. Such an interpretation can be a valid one because appeal to abrogation is recognized as a valid hermeneutic technique. Its validity follows from a hermeneutic principle to the effect that an abrogating statement is binding, and that an abrogated statement is not. Thus, as the third element in exegesis, hermeneutic principles specify how a particular type of rationale, such as appeal to abrogation, may or may not be used.

Two conclusions regarding the interpretation of the canon are worth restating. The first result is the nearly maximal hermeneutic flexibility of Ḥanafī interpretive standards. The Ḥanafīs used exegetic rationales with such flexibility that in principle almost any legal effect could be accommodated. When I say "any legal effect," I include the tough test cases of legal effects that go against the apparent meaning of the canon. In other words, the hermeneutic principles (i.e., the rules that govern the use of exegetic rationales) are so flexible that the canon can be interpreted in such a way as to accommodate even legal effects that go against its apparent meaning. Consider these two examples: First, the canon includes the command of the Prophet, "Do not prevent women from going out to the mosque." Nevertheless, the Ḥanafīs prohibited women from going out to the mosque. They initially banned young women and eventually the old and the infirm as well. Second, there are some half a dozen reports that the Prophet's wives led other women in group prayers, but again, the Ḥanafīs forbade women to lead other women in prayers. In both cases, the Ḥanafīs devised interpretations to reconcile their laws with the words of the Prophet and the practices of his wives.

To briefly review the case of women-only group prayers, the Ḥanafīs explain the reports about 'Ā'isha, Umm Salama, and the Companion Umm Waraqa by saying that they describe a practice that was eventually abrogated. But then they have to deal with the statement of the Companion Ibn 'Abbās that when a woman leads a prayer she should stand in the middle of the row. They explain this by arguing that Ibn 'Abbās is not implying that a woman may lead others; he is just saying what she should do in case she does lead others. In other words, there are degrees of evil, and while it is wrong for a woman to lead other women in prayer, it is even worse if she does so by standing in front of them rather than in the row. As evidence for abrogation, they argue that it is forbidden for the prayer leader to stand in the row of worshippers, but since that is the only way a woman may lead prayers, female leadership of prayers must be forbidden. They also cite the *ḥadīth* that it is better for a woman to pray in the remotest spot in her house.

In the case of the question of whether a woman may go out to pray in the mosque, a number of different justifications were offered throughout the centuries, and the most sophisticated one is that of Ibn al-Humām. He acknowledges the command of the Prophet not to prevent women from going out to the mosque but asserts that there are preconditions attached to this command. In particular, the Prophet also said that women must not go out perfumed. Now, the reason behind the perfume prohibition was the prevention of temptation and misdeeds. In our day, he says, mosques are very crowded and there is jostling, which can lead to temptation and misdeeds. Also, there are bands of lascivious men who are out to abuse women. So, by analogy with the case of perfume, we can prohibit women today from going out.

The second result bearing on formal exegesis, which holds true also in the case of reasoning with legal principles, is that the starting point for the Ḥanafī jurist is the canon-blind law, and an interpretation of the canon in the form of specific exegetic rationales is the end result. That is to say, the interpretation is contrived to accommodate the needed legal outcome. This can be seen by analyzing the arguments of jurists in detail. Such analysis points to the hermeneutic flexibility of Ḥanafī exegesis and leads to the conclusion that textual interpretation does not determine the laws; rather, it justifies them. Another indication of the secondary status of legal reasons is the frequent use of ad hoc justifications: one repeatedly encounters principles that are created to justify the legal outcome in the case at hand – principles that can be shown to serve no other purpose, since no other legal outcome is derived from them and since they were never mentioned previously in any context. Yet another indication is the use of stretched and convoluted arguments.

Aside from analyzing the logical structure of Ḥanafī reasons, one can support the same conclusion by noting the broad historical pattern of the relative stability of laws compared to legal reasons and exegetic rationales. This can be seen in a number of ways, as discussed in greater detail in the previous chapter (Section 7.3): Chronologically, laws tend to precede the reasons given for them, which can be numerous and variable. Sometimes a jurist is sure of the law, but unsure about the reason behind it. And when a standard rationale given for a law is disqualified for some reason, jurists create new and better rationales for it rather than give up the law. This pattern of the relative stability of laws compared to rationales is ubiquitous. To give an example, through the centuries, Ḥanafīs offered five different reasons for the adjacency principle, including four that employed exegetic rationales, and none of these gives the original cause of the genesis of the adjacency rule.

Legal reasons adapt to accommodate canon-blind law; but what form does adaptation take in the type of reasoning that involves exegetic rationales? One thing formal exegesis has in common with reasoning with principles is that the legal effect is in the conclusion of the deduction. So, by *modus tollens*, to ensure an acceptable legal outcome, one makes adjustments in the premises. The question is where in the premises. Exegetic rationales are relatively dispensable; and that is thus where changes are made. Hermeneutic principles, which tend to be more general, are relatively more stable. But change does not just take the form of amendments, which are more suited to legal principles; instead it more often involves replacing one set of rationales with another set. Hence, this type of reasoning is less accumulative and less conducive to the rise of seemingly unnecessary complexity.

8.3.1. *Exegetic Rationales and Hermeneutic Flexibility in Practice*

In Section 1.3, I explained how the degree of hermeneutic flexibility depends on the standards governing the use of exegetic rationales involving abrogation, qualification, analogy, and so on. The case studies have illuminated how such techniques are used.

Abrogation is used in a loose and ad hoc way in order to justify the canon-blind law. Its manner of application leaves, in general, a high degree of indeterminacy. Initially, it could be invoked without any justification at all. In the case of the law on women-only prayers, as far as my sources allow me to determine, it was not until the seventh/thirteenth century that some justification came to be offered. But even then the standards of evidence required for showing that a law was abrogated were lax. It was enough to adduce a tradition or verse "going against" the putatively abrogated law. It was not necessary to show that this tradition or verse dated from a period after the abrogated law. Moreover, "going against" could be construed in a loose manner. For example, in the case of women-only prayers, a number of textual indications of abrogation were proposed, the strongest of which was the tradition praising women's prayers in the storage room or in the remotest spot in the house.

Qualification is one of the tools used most readily. The main use of qualification is to limit the scope of a general statement that would go against the canon-blind law if it were taken literally (i.e., if applied as a universally applicable, unqualified rule). One source of flexibility lies in the choice of which statement qualifies which in the case of two seemingly contrary statements. For example, do *ḥadīths* discouraging women from leaving their homes qualify those permitting them to go out to the mosque, as al-Ṭaḥāwī holds? Or is it the other way around?

More flexibility can be injected into qualification by means of analogy. Suppose there is a general statement in the canon going against the canon-blind law that one wants to neutralize using qualification. Obviously, one starts by looking for a statement from the canon that is contrary to it. But what if one does not find such a statement? In this case, one could try to use analogy to create a "virtual" contrary principle. For example, there is nothing in the canon to the effect that the existence of crowds at communal prayers can be a cause for barring women. But such a "virtual" principle can be created by drawing an analogy with the use of perfume, which the canon does name as an impediment to women's going out. Once created, the virtual principle is used to qualify the permissive traditions.

In a similar vein, in the case of *ʿĪd* prayers, it was assumed, without direct evidence, that the Prophet had allowed women's attendance only at the beginning of his mission, when the Muslims were weak and oppressed, in order to impress upon the enemy that the Muslims were numerous. Thus, it was implicitly posited that the small number of Muslims and their need to appear larger is a precondition for women's attendance at the *ʿĪd*s. The permissibility of women's attendance was thus qualified almost out of existence.

Another way a "virtual" qualifier can be created is by using "reverse implication" in the manner of the following example. There is nothing in the canon to indicate that women are barred from daytime prayers. There are traditions of quite general purport saying that women must not be barred from mosques, and then there are traditions of more limited scope saying that women must not be barred at night. Now, one may choose to read the tradition about acceptability at nighttime as no more than an instance of acceptability in general, at all times. On this reading, the nighttime prayers may have been mentioned separately for the sake of emphasis, for example, to remind people who may have been keeping women away specifically from nighttime prayers. Alternatively, they may have represented the first stage of a gradually broadening affirmation of permission. However, the early Ḥanafīs preferred a different solution that better conformed to the canon-blind law: by "reverse implication," traditions saying that women may attend prayers at nighttime mean that they cannot do so in daytime. This "virtual" principle could then be used to qualify the traditions that permit women's attendance in general, unrestricted terms.[4]

Analogical reasoning itself provides additional flexibility. In the two main instances of analogy encountered in this book (namely, the barring of women from mosques and the justification for the adjacency law), there are several sources of indeterminacy. One is in the very choice of whether or not analogy ought to be used. Another source of uncertainty is the choice of the case to which one should analogize. Further flexibility results from the often inevitable uncertainty over the choice of the true effective cause among the range of feasible candidates.

All of this suggests that the hermeneutic principles used by jurists remained limited in scope and number. Now, the task of hermeneutic principles is to regulate the use of exegetic rationales. The fact they were limited resulted in exegetic rationales being underdetermined by the hermeneutic principles. That is, the hermeneutic principles did not determine the exegetic rationales; they put at best rather loose constraints on the choice of exegetic rationales. Consequently, a variety of exegetic rationales could be selected, leading to a variety of potential legal outcomes. The hermeneutic principles, therefore, were inherently incapable of mapping the evidence of the canon onto unique law, making for a nearly maximally flexible hermeneutic approach. This flexibility made it possible to maintain the canon-blind laws by surrounding them with a protective cushion of rationales. The exegetic rationales – undetermined and highly malleable, dispensable, and revisable – shielded the laws, absorbing the impact of contrary evidence, such as any apparently unfavorable *ḥadīths*. Since most of the time, in the interest of continuity, the canon-blind law equaled the received law, the laws remained stable. When, however, the canon-blind law differed from the received law, it could be accommodated thanks to hermeneutic flexibility.

[4] To illustrate the issue with a simple example, suppose a physician's instructions were: "Eat fruit. Eat apples" (or "Take medicine. Take aspirin."). Apples are particular examples of fruit (as is aspirin of medicine). We may understand the instruction in two different ways. In his first sentence, in which the physician uses the general term "fruit" (or "medicine"), the physician might have had in mind only apples (or only aspirin pills), not other fruits (or medicine). In this case, the general term "fruit" (or "medicine") is construed as having only a particular reference, namely apples (aspirin). Alternatively, the physician may have meant fruit generally, i.e., any fruit (any medicine), and mentioned apples (aspirin) only as an example. I mention the two different examples because in these two cases the mind tends to leap to different conclusions: to a general construal in the first example (fruit), and a particular construal in the second example (aspirin).

Appendix

The Authenticity of Early Ḥanafī Texts: Two Books of al-Shaybānī

Introduction

The *Kitāb al-Āthār*[1] has the appearance of a direct record of the teachings of Muḥammad b. al-Ḥasan al-Shaybānī[2] in which he compares his legal rulings with those of various predecessors. That appearance, it has been recently argued, is at variance with the reality. The authenticity of the works attributed to second- and third-century Muslim scholars has been questioned. With regard to al-Shaybānī, the article in the second edition

[1] For information on the manuscripts of the *Kitāb al-Āthār* and brief biographical sketches of al-Shaybānī, see Carl Brockelmann, *Geschichte der Arabischen Litteratur* (Leiden: Brill, 1937), 1:288–291; Brockelmann, *Geschichte* (Leiden: Brill, 1943), 1:178–80; Fuat Sezgin, *Geschichte des arabischen Schrifttums* (Leiden: Brill, 1967), 1:421–433. Abū al-Wafā' al-Afghānī, in the introduction to his edition of the *Kitāb al-Āthār*, provides information on a number of manuscripts of the book. See al-Shaybānī, *Kitāb al-Āthār* (Karachi: al-Majlis al-'Ilmī, 1385), 1:10–11. However, I have used the previously cited edition from AH 1410. For more on manuscripts of the *Muwaṭṭa'*, see 'Abd al-Wahhāb 'Abd al-Laṭīf's introduction in Mālik b. Anas, *Muwaṭṭa' … al-Shaybānī*, 2nd ed. (Cairo: al-Majlis al-A'lā li-al-Shu'ūn al-Islāmiyya, 1967). For a study of the *isnād*s of the manuscripts, see the postscript at the end of this appendix.

[2] Several features give this impression. First, unlike other authorities, al-Shaybānī is almost always quoted in the first person (and occasionally in the third). In early Arabic prose the first person in quotations is usually interchangeable with the third. Therefore, normally one should not set much store by direct quotes. But if a regularity does emerge in a book of a thousand or so quotations, that must mean something. Second, the recurring phrases "Says Muḥammad [al-Shaybānī]" and "Muḥammad [al-Shaybānī] says" are not preceded with the name of an intermediary. Third, al-Shaybānī is the first person named in all the *isnād*s, without exception.

This appendix is an improved version of the following essay: Behnam Sadeghi, "The Authenticity of Two 2nd/8th-Century Legal Texts: the *Kitāb al-Āthār* and *al-Muwaṭṭa'* of Muḥammad b. al-Ḥasan al-Shaybānī," *Islamic Law and Society* 17.3 (Nov. 2010): 291–319.

of the *Encyclopaedia of Islam* by E. Chaumont states that "al-Shaybānī cannot really be considered in anything other than a remote sense the real author of the corpus attributed to him." Chaumont follows Norman Calder, who sees neither fixed books nor unique authors in the initial centuries of Islam, but rather growing texts reflecting the collective and continuous authorship of whole communities.[3] Christopher Melchert, another scholar who is impressed by Calder, seems to believe that the *Kitāb al-Āthār* and the recension of *Muwaṭṭa'* ascribed to al-Shaybānī do not have the same author(s). The *Kitāb al-Āthār*, he writes, is "entirely independent of ... Shaybānī's *Muwaṭṭa'*."[4]

Against these theories, I will argue that the *Kitāb al-Āthār* of al-Shaybānī has a single redactor who heard and recorded al-Shaybānī's lectures, except for the equivalent of a one-hour lesson amounting to six pages of the printed text, the contents of which were recorded by another person. These conclusions are based on considerations of style and vocabulary that preclude alternative scenarios. A key methodological assumption here is that while an irregular style and usage of vocabulary may or may not result from collective and piecemeal authorship, a highly regular and distinctive style may not. This assumption offers a simple and plausible explanation for the two highly distinct styles observed in the *Kitāb al-Āthār*.

[3] Calder does not mention the *Kitāb al-Āthār*; he discusses the *Muwaṭṭa'*. Yet clearly he would have taken a similar stance toward the *Kitāb al-Āthār*. See Norman Calder, *Studies in Early Muslim Jurisprudence* (Oxford: Clarendon Press, 1993), 39–66, for his discussion of early Ḥanafī texts. It would be a fair characterization of Calder's discussion to say that he puts a certain interpretation on the evidence without trying to show that competing theories fail to explain the evidence equally well (despite the fact that the burden of proof is generally on those who maintain that things are not as they appear, hence on Calder in this case). By contrast, my approach is to argue that one interpretation fits the evidence better than others.

In the last two decades, a number of other works have dealt with early Muslim literature. The following list is far from exhaustive: Jonathan Brockopp, *Early Mālikī Law* (Leiden: Brill, 2000); Dutton, *The Origins of Islamic Law*; Andreas Görke and Gregor Schoeler, *Die ältesten Berichte über das Leben Muhammads* (Princeton, NJ: Darwin Press, 2008); Wael Hallaq, "On Dating Mālik's *Muwaṭṭa'*," *UCLA Journal of Islamic and Near Eastern Law*, 1 (Fall 2001-Winter 2002): 47–65; Harald Motzki, "The Author and His Work in Islamic Literature of the First Centuries: The Case of 'Abd al-Razzāq's *Muṣannaf*," *Jerusalem Studies in Arabic and Islam* 28 (2003): 171–201; Ahmed El Shamsy, "The First Shāfi'ī: The Traditionalist Legal Thought of Abū Ya'qūb al-Buwayṭī (d. 231/846)," *Islamic Law and Society* 14 (Nov. 2007): 301–41.

[4] Christopher Melchert, "The Early History of Islamic Law," in *Method and Theory in the Study of Islamic Origins*, ed. Herbert Berg (Leiden: Brill, 2003), 323.

The evidence indicates that the *Kitāb al-Āthār* represents the lecture notes of two students of a single teacher who is alleged by the two students to be al-Shaybānī. These two attempted to write down in a verbatim fashion the traditions quoted by the teacher; however, when the teacher compared his views with those of other jurists, one or both students felt free to write down the comparisons in their own, personal styles. This discrepancy, I will argue, confirms that the teacher was not a scholar who projected his own views back onto al-Shaybānī; the teacher was indeed al-Shaybānī.

Moreover, it will be shown that the person whose style characterizes the book was its first redactor. In other words, the stylistic distinctiveness of the book did not result from the redactor's rewriting a text that had emerged through a messy process of organic growth. The book as we have it today is the original text.

I will argue for a similar conclusion in the case of the *Muwaṭṭa'* of al-Shaybānī and demonstrate its shared origin with the *Kitāb al-Āthār*. And having established the authorship of both books, I will discuss the authenticity of the material ascribed in the *Kitāb al-Āthār* to al-Shaybānī's Kūfan master, Abū Ḥanīfa, and to the late first/seventh-century Kūfan jurist, Ibrāhīm b. Yazīd al-Nakha'ī, as well as the material ascribed in the *Muwaṭṭa'* to Mālik b. Anas (d. 179/795–6).

The Corpora in the *Kitāb al-Āthār* and Their Common Features

Analyzed for style and vocabulary, the contents of the *Kitāb al-Āthār* unmistakably divide into two corpora, which will be called the P-corpus and the Q-corpus. The P-corpus consists of everything but the Q-corpus. The Q-corpus consists of a contiguous segment of about six pages in the printed edition and comprises twenty-three traditions. It is located about two-thirds into the book, where criminal law is treated, without evincing any thematic dislocation or discontinuity.[5] Internally, each corpus has certain highly regular and distinctive features of vocabulary and style that unequivocally point to unique redactors, whom I designate respectively P and Q.

[5] The P-corpus stops at the end of *bāb man wujida fī dārih qatīl*. At this point, the Q-corpus begins with the *bāb al-li'ān wa-intifā' min al-walad*, on page 305, no. 548, and goes on to cover several other headings dealing with penal law, through the end of *bāb dar' al-ḥudūd*, i.e., through page 311, no. 625. Then the P-corpus resumes with the *bāb ḥadd al-sakrān*.

Before discussing what makes the two corpora distinctive, it is necessary to examine their common features that characterize the book as a whole. The book is built around a core of traditions. The traditions typically alternate with commentaries that in turn may quote other traditions or authorities. A tradition that is quoted with an *isnād* is typically introduced by the formula *Muḥammad qāla* ("Says Muḥammad"). This phrase is distinctive for its inversion of the verb and the subject, as is the consistent use of the verb *qāla* (among other verbs that could have been used, such as *akhbaranā*, *ḥaddathanā*, *anba'anā*, *sami'tu*, etc.) This introductory formula almost always precedes an *isnād,* which in turn is followed by the text of the tradition. There are some 916 such traditions. In the great majority of them, Abū Ḥanīfa is the authority from whom al-Shaybānī relates. Thus, the most typical introductory formula is: *Muḥammad qāla akhbaranā Abū Ḥanīfa* ("Says Muḥammad: Abū Ḥanīfa informed me"). Abū Ḥanīfa, in turn, speaks mostly of Ḥammād (d. 120/737–8), who speaks mostly of Ibrāhīm al-Nakha'ī, at which point either the *isnād* ends and Ibrāhīm's own doctrine is related, or it continues with Ibrāhīm relating someone else's doctrine, act, or saying. Thus, the most common *isnād* or *isnād* segment is Abū Ḥanīfa—Ḥammād—Ibrāhīm.

A tradition thus quoted introduces the legal question at hand, whereupon al-Shaybānī's commentary provides his own position and that of Abū Ḥanīfa. Occasionally, opposing traditions from different earlier authorities are quoted, followed, again, by the positions of al-Shaybānī and Abū Ḥanīfa. The need to describe the relationships between the views of the different authorities – including al-Shaybānī, Abū Ḥanīfa, and at least one other person – necessitates the constant use of formulae to express the agreement or disagreement of one person with another. In addition to clarifying who (dis)agrees with whom, al-Shaybānī often elaborates on the legal points or the quoted traditions by way of explication or expansion.

In addition to this basic structure, the two corpora share a number of other features. They include the use of the same types of *isnād*s and of the same formulae to link the persons named in them. The frequencies of agreement or disagreement between the different authorities are consistent in the two corpora. In both, a second, redundant *qāla* ("he said") sometimes punctuates a tradition. More remarkably, in both one finds that when al-Shaybānī agrees with another authority "except in one respect," he uses the distinctive phrase *illā fī khaṣla wāḥida*. The distinctiveness of the phrase means that P and Q are unlikely to have thought of it independently. There is also another important similarity. In the Q-corpus, in exactly one case, al-Shaybānī rejects a view shared by Ibrāhīm and Abū Ḥanīfa. The formula he uses in this case is *wa-ammā fī qawlinā*. In the P-corpus, in similar cases of dissent, al-Shaybānī uses the exact same phrase half of the time, that is, in sixteen of the thirty-two cases. In light of the fact that – as will emerge soon – the two corpora are independent, these shared phrases must have come from the common source of P and Q.

One may now examine what makes the two corpora distinct by focusing on the phrases used to distinguish who agrees or disagrees with whom.

The P-Corpus

The most common situation, occurring hundreds of times, is that al-Shaybānī, Abū Ḥanīfa, and the authority cited in a tradition all agree. In P-corpus, the typical expression used in these cases follows this pattern, where brackets enclose optional elements and a forward slash separates alternative choices:

Muḥammad qāla: (the tradition). *Qāla Muḥammad* (*wa-bihi*/*wa-bi-hādhā* [*kullihi*]) *na'khudhu*. [Explanatory comment.] *Wa-huwa* [*kulluhu*] *qawl Abī Ḥanīfa*.

Translation:

Says Muḥammad: (the tradition). Muḥammad says: I follow [all of] this. [Explanatory comment.] And [all of] that is the position of Abū Ḥanīfa.

Infrequently, one sees *wa-hādhā qawl Abī Ḥanīfa* instead of *wa-huwa qawl Abī Ḥanīfa*.

Despite variations, this pattern holds in the overwhelming majority of cases in which the three people agree. When there are variations, it is more often in the order of elements or choice of material included (e.g., whether Abū Ḥanīfa is actually quoted) rather than in the choice of words. The choice of words, for example, the use of the verb *na'khudhu* or its cognates, is extremely distinctive, especially as it is repeated several hundred times. There are numerous ways to describe the same things (e.g., *'indanā, nadhhab ilā, fī ra'yinā, fī ra'yī, wa-innā narā anna, arā anna, 'alā qawlinā, wa-hādhā qawlī, wa-naqūlu inna*, etc.); the fact that only a single choice is adopted so often rules out chance altogether, indicating that a single redactor's style characterizes the P-corpus.

So far, the discussion of the vocabulary has covered cases of agreement with other authorities, which constitute the majority of the cases.

However, verbal and structural regularities are found also in the ways in which disagreements are described. Now, given the relatively small number of such instances, one would not expect a redactor to settle on a formula for expressing disagreement as readily as for expressing agreement. In other words, one must expect relatively greater variation in the formulae used. Indeed, one does find greater variation, alongside significant regularities. For analysis, I will focus only on the cases in which Ibrāhīm's views are reported. There are, by a rough estimate, 470 such cases (not including cases in which Ibrāhīm quotes or describes someone else's view or practice). Within this subset, I examine how al-Shaybānī's differences with Ibrāhīm and Abū Ḥanīfa are expressed. By my count, al-Shaybānī disagrees with Ibrāhīm forty-seven times. In all but five of these cases, al-Shaybānī points out that Abū Ḥanīfa agrees with him (i.e., both are against Ibrāhīm). The expression he uses to indicate this is almost always *wa-huwa qawl Abī Ḥanīfa*. His manner of differing with Ibrāhīm is more varied, but still highly distinctive, as well as familiar, given his frequent use of the verb *na'khudhu* and its cognates.[6] At times (sixteen cases), he says that he agrees with Ibrāhīm, but then makes a comment that reveals a partial disagreement; in fourteen of these sixteen cases, he uses the phrase *wa-bihi na'khudhu*. In thirty-one cases, he uses an expression to indicate disagreement rather than agreement. Two-thirds of the time, this expression is the distinctive *lasnā na'khudhu bi-hādhā*. In the remaining one-third of the cases, the expression varies, but involves *wa-ammā* in all cases but one.

I have counted thirty-two cases in which al-Shaybānī disagrees with Abū Ḥanīfa. He typically distinguishes his views from those of Abū Ḥanīfa by employing two phrases: (1) one that describes Abū Ḥanīfa's agreement with a tradition quoted, and (2) another phrase that introduces al-Shaybānī's own dissenting point of view. For (1), he uses the verb *ya'khudhu* fourteen times, doing so in the expression *bi-hādhā/bi-hi [kullihi] [kāna] ya'khudhu Abū Ḥanīfa* in twelve of these fourteen cases (bracketed words are optional). He uses the following expression eight times: *huwa/hādhā [kulluhu] qawl Abī Ḥanīfa*. For (2), he uses *wa-ammā fī qawlinā* sixteen times and *na'khudhu* sixteen times.

The Q-Corpus

The Q-corpus manifests its distinctive character with its very first tradition. Here, the saying of Ibrāhīm is followed by the opposing doctrine

[6] See the previous paragraph on *na'khudhu*.

of Abū Ḥanīfa. Then follow the words *kadhālik qāla Muḥammad* ("Muḥammad held the same view"). If you have read the book up to this point, you are startled by this expression, which occurs nowhere else. Your wonderment is compounded when you come to the next tradition, and then the one after that, and so on, as unfamiliar features appear in every one of them. Six pages later, when encountering *wa-bi-hādhā na'khudhu … wa-huwa qawl Abī Ḥanīfa*, you are once again on familiar grounds: P has returned.

In exactly twenty instances, after quoting traditions from Ibrāhīm in the Q-corpus, al-Shaybānī expresses either full agreement or agreement "except in one respect" both with the tradition of Ibrāhīm and with Abū Ḥanīfa. In the first three instances, he uses this locution: *wa-hādhā/huwa qawl Abī Ḥanīfa wa-Muḥammad* (he uses *huwa* once and *hādhā* twice). From this point on, he settles on one expression with which he stays through the end of the corpus, using it a total of fifteen times. The expression is:

Qāla Muḥammad hādhā [*kulluhu*] *qawl Abī Ḥanīfa wa-qawlunā* [*illa* [*fī khaṣla wāḥida*]].

None of the above expressions ever appear in the P-corpus. Compare them with the standard expression P uses:

wa-bihi na'khudhu … wa-huwa qawl Abī Ḥanīfa.

The differences are comprehensive, down to the tendency to use *hādhā* in one corpus and *huwa* in the other, two words that are normally interchangeable. Moreover, the verb *na'khudhu* and its cognates, which P uses hundreds of times, do not appear once in the Q-corpus.

Thus, the P-corpus has a single redactor, the Q-corpus has a single redactor, and the two redactors are not the same person.

The Relationship between P and Q

It has been shown that the P-corpus and the Q-corpus are two independent writings that draw on the same source. How does one explain their integration into one book? Could the Q-corpus represent a separate manuscript tradition of the book, a fragment of which found its way into a P-tradition? For example, could it be that after six pages of a manuscript were accidentally destroyed, the owner copied them from another manuscript, creating the hybrid version that has reached us?

A remarkable phenomenon weakens the above possibility. I already mentioned that Q begins with a locution (*kadhālik* …) that is uncharacteristic of either corpus. I also noted that it is with the fourth tradition that, after some hesitation, Q settles on one expression, which is thereafter used consistently. Indeed, a similar phenomenon is observed at the beginning of the P-corpus, which shows an even longer period of instability and vacillation (about five pages) before reaching the steady state.

The apparent explanation for the phenomenon is that as P and Q were taking notes, it took them a little experimentation, a degree of getting their feet wet, before they settled on locutions with which they felt comfortable. The Q-corpus, therefore, is not a chunk removed from a larger manuscript. It is complete. It originally began in the same place that the Q-corpus as we have it begins today. But why would anyone begin taking notes at such a late stage and, for such a short time; and how would his notes come to be incorporated in P's work? The answer may have already leaped to your mind. One day, P could not attend class. Perhaps he was sick, perhaps suffering from heartbreak. The cause is beside the point; the important thing is that either he or the lecturer asked Q to take notes for that day. Q may or may not have been P's classmate, but it appears that Q had not been taking down the lectures before, and that he was doing this as a favor. It is thanks to his act of kindness that we have the record of the lectures seamless and complete.

It should be noted, however, that the arguments regarding dating in the following sections do not depend on the knowledge that Q had started afresh. So, the overall conclusion of authenticity does not turn on the validity of the current section.

The Date of P and Q

Was P a student of al-Shaybānī? Or was the teacher one of the names in the long list that constitutes the *isnād* of the book, perhaps one who lived hundreds of years after al-Shaybānī? A clue to the answer is provided by comparing the traditions quoted in the two corpora with the variants in other collections of traditions, such as the *Kitāb al-Āthār* of Abū Yūsuf, the other famous student of Abū Ḥanīfa. The shared traditions are remarkably close in wording.[7] This means that the wording of the traditions in

[7] To establish the relative verbal fidelity of P, a quick-and-dirty test is to find those Prophetic *ḥadīth*s that both al-Shaybānī, as quoted by P, and Abū Yūsuf relate from Abū Ḥanīfa, and to examine whether they are worded similarly. This procedure readily confirms relative verbal uniformity, securing P's fidelity. However, the procedure cannot be repeated for the Q-corpus, which, short as it is, offers no traditions in common with Abū Yūsuf. Fortunately, to check the fidelity of Q, one may expand the search for parallels beyond

the *Kitāb al-Āthār* preserves the wording of the common source of P and Q. Thus, P or Q did not put the traditions in their own words. The key observation that will prove crucial for dating the book is as follows. The relative stability of the wording of the traditions contrasts unmistakably with the instability of the expressions P and Q used to denote the relationships among the views of al-Shaybānī, Abū Ḥanīfa, and so on. These expressions vary significantly from the P- to the Q-corpus, and they also vacillate at the beginning of each of them. As a shorthand, I call these expressions *transitional locutions*. This discrepancy between the wording of traditions and that of transitional formulae can be explained in two distinct ways that both lead to the same conclusion.

those found in Abū Yūsuf. However, parallels found in sources other than Abū Yūsuf are genetically more distant since their *isnād*s converge on the *isnād*s of Q in transmitters preceding Abū Ḥanīfa. Since anyone in the *isnād*s after the shared links could cause verbal changes, one would expect greater verbal differences (as compared to the differences between P and Abū Yūsuf). Indeed, we find some parallels with moderate to substantial verbal differences. What is remarkable is that one also finds quite a few instances of verbal uniformity. This supports the fidelity of Q in his transmissions, and tends to absolve him of responsibility in cases where a parallel is verbally different.

Here are some parallels with significant verbal similarity to traditions in the Q-corpus (the list is not meant to be exhaustive):

For tradition no. 601 ('Umar: *idhā aqarra al-rajul bi-waladih ṭarfata 'ayn*, etc.), see 'Abd al-Razzāq, *Muṣannaf*, 7:100, footnote 4, and al-Bayhaqī, *al-Sunan al-kubrā* (Beirut: Dār al-Fikr, n.d.), 7:411–12 (in both cases the *isnād*s bypass Abū Ḥanīfa to converge on his immediate authority).

For no. 610 (Prophet: *man balagha ḥaddan fī ghayr ḥadd*, etc.), see al-Bayhaqī, *al-Sunan al-kubrā*, 8:327 (with an *isnād* converging on al-Shaybānī's immediate authority).

For no. 614 (Ibn Mas'ūd: *innahumā yujladāni wa-yunfayāni sanatan, 'Alī*: etc.), see 'Abd al-Razzāq, *Muṣannaf*, 7:315, no. 13,327 ('Abd al-Razzāq—Abū Ḥanīfa—etc.: *yujladāni mi'atan wa-yunfayāni, 'Alī*: etc.).

For no. 616 (Ḥammād—Ibrāhīm: *al-lūṭī bi-manzilat al-zānī*), see Ibn Abī Shayba, *Muṣannaf*, 6:495, no. 8 (with entirely different *isnād* to Ibrāhīm yet same wording); cf. no. 6 (converges on Ḥammād—Ibrāhīm but has different wording).

For no. 619 (Ibrāhīm: *annahu su'ila 'an jāriyat imra'atih*, etc.), see al-Ṭaḥāwī, *Sharḥ ma'ānī al-āthār* (Beirut: Dār al-Kutub al-'Ilmiyya, 1416), 3:148 (with a different *isnād* to Ibrāhīm).

For no. 621 (Ḥammād—Ibrāhīm—'Umar: *idra'ū al-ḥudūd 'an al-muslimīn mā istaṭa'tum*, etc.), see 'Abd al-Razzāq, *Muṣannaf*, 10:116, no. 18,698 (with the *isnād* … al-Thawrī—Ḥammād—etc., thus bypassing Abū Ḥanīfa).

For no. 625 (Ibn 'Abbās: *man atā 'alā bahīma fa-lā ḥadd 'alayh*), see Ibn Abī Shayba, *Muṣannaf*, 6:516 (with an *isnād* converging on Abū Ḥanīfa's immediate authority).

It is true that occasionally one encounters *ḥadīth*s in al-Shaybānī's *Āthār* with highly aberrant wording, but the key point is that Abū Yūsuf reports the same aberrant wording, which points to Abū Ḥanīfa as the source of the wording. It appears that Abū Ḥanīfa reported some traditions word for word and paraphrased others, possibly due to reliance on a written source in the former case and on his memory in the latter case. Although transmission from Abū Ḥanīfa to his students appears to have involved careful dictation or written transmission, the same cannot always be said for the transmissions from all of Abū Ḥanīfa's authorities to him.

Scenario One. P and Q felt free to devise their own transitional locutions while they strove for exact quotation when it came to the actual traditions/doctrines. If so, what caused this discrepancy? It is not hard to explain. As a thought experiment, let us imagine ourselves as students taking notes. The professor first states a legal principle spoken by someone else, then says whether she and another famous jurist agree with it, in the process sometimes adding explanatory comments. In such a situation, we will tend to strive to accurately record information of two types: (1) the legal positions, principles and explanations, and (2) which position belongs to which authority. We will probably seek to record materials of the first type with high verbal fidelity. By contrast, we are not going to care as much about the exact wording (or symbols) we use to convey information of the second kind. Each one of us may concoct a different method, in other words a different set of transitional locutions or symbols. It would be different if our lecturer were not comparing her own views to those of others, that is, if instead she were merely dictating a dead person's book. In this case, both we and the lecturer could see the book as a finished product that no longer required our creative input; our task would simply be to replicate the book. We would then be likely to reproduce all elements of the book with equally good or poor accuracy. Obviously, that also would be the case if we copied the book from a master copy and then (possibly) read it back to the professor – a common method of transmission of finished works. Of these two thought experiments, the first corresponds to what we actually observe in the text. The discrepancy observed, therefore, originated not through later transmission, but at the moment a teacher gave lectures in which he compared *his own* views with those of others.

Scenario Two. The instability and vacillation at the beginning of the P-corpus originated with the common source of P and Q. On this hypothesis, P would not necessarily be an inexact transmitter: he could have transmitted with perfect fidelity. This in turn would raise two questions: what explains Q's vacillation and inaccuracy, and what explains the initial uncertainty of the common source? The first question takes us back to the first scenario and its solution. As for the second question, the initial uncertainty of the common source is expected if he is the person who originally composed the book through his lectures and dictations, but not if he is a later transmitter reciting a book.[8]

[8] Note that under the second scenario the text as we have it would represent the first (the only?) time the lecturer (al-Shaybānī) taught it; otherwise there would be less or no vacillation at its beginning.

Both scenarios indicate that the two corpora in their present form capture the moment when the work was first composed through lectures and dictations in that they preserve the reactions of two hearers of the lectures. At that moment, the book became the fixed text that has reached us. In sum, there is a lecturer, X, and the authentic texts of two independent redactors, P and Q, who heard X's lectures from him in a direct, unmediated fashion. Now, this X compared his own opinions to those of authorities before Muḥammad al-Shaybānī. Furthermore, P and Q both identified X, in the third person, as Muḥammad al-Shaybānī. What all this establishes is that the immediate hearers of X's lectures identified him as Muḥammad al-Shaybānī, and that this claim is consistent with the way X speaks of other authorities. It follows that al-Shaybānī was the common source of P and Q.

But could the material attributed to al-Shaybānī be the work of a later teacher, X, who lectured P and Q? After all, is it not easy to imagine that later Ḥanafī views would be projected back onto al-Shaybānī? In this scenario, X used the phrase "says Muḥammad" to introduce his own positions. Actually, this scenario would not account for the data. Before explaining why, one needs to remember the structure of the work. Typically, a section in either P or Q has the following structure: the third-person formula "Says Muḥammad" is followed by text that is composed of two types of material, (1) traditions about figures other than al-Shaybānī, and (2) transitional locutions (stated usually in the first person) comparing the speaker's own views to those of other figures, including those whose traditions were quoted. This is where the scenario runs into a problem: if the material ascribed to al-Shaybānī were the words of X, a figure later than al-Shaybānī, then both types of material introduced by "Says Muḥammad" would have the same status. The words ascribed only to al-Shaybānī himself, that is, the transitional locutions, would now be traditions about an earlier authority figure, al-Shaybānī, and as such would have the same status as other traditions. There would be no reason for either P or Q to treat the transitional formulae uttered by X any differently than the traditions, no reason for them to transmit one type of material verbatim while putting the other type in their own words. Yet, one finds that the two types of material were transmitted differently. If the common source were a later figure, then all the material after "Says Muḥammad" would have been transmitted with equally good or poor verbal fidelity, since now everything X stated would have been reports about past authorities; X would not be comparing his own views with those of other figures. What the data shows, however, is that P and Q treated the transitional formulae differently than the traditions.

As explained earlier in this section, this is compatible with their common source being a person who explicitly compared his own views with those of other figures. But in the hypothetical scenario, X would not be openly speaking of his own views; he would only be speaking of earlier authorities: al-Shaybanī, Abū Ḥanīfa, and so on.

Comparisons with *al-Muwaṭṭa'*

These conclusions are corroborated by the analysis of another work of al-Shaybānī, namely, his *Muwaṭṭa'*, a book in which he alternates the traditions of the Medinan jurist Mālik b. Anas with his own commentary and traditions. This is a more complex and subtle book than *al-Āthār*. It describes the precedents of more scholars and negotiates the disagreements between Mālik and the Kūfans, often bolstering the latter. This book has its own set of recurrent structures and phrases. There are very few comments of al-Shaybānī that do not use some of the following expressions:

qad balaghanā hādhā,
wa-balaghanā 'an fulān khilāf dhālik,
wa-bi-hādhā [*kullihi*] *na'khudhu*,
wa-huwa[9] [*kulluhu*] *qawl* [*fulān wa-*] *Abī Ḥanīfa* [*wa-fulān*] [*wa-al-'āmma* [*min fuqahā'inā*]/[[*min*] *qablinā*]],
wa-bi-qawl fulān na'khudhu,
lasnā na'khudhu bi-hādhā,
wa-ammā Abū Ḥanīfa [*fa-qāla*][*fa-innahu kāna ya'khudhu bi-qawl fulān*],
wa-kāna [*fulān*][*lā*] *ya'khudhu bi-*,
wa-ammā fī qawl [*fulān*],
ikhtalafa[*t*] *al-nās fī* …,
illā [*fī khaṣla wāḥida*],
[*wa-fī dhālik/hādhā*]/[*bi-dhālik jā'at*] *al-āthār/āthār kathīra/'āmmat al-āthār*,
[[*kull*] *hādhā/huwa*] [*hādhā* [*kulluhu*]] [*kull*] *ḥasan* [*jamīl*] [used for nonobligatory deeds],
[*wa-hādhā*] *lā ba'sa bi-*,
lā narā bi-hādhā ba'san/fa-kāna lā yarā bihi ba'san, and so forth,
afḍal,
[*lā*] *yanbaghī* …,
[*wa-huwa*] *aḥabb ilaynā*.

Thus, this book, too, is characterized by a distinctive, personal style.

Both the Q- and the P-corpus share some structural features with *al-Muwaṭṭa'* as well as the distinctive phrases *fī khaṣla wāḥida* and

[9] Much less frequently: *wa-hādhā*.

TABLE 1. *Distribution of additions to* wa-huwa qawl Abī Ḥanīfa

	Number of times followed by *wa-al-'āmma min fuqahā'inā*	Number of times followed by *wa-al-'āmma*	Number of times followed by *wa-al-'āmma [min] qablinā*	Number of times not followed by anything at all
1–50	3 (6%)	1	0	46
51–100	1 (2%)	0	0	49
101–150	17 (34%)	5	7	21
151–200	34 (68%)	5	0	11
201–250	35 (70%)	3	0	12
251–300	36 (72%)	4	0	10
301–350	36 (72%)	2	0	12
Whole-corpus (1–350) totals:	162 (46.3%)	20 (5.7%)	7 (2%)	161 (46%)

wa-ammā fī qawlinā, the use of *akhbaranā* to quote al-Shaybānī's informants, and the use of *qāla* to quote al-Shaybānī. More to the point, *al-Muwaṭṭa'* is intimately related to the P-corpus, as indicated by the constant use of the verb *na'khudhu*, other conjugations of the verb *akhadha*, and the ubiquitous phrases *wa-bi-hādhā [kullihi] na'khudhu* and *wa-huwa qawl Abī Ḥanīfa*. Other common *al-Muwaṭṭa'* phrases that make a debut in the P-corpus include *jā'a fī … āthār kathīra*[10] and the word *al-'āmma*.[11] The stylistic similarities of *al-Muwaṭṭa'* to the P-corpus can be plausibly explained by only two scenarios. Either the same hearer wrote down both the *Muwaṭṭa'* and the P-corpus (in which case he and/or al-Shaybānī would be responsible for the shared features), or different hearers wrote them down, doing so in a verbatim manner (in which case only al-Shaybānī would be responsible for the common features, and Q-corpus would be a nonverbatim reproduction). In any case, it is clear that *al-Muwaṭṭa'* and *al-Āthār* have a common source and date from the same period, as could be expected if al-Shaybānī played a role in creating both. To be sure, the style of *al-Muwaṭṭa'* does differ slightly from that of the P-corpus, but this is not surprising: it is common for an author's style to evolve over time and between different works.

One can learn even more about the composition of the *Muwaṭṭa'* and its relationship with *al-Āthār* by examining how its style evolves in the

[10] Al-Shaybānī, *Āthār*, 359, no. 818.

[11] For example, al-Shaybānī, *Āthār*, 262, no. 430.

course of the book: it seems that the *Muwaṭṭa'* was composed via lecturing after *al-Āthār*, and it is clear that its creator did not edit it significantly after the lectures.

The expression *wa-huwa [kulluhu] qawl Abī Ḥanīfa* occurs 350 times in the *Muwaṭṭa'*. About half the time, it is followed by another expression. One might think that the distribution of the additional expression would be about even throughout the book, but this is not so. At the beginning of the *Muwaṭṭa'*, the recurrent expression *wa-huwa [kulluhu] qawl Abī Ḥanīfa* is rarely followed by *wa-al-'āmma min fuqahā'inā*, that is, only about 2 to 6 percent of the time. Then the frequency of this addition rises smoothly to about 70 percent and remains fairly steady thereafter. This is shown in Table 1, where the 350 occurrences in the book of *wa-huwa [kulluhu] qawl Abī Ḥanīfa* are divided into seven groups of fifty each. For each group, the number of times a given phrase (or no phrase) follows is recorded. It can be seen that the transition occurs smoothly, mainly between the 50th and 100th instances (third row in the table). In this transitional phase, one also observes some vacillation and experimentation, as shown by the introduction of the short-lived alternatives *wa-al-'āmma qablanā* (see the table) and *wa-'alayh al-āmma 'indanā*. The vacillation indicates that, in the transitional phase, the "author" is experimenting with different ways of conveying information that he did not formerly think to include – namely whether the Kūfan consensus matched Abū Ḥanīfa's doctrine. As one reads on, one sees how he settles on one formula.

What does this pattern mean? First, note that *al-Muwaṭṭa'* begins with a style almost identical to that of the P-corpus in *al-Āthār*, and then it drifts away slightly. This suggests that the *Āthār* came before the *Muwaṭṭa'*. That conclusion fits with another fact: there is no vacillation at the beginning of *al-Muwaṭṭa'*. It is a sign of prior experience that this time, unlike in the case of *al-Āthār*, there was no need for the redactor or lecturer to get his feet wet. This provisional relative chronology of the texts happens to fit their contents: al-Shaybānī defines his doctrine relative to the legal tradition he is a part of in Iraq before expanding his horizons.

Second, the pattern indicates that the creator of the book did not go back and edit earlier parts of the book. The book was a "one-shot" undertaking. (Had he gone back, he would have added the phrase *wa-al-'āmma min fuqahā'inā* where appropriate.) This approach is what one would expect from composition by lectures, even though it is not incompatible with written composition. An author, working with written material that allowed him to go back and forth in the text with ease, could have systematically added *wa-al-ʿāmma min fuqahāʾinā* where appropriate in the early part of the book. Composition by lecturing does not afford this possibility.

The Question of Later Editing or Rewriting

How much did P edit the Q-corpus in the *Kitāb al-Āthār*? And how much did others edit the corpora once they were put together? Not much, the next paragraph will argue. But first, in this paragraph, I consider the one candidate for later editing that most readily suggests itself. The most conspicuous distinctive feature of the *Kitāb al-Āthār*, namely the ubiquitous expression *Muḥammad qāla* found in both corpora, cannot have been chosen by P and Q independently. Nor could the common source of P and Q be credited with it. Either its appearance in Q represents P's editorial hand, or its addition to the Q-corpus, or to both corpora, is the work of a later transmitter. Indeed, the lack of vacillation with regard to this expression at the beginning of the P-corpus may be a sign of its systematic addition after the completion of the first draft. It is not difficult to see why one would want to edit the text in this manner. The expression stands out in a written page, marking each tradition. It is akin to a modern editor's marking the traditions by adding numbers or bullets, or indenting paragraphs.

This is the sum total of probable significant editorial changes to the original text. Had P edited the Q-corpus any further, at some point in the Q-corpus he definitely would have used the verb *naʾkhudhu* or a cognate of it. And had later figures rewritten or edited the text, the two corpora would not have remained so different and distinct from each other. (If later redactors, say C and D, had altered the work of P and Q, the pure styles of P and Q would have ended up as P-C-D and Q-C-D, that is, each would have acquired a bit of C's and D's styles. That would have diluted the distinctness of the pure P and Q sections and, in this sense, would have made the book as a whole more uniform.) Moreover, editing and rewriting would have made the initial vacillation of each corpus less conspicuous.

In the case of the *Muwaṭṭaʾ* as well, later redaction is unlikely: First, *al-Muwaṭṭaʾ* and the P-corpus have a common origin, and what is sauce for the goose is sauce for the gander. Second, the style of the *Muwaṭṭaʾ* is extremely regular, and deviations are rare. Later redaction, especially by many people, would have introduced a significant number of deviations. Third, the phenomenon of stylistic drift, represented in the evolving frequency of the phrase *wa-al-ʿāmma min fuqahāʾinā*, suggests that the text is pristine (as discussed in the final paragraph of the last section).

The Traditions about Abū Ḥanīfa and Ibrāhīm

The bulk of the traditions in *al-Āthār* are transmissions by or about Ibrāhīm al-Nakhaʿī. The question arises whether these traditions really go back to Ibrāhīm or whether they were incorrectly projected back onto him. I will use the word "authenticity" to refer to the scenario in which Ibrāhīm really said these sayings. Thus, "authenticity" does not refer to the genuineness of what Ibrāhīm may have said about earlier authorities in the traditions ascribed to him.

Schacht has dismissed the authenticity of the material ascribed to Ibrāhīm on subjects other than ritual. A full investigation of the matter requires comparing the traditions of Ibrāhīm in the *Kitāb al-Āthār* with those found in many other sources – a task not attempted here. Rather, I will limit myself to the book at hand, and will criticize Schacht's refutation of authenticity. My criticism will not prove authenticity. But by refuting Schacht's disproof of authenticity, it will help restore the plausibility of authenticity pending further investigation. In the process, I will also consider Abū Ḥanīfa's corpus, and here I will offer positive evidence for the veracity of al-Shaybānī's accounts of Abū Ḥanīfa's doctrines.

The bulk of the Ibrāhīm traditions in the *Kitāb al-Āthār* are related by his student, Ḥammād. It is Ḥammād, "or someone using his name," who Schacht considers as the true author of the material ascribed to Ibrāhīm.[12] One of the arguments he offers is this:

> It is, moreover, part of a literary convention which found particular favor in Iraq and by which a legal scholar or author put his own doctrine or work under the aegis of his master. Shaibānī, for instance, refers at the beginning of every chapter of his *Jāmiʿ al-Ṣaghīr* and at the beginning of his *Kitāb al-Makhārij fīl-Ḥiyal* to the final authority of Abū Ḥanīfa as transmitted to him through Abū Yūsuf; this does not mean that the books in question were in any way based on works or lectures of Abū Ḥanīfa and Abū Yūsuf, but implies only the general relationship of pupil to master. We must take the standing reference of Ḥammād to Ibrāhīm as meaning the same.

Thus, Schacht suggests that the relationship of Ḥammād to Ibrāhīm is analogous to that of al-Shaybānī to Abū Ḥanīfa: Ḥammād's attributions to Ibrāhīm are just as valid or invalid as those of al-Shaybānī to Abū

[12] Schacht, *Origins*, 236.

Ḥanīfa. Let us accept such an equivalence and see where it leads. The obvious question is: how does one know that the abovementioned works of al-Shaybānī were in no way based on the work of Abū Ḥanīfa, despite al-Shaybānī's claim? Schacht does not say how he arrived at that conclusion. In assessing the validity of al-Shaybānī's attributions in the *Kitāb al-Āthār*, I propose that we take the lead from a method Schacht uses in his footnote to the above-quoted paragraph. He writes perceptively:

> But Abū Ḥanīfa did not, as a rule, project his own opinions back to Ḥammād and, through Ḥammād, to Ibrāhīm; this appears from the considerable differences as regards technical legal thought which exist between the authentic opinions dating from the time of Abū Ḥanīfa and those introduced by the *isnād* of Abū Ḥanīfa—Ḥammād—Ibrāhīm.

Therefore, if it were shown that there are considerable differences between al-Shaybānī and the opinions he attributes to Abū Ḥanīfa, it would follow from Schacht's method that al-Shaybānī did not, as a rule, project his own positions back to Abū Ḥanīfa. It happens that there are a good number of such cases. In the *Kitāb al-Āthār,* I have counted twenty-seven cases in which al-Shaybānī disagrees with Abū Ḥanīfa. By comparison, Abū Ḥanīfa disagrees with Ibrāhīm forty-seven times. However, a more meaningful comparison would be based on the ratio of disagreements to the total number of transmitted opinions. For Ibrāhīm, the latter number is roughly 470. For Abū Ḥanīfa, that number is greater by a factor of less than two. If, conservatively, one takes the factor to be two, then al-Shaybānī disagrees with Abū Ḥanīfa roughly a third as often as Abū Ḥanīfa with Ibrāhīm (i.e., in respectively 3 percent and 10 percent of the reported opinions).

In addition to the consequences of Schacht's method, there are other indications that al-Shaybānī did not automatically project his own views back to Abū Ḥanīfa as a matter of literary convention. In a number of cases, al-Shaybānī gives his opinion without saying if Abū Ḥanīfa held the same or an opposite view.[13] Moreover, in a couple of cases he reports Abū Ḥanīfa's response to a question posed by him.[14] And, in one case, he reports Abū Ḥanīfa's initial view and final view on a matter, declaring his preference for the former.[15]

[13] This is a partial list: al-Shaybānī, *Āthār*, nos. 50, 132, 333, 224, 225, 231, 235, 275, 278, 300, 367, 369, 375, 389, 424, 428, 463, 466, 521, 558, 616, 617, 642–3.

[14] Al-Shaybānī, *Āthār*, nos. 540, 614–5.

[15] Al-Shaybānī, *Āthār*, no. 568.

Now, given that – as observed by Schacht – Abū Ḥanīfa did not project his own positions back, and – as shown here using similar methods – al-Shaybānī did not do so either, doing so must have been less of a "literary convention" than Schacht assumes. Consequently, one cannot, without a positive indication, consider Ḥammād as the original author of the material he transmits on the authority of Ibrāhīm. However, Schacht holds that such positive indication does exist:

> [Much of] the information about Ibrāhīm can be positively shown to be spurious, because the opinions attributed to him express secondary stages in the development of the Iraqian doctrines, or because the reasoning ascribed to him presupposes the discussions of a later period, or because the legal thought with which he is credited is too highly developed for it to be possible in the first century.[16]

In the third category mentioned in this quotation, Schacht cites two alleged opinions of Ibrāhīm that he asserts are too sophisticated for his era and must date from the time of Ḥammād, who died just twenty-four years after Ibrāhīm. Such an argument requires that Schacht have a good idea of what legal thought was like one generation before Ḥammād, that is, toward the end of the first century AH. Indeed, he says exactly what it was like then: simply, legal thought in areas other than ritual was nonexistent at the time of Ibrāhīm.[17] From such a premise, it surely follows that the two traditions he adduces were too advanced for Ibrāhīm's time; but it also follows that so were hundreds of other traditions that are not related to rituals, roughly 80 percent of Ibrāhīm's alleged corpus. Clearly, it is Schacht's outline of the development of Islamic law that determines his dating of these traditions, not the other way around. But the evidentiary basis of that outline is unclear: it is hard to see how he forms such a precise idea of the quality of Ibrāhīm's legal thought, especially considering that he does not acknowledge the authenticity of the traditions purporting to describe that thought. The scheme may be said to rest on a circularity: one knows that the Ibrāhīm traditions on matters other than ritual are spurious because such thought was too advanced for his time; and one knows such thought was too advanced for his time because one has no authentic legal traditions about or from Ibrāhīm in areas other than ritual. The scheme also draws an unfounded distinction between the development of rituals and that of other laws.

[16] Schacht, *Origins*, 235.

[17] Schacht, *Origins*, 234, 237, etc. He makes the astonishing claim: "It is safe to conclude that the historical Ibrāhīm gave opinions on questions of ritual … but not on law proper. This is all that we can expect of a specialist in religious law toward the end of the first century" (237).

It would be outside the scope of this essay to analyze in detail each of the several corroborating examples adduced by Schacht for the first two categories mentioned in the quotation given above; but it can be said in general terms that his judgments of inauthenticity in these cases, too, depend on his chronology of the origins of the law, *ḥadīth*s, and legal maxims in the first two centuries of Islam – a chronology that is insufficiently corroborated.[18]

The Traditions of Mālik b. Anas

A similar argument applies, only more obviously, to the traditions that al-Shaybānī ascribes in his *al-Muwaṭṭa'* to Mālik b. Anas. Schacht did not doubt the validity of their ascription, but Calder did. Yet the fact that al-Shaybānī often disagrees with Mālik shows that he did not put his own positions in the mouth of Mālik.[19]

Conclusion

The arguments may be summarized as follows.

The P- and Q-corpus in the *Kitāb al-Āthār* employ different sets of transitional formulae in describing the teachings of a common source, and in both corpora the transitional formulae vacillate initially. By contrast, P and Q quote the traditions purveyed by that source with relative

[18] See, for example, Harald Motzki, *The Origins of Islamic Jurisprudence* (Leiden: Brill, 2002).

[19] This argument adds to the already powerful evidence for the historicity of the ascriptions to Mālik based on the correlation of *matn*s and *isnād*s. The basic idea is that just as one can analyze Greek manuscripts to draw tree diagrams (stemmas) depicting the descent and genetic relationships of the manuscripts, so too one can analyze *matns*, and when one does so, one generally observes a close correlation with the *isnād* tree, thus confirming that transmission took place through the channels specified by the *isnād*s. This method has been applied most extensively by Harald Motzki and Gregor Schoeler. See, for example, Motzki et al., *Analysing Muslim Traditions* (Leiden: Brill, 2010); Schoeler, *Charakter und Authentie der muslimischen Überlieferung über das Leben Mohammeds* (Berlin, New York: de Gruyter, 1996); cf. Andreas Görke et al., *Die ältesten Berichte über das Leben Muhammads*; cf. Iftikhar Zaman, "The Evolution of a Hadith: Transmission, Growth, and the Science of *Rijal* in a Hadith of Sa'd b. Abi Waqqas" (PhD diss., University of Chicago, 1991); Iftikhar Zaman, "The Science of *Rijāl* as a Method in the Study of Hadiths," *Journal of Islamic Studies* 5.1 (1994): 1–34.

Just as with Greek manuscripts one may reconstruct prototypes, so too it is often possible to reconstruct older versions of a tradition. A glance at the data used by Zaman in his dissertation shows that 100 percent of Mālik's wording can be reconstructed. In fact, one can also reconstruct more than 75 percent of the words of Mālik's informant, al-Zuhrī, as well as the full meaning of the remaining 25 percent of the tradition as it left the mouth of al-Zuhrī.

verbal fidelity. These features mean that the common source conveyed his teachings orally, and the text as we have it consists of the lecture notes of two students of the teacher. Therefore, identifying the teacher fixes the date of the text. Now, this lecturer was one who compared *his own* views with those of Abū Ḥanīfa and other jurists, including Zufar b. al-Hudhayl and Abū Yūsuf, and related traditions from a variety of second-century figures. This person was identified independently by both P and Q as al-Shaybānī, and his words were often recorded in the first person. All this points to al-Shaybānī as the lecturer. I ruled out the hypothesis of the common source being a later figure, X, since in that scenario (1) X could not be said to be comparing his own views with those of earlier authorities; and (2) P and Q would have no reason to treat transitional locutions differently from the traditions.

The authenticity of the *Kitāb al-Āthār* is thus established. The next question is: did the text, once written by P and Q, undergo any substantial editing/revision? The answer is negative, for otherwise the stylistic distinctiveness of the two corpora would have been blurred.

The so-called blemishes in the *Kitāb al-Āthār* that allow one to establish its authenticity are by comparison absent from *al-Muwaṭṭa'*. Nonetheless, the authenticity of *al-Muwaṭṭa'* can be established indirectly with equal confidence. Stylistically, this book is exceedingly regular, and it was quite clearly redacted by a single person. It has, in fact, the same style as that of the P-corpus, pointing to common origins. Since the *Kitāb al-Āthār* is authentic, so is al-Shaybānī's *Muwaṭṭa'*. Moreover, the possibility of substantial editorial or redactional revisions subsequent to the time of P can be discounted, not only because of the tightness and regularity of the style, but also because of the phenomenon of stylistic drift.

The *Kitāb al-Āthār* and the *Muwaṭṭa'* not only are authentic works of al-Shaybānī, but they also contain accurate reports of Abū Ḥanīfa's and Mālik's doctrines and traditions. Moreover, the ascriptions to Ibrāhīm al-Nakha'ī contained in the *Kitāb al-Āthār* are not yet demonstrably apocryphal as Schacht thought. Unless further evidence is brought into play, it is not implausible that they are accurate reports of Ibrāhīm's views and sayings. The dates of Ibrāhīm al-Nakha'ī's reports deserve further research.

Postscript: Later Trajectories

Their shared distinctive style shows that the *Kitāb al-Āthār* and the *Muwaṭṭa'* had common origins. Yet the two books followed very different trajectories. They inhabited different cities and were handed down in different milieus. According to the story told by its *isnāds*, the *Kitāb al-Āthār* reached Bukhārā already in al-Shaybānī's lifetime, which is remarkable but not surprising, considering that Ḥanafism had spread to Khurāsān already in the time of Abū Ḥanīfa.[20] The book was subsequently handed down among the Ḥanafī jurists and judges of Bukhārā on account of the importance they attached to al-Shaybānī and Abū Ḥanīfa. On the other hand, the *Muwaṭṭa'* of al-Shaybānī was transmitted in Baghdad by *ḥadīth* specialists with Ḥanbalī rather than Ḥanafī connections, perhaps because of the importance they attached to Mālik b. Anas.

In his introduction to the *Kitāb al-Āthār*, al-Nu'mānī gives an *isnād* for the book, the earliest part of which runs as follows:

> 'Abd al-Raḥmān b. Muḥammad al-Kirmānī (d. 543/1148–9, Marw, chief Ḥanafī jurist)—Abū Bakr [Muḥammad] b. al-Ḥusayn al-Arsābandī (d. 512/1118–9, Marw, Ḥanafī judge)—Abū 'Abd Allāh [al-Ḥusayn b. Aḥmad] al-Zūzanī (d. 486/1093–4, judge and grammarian)—Abū Zayd ['Abd Allāh b. 'Umar b. 'Īsā] al-Dabūsī (d. 430/1038–9, Bukhārā and Samarqand, Ḥanafī jurist)—Abū Ja'far [Muḥammad b. 'Amr b. al-Sha'bī] al-Usrūshanī[21] (in 440/1048–9 he was a Ḥanafī judge, Bukhārā or Samarqand)—Abū 'Alī al-Ḥusayn b. [al-] Khaḍir al-Nasafī (d. 424/1032–3, from Bukhārā, judge and Ḥanafī jurist)—Abū Bakr Muḥammad b. al-Faḍl [al-Faḍlī al-Kamārī] (d. 381/991–2, Bukhārā)—Abū Muḥammad 'Abd Allāh b. Muḥammad b. Ya'qūb al-Ḥārithī (b. 258/871–2, d. 340/951 or 345/956, Bukhārā, Ḥanafī jurist)—Abū 'Abd Allāh Muḥammad b. Abī Ḥafṣ al-Kabīr (Aḥmad b. Ḥafṣ, d. *ca.* 270/883, Bukhārā)—*abī* [i.e., Abū Ḥafṣ al-Kabīr Aḥmad b. Ḥafṣ, d. 217/832–3, Bukhārā, student of al-Shaybānī]—al-Imām Muḥammad b. al-Ḥasan al-Shaybānī.

The authority immediately after al-Shaybānī, Abū Ḥafṣ, must have been a prolific transmitter of the works of al-Shaybānī. This seems to be the case because al-Sarakhsī comments that Abū Ḥafṣ never related al-Shaybānī's *Siyar* from him, since this was al-Shaybānī's last book of law, composed when Abū Ḥafṣ had already left Iraq.[22] This indicates that the *Kitāb al-Āthār* had reached Bukhāra already in al-Shaybānī's lifetime.

The edition of *al-Muwaṭṭa'* by 'Abd al-Wahhāb 'Abd al-Laṭīf is based on four manuscripts as well as previous printings of the book. The editor

[20] Madelung, *Religious Trends in Early Islamic Iran*, 18–9.
[21] Read thus for al-Ustrūshanī. The *nisba* al-Usrūshanī refers to a region near Samarqand.
[22] Al-Sarakhsī, *Sharḥ kitāb al-Siyar al-kabīr* (Egypt: Maṭba'at Miṣr, 1960), 1.

quotes the *isnāds* that two manuscripts give for *al-Muwaṭṭa'*. Moreover, various sources give *isnāds* either for the whole *Muwaṭṭa'* or for individual traditions.[23] All of these *isnāds* have their earliest part in common, which is as follows:

Abū Ṭāhir 'Abd al-Ghaffār b. Muḥammad b. Ja'far b. Zayd al-Mu'addib (b. 345/956, d. 428/1036, Baghdad)—Abū 'Alī Muḥammad b. Aḥmad b. al-Ḥasan b. Isḥāq b. al-Ṣawwāf (b. *ca.* 270/883, d. 359/969, Baghdad)—Abū 'Alī Bishr b. Mūsā b. Ṣāliḥ b. Shaykh b. 'Amīra al-Asadī (b. 190–1/805–6, d. 288/900, Baghdad) —Abū Ja'far Aḥmad b. Muḥammad b. Mihrān al-Nasā'ī *qāla akhbaranā* Muḥammad b. al-Ḥasan [al-Shaybānī].

Unfortunately, nothing more is known about the first transmitter listed after al-Shaybānī, Aḥmad b. Muḥammad b. Mihrān.[24] The others were *ḥadīth* transmitters and scholars. The same *isnād*, down to Bishr b. Mūsā, carries the *Musnad* of 'Abd Allāh b. al-Zubayr al-Ḥumaydī (d. 219/834–5). Moreover, Abū 'Alī al-Ṣawwāf transmitted the *'Ilal* of Ibn Ḥanbal from the latter's son. (The text of the *'Ilal* was recited back to him, *quri'a 'alayh*, in the year 343.[25]) Interestingly, al-Ṣawwāf is not the only name in the *isnād* with a connection to Ibn Ḥanbal. Another one is Bishr b. Mūsā, an important traditionist whom Ibn Ḥanbal held in high esteem.[26] Moreover, Abū Ṭāhir related a number of traditions about Ibn Ḥanbal.

Let us see what happens beyond the common part quoted above. Those independently relating from the common link, Abū Ṭāhir 'Abd al-Ghaffār, are as follows:

1. Abū al-Ḥasan 'Alī b. al-Ḥusayn b. 'Alī b. Ayyūb al-Bazzāz (b. 410/1019, d. 492/1097, Baghdad, traditionist)
2. Abū Ṭāhir Aḥmad b. al-Ḥasan al-Bāqillānī (b. 416/1025, d. 489/1096, Baghdad, traditionist)

[23] See, e.g., al-Majlisī, *Biḥār al-anwār* (Beirut: Mu'assasat al-Wafā', 1403), 104:90–1, 106:52; Ibn 'Asākir, *Ta'rīkh madīnat Dimashq*, 36:454–5, 44:267.

[24] The fact that the first transmitters after al-Shaybānī in the two *isnāds* are different may suggest that the shared regularities in the transitional formulae entirely reflect al-Shaybānī's own style: thus, we have two redactors who stayed close to al-Shaybānī's wording. However, a different scenario seems possible as well. It could be that a single student, P, initially wrote down both books. Subsequently, another student made a copy of one of the books, and recited it back to al-Shaybānī, which allowed him to transmit the book without naming P as an intermediary. On this scenario, it would not be necessary to assume that the transitional formulae reflect al-Shaybānī's style (although they could).

[25] See the detailed remarks of the editor in Ibn Ḥanbal, *Kitāb al-'Ilal wa-ma'rifat al-rijāl* (Beirut: al-Maktab al-Islāmī, 1408), 1:101–6.

[26] See al-Dhahabī, *Siyar* (Beirut: Mu'assasat al-Risāla, 1413), 13:353–4.

3. Abū al-Faḍl Aḥmad b. al-Ḥasan[27] b. Khayrūn (d. 488/1095–6, Baghdad, major traditionist)

Thus, the book stayed with the traditionists of Baghdad through the fifth century AH. The branching *isnād*s in this century indicate the spread of awareness of the book. And the *isnād*s reveal the increasing interest of Ḥanafī jurists in the book shortly thereafter. The earliest Ḥanafī I have identified in the *isnād*s (other than al-Shaybānī and possibly his student) is al-Ḥusayn b. Muḥammad b. Khusraw al-Balkhī (d. 523/1128–9, Balkh and Baghdad), who received and transmitted the book in Baghdad. In due course, the names of several eminent Ḥanafī jurists would grace some *isnād*s of the book.

[27] Read thus for al-Ḥusayn.

Bibliography

Ḥanafī Legal Texts

Abū Ḥanīfa, al-Nuʿmān b. Thābit. *Kitāb al-Āthār … riwāyat … Muḥammad b. al-Ḥasan al-Shaybānī*. Karachi: al-Raḥīm Ākīdimī, 1410.

Abū al-Layth al-Samarqandī, Naṣr b. Muḥammad. *Khizānat al-fiqh wa-ʿUyūn al-masāʾil*. Ed. Ṣalāḥ al-Dīn al-Nāhī. Baghdad, 1385–6/1965–7.

Fatāwā al-nawāzil. Ḥaydarābād: Maṭbaʿat Shams al-Islām, 1355.

Abū al-Suʿūd, Muḥammad b. ʿAlī b. ʿAlī al-Ḥusaynī. *Fatḥ al-muʿīn ʿalā sharḥ al-Kanz, ḥāshiyat Muḥammad Abī al-Suʿūd al-Miṣrī al-Ḥanafī*. Karachi: H. M. Saʿīd, 1303.

Abū Yūsuf, Yaʿqūb b. Ibrāhīm. *Kitāb al-Āthār*. Ed. Abū al-Wafāʾ. Ḥaydarābād: Lajnat Iḥyāʾ al-Maʿārif al-Nuʿmāniyya, 1355.

Afghānī, ʿAbd al-Ḥakīm al-Qandahārī al-. *Kashf al-ḥaqāʾiq sharḥ Kanz al-daqāʾiq, wa-bi-ḥāmishih sharḥ al-Wiqāya li-… Ṣadr al-Sharīʿa ʿUbayd Allāh b. Masʿūd*. Karachi: Idārat al-Qurʾān wa-al-ʿUlūm al-Islāmiyya, 1987.

Āydīnī, Muḥammad al-Güzelḥiṣārī al-. "*Risāla fī dawām al-ḥukm*." In Kevin Reinhart, "When Women Went to Mosques." In *Islamic Legal Interpretation: Muftis and their Fatwas*, edited by Muhammad Khalid Masud, Brinkley Messick, and David Powers, 116–27. Cambridge: Harvard University Press, 1996.

ʿAynī, Badr al-Dīn Maḥmūd b. Aḥmad al-. *Al-Bināya sharḥ al-Hidāya*. 2nd ed. Annotated by Nāṣir al-Islām al-Rāmafūrī. Beirut: Dār al-Fikr, 1411/1990.

Bābirtī, Akmal al-Dīn Muḥammad b. Maḥmūd al-. *Sharḥ al-ʿInāya ʿalā al-Hidāya*. Printed with Muḥammad b. ʿAbd al-Wāḥid Ibn al-Humām. *Sharḥ Fatḥ al-qadīr*. Egypt: Maktabat Muṣṭafā al-Bābī al-Ḥalabī, 1389/1970.

Dabūsī, ʿUbayd Allāh b. ʿUmar b. ʿĪsā al-. *Kitāb Taʾsīs al-naẓar*. Egypt: al-Maṭbaʿa al-Adabiyya, n.d.

Ḥalabī, Ibrāhīm b. Muḥammad al-. *Multaqā al-abḥur*. Ed. Wahbī Sulaymān Ghāwijī al-Albānī. Beirut: Muʾassasat al-Risāla, 1409/1989.

Ghunyat al-mutamallī sharḥ al-kabīr li-Munyat al-muṣallī. Istanbul, 1295.

Ḥaṣkafī, Muḥammad b. ʿAlī al-. *Sharḥ al-Durr al-mukhtār*. Egypt: Maktabat Muḥammad ʿAlī Ṣubayḥ, n.d.

Ibn ʿĀbidīn, Muḥammad Amīn b. ʿUmar. [*Ḥāshiyat*] *Radd al-muḥtār ʿalā al-Durr al-mukhtār fī sharḥ Tanwīr al-abṣār*. Ed. ʿĀdil Aḥmad ʿAbd al-Mawjūd and ʿAlī M. Muʿawwaḍ. Beirut: Dār al-Kutub al-ʿIlmiyya, 1415-/1994-.

Minḥat al-Khāliq ʿalā al-Baḥr al-rāʾiq. Printed in Zayn al-Dīn b. Ibrāhīm Ibn Nujaym. *Al-Baḥr al-rāʾiq sharḥ Kanz al-daqāʾiq*. Cairo, n.d.

Ibn al-Humām, Muḥammad b. ʿAbd al-Wāḥid. *Sharḥ Fatḥ al-qadīr*. Egypt: Maktabat Muṣṭafā al-Bābī al-Ḥalabī, 1389/1970.

Ibn al-ʿImād, ʿAbd al-Raḥmān b. Muḥammad al-ʿImādī. *Hadīyat Ibn al-ʿImād li-ʿubbād al-ʿibād*. Printed in ʿAbd al-Ghanī b. Ismāʿīl al-Nābulusī, *Nihāyat al-murād fī sharḥ Hadīyat Ibn al-ʿImād*. Ed. ʿAbd al-Razzāq al-Ḥalabī. Dubai: Markaz Jumʿa al-Mājid, 1414/1994.

Ibn Nujaym, Sirāj al-Dīn ʿUmar b. Ibrāhīm. *Al-Nahr al-fāʾiq sharḥ Kanz al-daqāʾiq*. Beirut: Dār al-Kutub al-ʿIlmiyya, 1992.

Ibn Nujaym, Zayn al-Dīn Zayn b. Ibrāhīm. *Al-Baḥr al-rāʾiq sharḥ Kanz al-daqāʾiq*. Beirut: Dār al-Kutub al-ʿIlmiyya, 1418/1997.

Kākī, Muḥammd b. Muḥammad al-. *Miʿrāj al-dirāya fī sharḥ al-Hidāya*. Princeton, Islamic Manuscripts, ms. Garrett no. 97Y.

Karkhī, ʿUbayd Allāh b. al-Ḥusayn b. Dallāl al-. *Risāla fī al-uṣūl allatī ʿalayhā madār furūʿ al-Ḥanafiyya*. Printed with ʿUbayd Allāh b. ʿUmar al-Dabūsī, *Kitāb Taʾsīs al-naẓar*. Egypt: al-Maṭbaʿa al-Adabiyya, n.d.

Kāsānī, Abū Bakr b. Masʿūd al-. *Kitāb Badāʾiʿ al-ṣanāʾiʿ fī tartīb al-sharāʾiʿ*. Egypt: Maṭbaʿat Shirkat al-Maṭbūʿāt al-ʿIlmiyya, 1327-/1909-.

Khwārazmī, Muḥammad b. Maḥmūd al-. *Jāmiʿ masānīd al-imām al-aʿẓam*. Ḥaydarābād: Majlis Dāʾirat al-Maʿārif, 1332.

Laknawī, Muḥammad ʿAbd al-Ḥayy b. Muḥammad al-. *Tuḥfat al-nubalāʾ fī jamāʿat al-nisāʾ*. Ed. Ṣalāḥ Muḥammad Sālim Abū al-Ḥājj. ʿAmmān: Muʾassasat al-Risāla, Dār al-Bashīr, 2002.

Mālik b. Anas. *Muwaṭṭaʾ … riwāyat Muḥammad b. al-Ḥasan al-Shaybānī*. 2nd ed. Ed. ʿAbd al-Wahhāb ʿAbd al-Laṭīf. Cairo: al-Majlis al-Aʿlā li-al-Shuʾūn al-Islāmiyya, 1967.

Manbijī, ʿAlī b. Zakarīyā al-. *Al-Lubāb fī al-jamʿ bayna al-sunna wa-al-kitāb*. Jeddah: Dār al-Shurūq, 1983.

Marghīnānī, ʿAlī b. Abī Bakr al-. *Al-Hidāya sharḥ Bidāyat al-mubtadiʾ*. Ed. Muḥammad Muḥammad Tāmir and Ḥāfiẓ Āshūr Ḥāfiẓ. Cairo: Dār al-Salām, 1420/2000.

Mawṣilī, ʿAbd Allāh b. Maḥmūd al-. *Al-Ikhtiyār li-taʿlīl al-Mukhtār*. Beirut: Dār al-Maʿrifa, 1395/1975.

Minlā [Mullā] Khusraw, Muḥammad b. Farāmurz. *Durar al-ḥukkām fī sharḥ Ghurar al-aḥkām*. Istanbul: Muḥammad Asʿad, 1300.

Murtaḍā al-Zabīdī, Muḥammad b. Muḥammad. [*Kitāb*] *ʿUqūd al-jawāhir al-munīfa*. Ed. Wahbī Sulaymān Ghāwijī al-Albānī. Beirut: Muʾassasat al-Risāla, 1406/1985.

Nābulusī, ʿAbd al-Ghanī b. Ismāʿīl al-. *Nihāyat al-murād fī sharḥ Hadīyat Ibn al-ʿImād*. Ed. ʿAbd al-Razzāq al-Ḥalabī. Dubai: Markaz Jumʿa al-Mājid, 1414/1994.

Nasafī, 'Abd Allāh b. Aḥmad al-. *Kanz al-daqā'iq*. Printed with 'Uthmān b. 'Alī al-Zayla'ī. *Tabyīn al-ḥaqā'iq*. Ed. Aḥmad 'Izzū 'Ināya. Beirut: Dār al-Kutub al-'Ilmiyya, 1420/2000.

Qāḍī Khān, al-Ḥasan b. Manṣūr. *Fatāwā*. Printed on the margin of Shaykh Niẓām, al-, et. al. *Al-Fatāwā al-'Ālamgīrīya: al-Fatāwā al-Hindiyya fī madhhab al-imām al-a'ẓam Abī Ḥanīfa al-Nu'mān*. 3rd ed. Diyār Bakr: al-Maktaba al-Islāmiyya, 1393/1973.

Qāri'ī, al-Mullā 'Alī b. Sulṭān Muḥammad al-. *Sharḥ Musnad Abī Ḥanīfa*. Beirut: Dār al-Kutub al-'Ilmiyya, n.d.

Qudūrī, Aḥmad b. Muḥammad al-. *Mukhtaṣar al-Qudūrī fī al-fiqh al-Ḥanafī*. Ed. Kāmil M. M. 'Uwayḍa. Beirut: Dār al-Kutub al-'Ilmiyya, 1418/1997.

Samarqandī, 'Alā' al-Dīn Muḥammad b. Aḥmad al-. *Tuḥfat al-fuqahā'*. Ed. Muḥammad Zakī 'Abd al-Barr. Damascus: Maṭba'at Jāmi'at Dimashq, 1377/1958.

Sarakhsī, Muḥammad b. Aḥmad al-. *Kitāb al-Mabsūṭ*. Beirut: Dār al-Ma'rifa, n.d.

Uṣūl. Beirut: Dār al-Kutub al-'Ilmiyya, 1414/1993.

Sharḥ kitāb al-Siyar al-kabīr. Ed. Ṣalāḥ al-Dīn al-Munajjid. Egypt: Maṭba'at Miṣr, 1960.

Shaybānī, Abū 'Abd Allāh Muḥammad b. al-Ḥasan al-. *Kitāb al-Āthār*. See Abū Ḥanīfa, *Kitāb al-Āthār*.

Kitāb al-Āthār. Ed. Abū al-Wafā' al-Afghānī. Karachi: al-Majlis al-'Ilmī, 1385.

Al-Jāmi' al-kabīr. Ḥaydarābād: Lajnat Iḥyā' al-Ma'ārif al-Nu'māniyya, 1356.

Shurunbulālī, al-Ḥasan b. 'Ammār al-. *Marāqī al-falāḥ sharḥ Nūr al-īḍāḥ wa-najāt al-arwāḥ*. Ed. 'Abd al-Jalīl al-'Aṭā. Damascus: Dār al-Nu'mān li-al-'Ulūm, 1411/1990.

Nūr al-īḍāḥ. Printed with al-Ḥasan b. 'Ammār al-Shurunbulālī, *Marāqī al-falāḥ sharḥ Nūr al-īḍāḥ wa-najāt al-arwāḥ*. Ed. 'Abd al-Jalīl al-'Aṭā. Damascus: Dār al-Nu'mān li-al-'Ulūm, 1411/1990.

Ḥāshiya. Printed with Minlā [Mullā] Khusraw. *Durar al-ḥukkām fī sharḥ Ghurar al-aḥkām*. Istanbul: Muḥammad As'ad, 1300.

Ṭaḥāwī, Aḥmad b. Muḥammad b. Salāma al-. *Mukhtaṣar al-Ṭaḥāwī*. Ed. Abū al-Wafā' al-Afghānī. Cairo: Maṭba'at Dār al-Kitāb al-'Arabī, 1370.

Mukhtaṣar ikhtilāf al-'ulamā'. Printed with Aḥmad b. 'Alī al-Jaṣṣāṣ. *Mukhtaṣar ikhtilāf al-'ulamā' … Ikhtiṣār Abī Bakr Aḥmad b. 'Alī al-Jaṣṣāṣ*. Ed. 'Abd Allāh Nadhīr Aḥmad. Beirut: Dār al-Bashā'ir al-Islāmiyya, 1416/1995.

Sharḥ ma'ānī al-āthār. 3rd ed. Ed. Muḥammad Z. al-Najjār. Beirut: Dār al-Kutub al-'Ilmiyya, 1416/1996.

Ṭaḥṭāwī, Aḥmad b. Muḥammad b. Ismā'īl al-. *Ḥāshiyat al-Ṭaḥṭāwī 'alā al-Durr al-mukhtār*. Beirut: Dār al-Ma'rifa, 1395/1975.

Ḥāshiyat al-Ṭaḥṭāwī 'alā Marāqī al-falāḥ sharḥ Nūr al-īḍāḥ. Egypt: al-Maktaba al-Tijāriyya al-Kubrā, 1356.

Timurtāshī, Muḥammad b. 'Abd Allāh al-. *Kitāb matn Tanwīr al-abṣār wa-jāmi' al-biḥār*. [Cairo?]: Maṭba'at Ḥasan Aḥmad al-Ṭūkhī, 1298.

Zayla'ī, Jamāl al-Dīn al-. *Naṣb al-rāya*. Cairo: Dār al-Ḥadīth, 1415/1995.

Zayla'ī, 'Uthmān b. 'Alī b. Miḥjan al-. *Tabyīn al-ḥaqā'iq*. Ed. Aḥmad 'Izzū 'Ināya. Beirut: Dār al-Kutub al-'Ilmiyya, 1420/2000.

Other Premodern or Early Modern Sources

'Abd al-Razzāq b. Hammām, Abū Bakr al-Ṣan'ānī. *Al-Muṣannaf*. Ed. Ḥabīb al-Raḥmān al-A'ẓamī. Beirut: al-Majlis al-'Ilmī, 1970-.

'Ajlūnī, Ismā'īl b. Muḥammad al-. *Kashf al-khafā'*. Beirut: Dār al-Kutub al-'Ilmiyya, 1408/1988.

Bayhaqī, Abū Bakr Aḥmad b. al-Ḥusayn b. 'Alī al-. *Al-Sunan al-kubrā*. Beirut: Dār al-Fikr, n.d.

Bukhārī, Abū 'Abd Allāh Muḥammad b. Ismā'īl al-. *Ṣaḥīḥ al-Bukhārī*. Istanbul: Dār al-Ṭibā'a al-'Āmira, 1315.

Dhahabī, Abū 'Abd Allāh Shams al-Dīn Muḥammad b. Aḥmad b. 'Uthmān b. Qāymāz al-. *Siyar a'lām al-nubalā'*. 9th ed. Ed. Shu'ayb al-Arna'ūṭ et al. Beirut: Mu'assasat al-Risāla, 1413/1993.

Mīzān al-i'tidāl fī naqd al-rijāl. Ed. 'Alī Muḥammad al-Bajāwī. Beirut: Dār al-Ma'rifa, 1382/1963.

Tadhkirat al-ḥuffāẓ. Beirut: Dār Iḥyā' Turāth al-'Arabī, n.d.

Risāla fī al-ruwāt al-thiqāt. Printed with Ibn Quṭlūbughā. *Munyat al-Alma'ī*. Ed. Muḥammad Zāhid b. al-Ḥasan al-Kawtharī. Karachi: 1412.

Ḥājī Khalīfa, Muṣṭafā b. 'Abd Allāh Kātib Jalabī. *Kashf al-ẓunūn*. Ed. Muḥammad Sharaf al-Dīn Yāltaqāyā et al. Beirut: Dār Iḥyā' al-Turāth al-'Arabī, n.d.

Ḥumaydī, Abū Bakr 'Abd Allāh b. al-Zubayr al-. *Musnad al-Ḥumaydī*. Ed. Ḥabīb al-Raḥmān al-A'ẓamī. Beirut: Dār al-Kutub al-'Ilmiyya, 1409/1988.

Ibn Abī al-Wafā', Muḥyī al-Dīn Abū Muḥammad 'Abd al-Qādir b. Muḥammad b. Muḥammad al-Qurashī. *Al-Jawāhir al-muḍiyya fī ṭabaqāt al-Ḥanafiyya*. Ḥaydarābād: Maṭba'at Majlis Dā'irat al-Ma'ārif al-'Uthmāniyya,1988-

Ibn Abī Shayba, Abū Bakr 'Abd Allāh b. Muḥammad b. Ibrāhīm b. 'Uthmān. *Muṣannaf Ibn Abī Shayba fī al-aḥādīth wa-al-āthār*. Ed. Sa'īd al-Laḥḥām. Beirut: Dār al-Fikr, 1409/1989.

Ibn 'Adī, 'Abd Allāh. *Al-Kāmil*. 3rd ed. Beirut: Dār al-Fikr, 1409/1998.

Ibn 'Asākir, Abū al-Qāsim 'Alī b. al-Ḥasan b. Hibat Allāh. *Ta'rīkh madīnat Dimashq*. Ed. 'Alī Shīrī. Beirūt: Dār al-Fikr, 1415/1995.

Ibn al-Athīr, al-Mubārak b. Muḥammad. *Jāmi' al-uṣūl fī aḥādīth al-rasūl*. Ed. Ayman Ṣāliḥ Sha'bān. Beirut: Dār al-Kutub al-'Ilmiyya, 1418/1998.

Ibn Ḥajar al-'Asqalānī, Aḥmad b. 'Alī. *Tahdhīb al-tahdhīb*. Beirūt: Dār al-Fikr, 1404/1984.

Ibn Ḥanbal, Abū 'Abd Allāh Aḥmad b. Muḥammad. *Kitāb al-'Ilal wa-ma'rifat al-rijāl*. Ed. Waṣī Allāh b. Muḥammad 'Abbās. Beirut: al-Maktab al-Islāmī, 1408/1988.

Musnad. Beirut: Dār Ṣādir, n.d.

Ibn al-Jawzī, Abū al-Faraj 'Abd al-Raḥmān b. 'Alī b. Muḥammad. *Al-Muntaẓam fī ta'rīkh al-mulūk wa-al-umam*. Beirut: Dār al-Kutub al-'Ilmiyya, 1992.

Ibn Khuzayma, Abū Bakr Muḥammad b. Isḥāq. *Ṣaḥīḥ*. Ed. Muḥammad Muṣṭafā al-A'ẓamī. Beirut: al-Maktab al-Islāmī, 1412/1992.

Ibn Manẓūr, Muḥammad b. Mukarram. *Lisān al-'Arab*. Qum: Nashr Adab al-Ḥawza, 1406/ Sh.1363.

Ibn Quṭlūbughā, Abū al-'Adl Zayn al-Dīn al-Qāsim b. 'Abd Allāh. *Tāj al-tarājim fī ṭabaqāt al-Ḥanafiyya*. Baghdad: Maktabat al-Muthannā, 1962.

Munyat al-Alma'ī. Ed. Muḥammad Zāhid b. al-Ḥasan al-Kawtharī. Karachi: 1412.

Ibn Rushd, Abū al-Walīd Muḥammad b. Aḥmad. *Bidāyat al-mujtahid wa-nihāyat al-muqtaṣid*. Beirut: Dār al-Fikr, 1415/1995.

Ibn Sa'd, Abū 'Abd Allāh Muḥammad. *Al-Ṭabaqāt al-kubrā*. Beirut: Dār Ṣādir, 1968.

'Ijlī, Abū al-Ḥasan Aḥmad b. 'Abd Allāh b. Ṣāliḥ al-. *Ma'rifat al-thiqāt*. Ed. 'Abd al-'Alīm 'Abd al- 'Aẓīm al-Bastawī. Medina: Maktabat al-Dār, 1405/1985.

Ismā'īl Bāshā al-Baghdādī, b. Muḥammad Amīn b. Mīr Salīm. *Hadiyyat al-'ārifīn asmā' al-mu'allifīn wa-āthār al-muṣannifīn*. Istanbul: Wikālat al-Ma'ārif, 1951-.

Khaṭīb al-Baghdādī, Abū Bakr Aḥmad b. 'Alī b. Thābit al-. *Tārīkh Baghdād*. Ed. Muṣṭafā 'Abd al-Qādir 'Aṭā'. Beirut: Dār al-Kutub al-'Ilmiyya, 1417/1997.

Majlisī, Muḥammad Bāqir b. Muḥammad al-. *Biḥār al-anwār*. Beirut: Mu'assasat al-Wafā', 1403/1983.

Mizzī, Jalāl al-Dīn Abū al-Ḥajjāj Yūsuf b. 'Abd al-Raḥmān al-. *Tahdhīb al-Kamāl fī asmā' al-rijāl*. 4th ed. Ed. Bashshār 'Awwād Ma'rūf. Beirut: Mu'assasat al-Risāla, 1406/1985.

Qurṭubī, Abū 'Abd Allāh Muḥammad b. Aḥmad al-. *Tafsīr*. Ed. Aḥmad 'Abd al-'Alīm al-Bardūnī and Muṣṭafā al-Saqā. Beirut: Dār Iḥyā' al-Turāth al-'Arabī, 1405/1985.

Sam'ānī, Abū Sa'd 'Abd al-Karīm b. Muḥammad b. Manṣūr al-. *Al-Ansāb*. Ed. 'Abd Allāh 'Umar al-Bārūdī. Beirut: Dār al-Janān, 1408/1988.

Suyūṭī, 'Abd al-Raḥmān b. Abī Bakr al-. *Al-Durr al-manthūr fī al-tafsīr bi-al-ma'thūr*. Beirut: Dār al-Ma'rifa li-al-Ṭibā'a wa-al-Nashr, n.d.

Ṭabarānī, Sulaymān b. Aḥmad al-. *Al-Mu'jam al-kabīr*. 2nd ed. Ḥamdī 'Abd al-Majīd. Beirut: Dār Iḥyā' al-Turāth al-'Arabī, 1984-.

Ṭabarī, Abū Ja'far Muḥammad b. Jarīr al-. *Jāmi' al-bayān 'an ta'wīl āy al-Qur'ān*. Beirut: Dār al-Fikr, 1415/1995.

Ṭarsūsī, Najm al-Dīn Ibrāhīm b. 'Alī al-. *Kitāb Tuḥfat al-Turk: œuvre de combat Ḥanafīte à Damas au XIVe siècle*. Damascus: Institut français de Damas, 1997.

Tirmidhī, Abū 'Īsā Muḥammad b. 'Īsā al-. *Sunan*. 2nd ed. Ed. 'Abd al-Wahhāb 'Abd al-Laṭīf. Beirut: Dār al-Fikr, 1403/1983.

Modern Sources

Abd-Allah, U. F. "Abū Ḥanīfa." *Encyclopaedia Iranica*. London: Routledge, 1982-.

Abou el-Fadl, Khaled. *Rebellion and Violence in Islamic Law*. Cambridge: Cambridge University Press, 2001.

Abū Zahra, Muḥammad. *Abū Ḥanīfa*. Cairo: Dār al-Fikr al-'Arabī, 1366/1947.

Ahmad, Ahmad Atif. *Structural Interrelations of Theory and Practice in Islamic Law*. Leiden: E. J. Brill, 2006.

Ahmed, Leila. "Women and the Advent of Islam." *Signs* 2.4 (1986): 665–91.

Ali, Kecia. "Money, Sex, and Power: The Contractual Nature of Marriage in Islamic Jurisprudence of the Formative Period." PhD diss., Duke University, 2002.

"Progressive Muslims and Islamic Jurisprudence: The Necessity for Critical Engagement with Marriage and Divorce Law." In *Progressive Muslims: On Justice, Gender and Pluralism*, edited by Omid Safi, 163–89. Oxford: Oneworld, 2003.

Sexual Ethics and Islam. Oxford: Oneworld, 2006.

Allen, Prudence. *The Concept of Woman: The Aristotelian Revolution, 750 B.C. – A.D. 1250*. Grand Rapids, Michigan: William B. Eerdmans Publishing Company, 1985.

Andersson, Gunnar. *Criticism and the History of Science: Kuhn's, Lakatos's and Feyerabend's Criticisms of Critical Rationalism*. Leiden: E. J. Brill, 1994.

Azami, Muhammad Mustafa al-. *On Schacht's Origins of Muhammadan Jurisprudence*. Oxford: Oxford Centre for Islamic Studies, 1996.

Bell, Catherine. *Ritual Theory, Ritual Practice*. New York: Oxford University Press, 1992.

Belo, Catarina. "Some Considerations on Averroes' Views Regarding Women and their Role in Society." *Journal of Islamic Studies* 20.1 (2009): 1–20.

Brockelmann, Carl. *Geschichte der arabischen Litteratur*. Leiden: E. J. Brill, 1937 (Erster Supplementband), 1938 (Zweiter Supplementband), 1942 (Dritter Supplementband).

Geschichte der arabischen Litteratur, Zweite den Supplementbänden angepasste Auflage. Leiden: E. J. Brill, 1943 (Erster Band), 1949 (Zweiter Band).

Brockopp, Jonathan. *Early Mālikī Law: Ibn 'Abd al-Ḥakam and his Major Compendium of Jurisprudence*. Leiden, Boston: E. J. Brill, 2000.

Calder, Norman. *Studies in Early Muslim Jurisprudence*. Oxford: Clarendon Press, 1993.

Carlson, David. "The Traumatic Dimension in Law." *Cardozo Law Review* 24.6 (2003): 2287–329.

Chaumont, E. "Shaybānī." *Encyclopaedia of Islam*. New ed. Leiden: E. J. Brill, 1960-.

Cohn, Haim. "Legal Change in Unchangeable Law: The Talmudical Pattern." In *Legal Change: Essays in Honour of Julius Stone*, ed. A. R. Blackshield, 10–33. Sidney: Butterworths, 1983.

Dickinson, Eerik. "Aḥmad b. al-Ṣalt and his Biography of Abū Ḥanīfa." *Journal of the American Oriental Society* 116.3 (1996): 406–17.

Dutton, Yasin. "*'Amal* v. *Ḥadīth* in Islamic Law: The Case of *sadl al-yadayn* (Holding One's Hands by One's Sides) when Doing the Prayer." *Islamic Law and Society* 3 (1996): 13–40.

The Origins of Islamic Law. Surrey: Curzon, 1999.

Fadel, Mohammed. "'*Istiḥsān* is Nine-Tenths of the Law': The Puzzling Relationship of *Uṣūl* to *Furū'* in the Mālikī *Madhhab*." In *Studies in Islamic Legal Theory*, edited by Bernard Weiss, 161–76. Leiden: E. J. Brill, 2002.

Fish, Stanley. "Play of Surfaces: Theory and the Law." In *Legal Hermeneutics: History, Theory, and Practice*, edited by Gregory Leyh, 297–316. Berkeley: University of California Press, 1992.

Friedman, Matt. "The Evolutionary Origin of Flatfish Asymmetry." *Nature* 454 (July 2008): 209–12.

Gleave, Robert. *Inevitable Doubt: Two Theories of Shī'ī Jurisprudence*. Leiden: E. J. Brill, 2000.

Görke, Andreas and Gregor Schoeler. *Die ältesten Berichte über das Leben Muhammads: das Korpus 'Urwa ibn az-Zubair*. Princeton, NJ: Darwin Press, 2008.

Gurāyā, Muḥammad Yūsuf. *Origins of Islamic Jurisprudence*. Lahore: Muḥammad Ashraf, 1985.

Hallaq, Wael. "Was the Gate of *Ijtihād* Closed?" *International Journal of Middle Eastern Studies* 16.1 (1984): 3–41.

"*Uṣūl al-fiqh*: Beyond Tradition." *Journal of Islamic Studies* 3.2 (1992): 172–202.

A History of Islamic Legal Theory. Cambridge: Cambridge University Press, 1997.

Law and Legal Theory in Classical and Medieval Islam. Cambridge: Cambridge University Press, 2001.

Authority, Continuity, and Change in Islamic Law. Cambridge: Cambridge University Press, 2001.

"On Dating Mālik's *Muwaṭṭa'*." *UCLA Journal of Islamic and Near Eastern Law* 1 (Fall 2001-Winter 2002): 47–65.

The Origins and Evolution of Islamic Law. Cambridge: Cambridge University Press, 2005.

Jackson, Sherman. *Islamic Law and the State: The Constitutional Jurisprudence of Shihāb al-Dīn al-Qarāfī*. New York: E. J. Brill, 1996.

"Islam, Muslims, and Socio-political Reality in the United States." *American Journal of Islamic Social Sciences* 17.3 (2000): 1–25.

"Kramer versus Kramer in a 10th/16th Century Egyptian Court: Postformative Jurisprudence between Exigency and Law." *Islamic Law and Society* 8.1 (2001): 27–51.

"Fiction and Formalism: Toward a Functional Analysis of *uṣūl al-fiqh*." In *Studies in Islamic Legal Theory*, edited by Bernard Weiss, 177–201. Leiden: E. J. Brill, 2002.

Johansen, Baber. *The Islamic Law on Land Tax and Rent: The Peasants' Loss of Property Rights as Interpreted in the Hanafite Legal Literature of the Mamluk and Ottoman Periods*. London: Croom Helm, 1988.

Kaḥḥāla, 'Umar Riḍā'. *Mu'jam al-mu'allifīn*. Beirut: Maktabat al-Muthannā, n.d.

Kamali, Mohammad Hashim. *The Principles of Islamic Jurisprudence*. Rev. ed. Cambridge: Islamic Texts Society, 1991.

Kant, Immanuel. "What is Enlightenment?" In *The Enlightenment: A Sourcebook and Reader*, edited by Paul Hyland, Olga Gomez, and Francesca Greensides, 54–8. London: Routledge, 2003.

Katz, Marion. *Body of Text: The Emergence of the Sunnī Law of Ritual Purity*. Albany: State University of New York Press, 2002.

"The Study of Islamic Ritual and the Meaning of *Wuḍū'*." *Der Islam* 82 (2005): 106–45.

"The 'Corruption of the Times' and the Mutability of the *Shari'a*." *Cardozo Law Review* 28.1 (2006): 171–85.

Khaṭīb, ʿAbd al-Laṭīf Muḥammad al-. *Muʿjam al-qirāʾāt*. Damascus: Dār Saʿd al-Dīn, 1422/2002.

Kīrawānī, Ḥabīb Aḥmad al-. *Abū Ḥanīfa wa-aṣḥābuh*. Beirut: Dār al-Fikr al-ʿArabī, 1989.

Knapp, Steven and Walter Benn Michaels. "Intention, Identity, and the Constitution: A Response to David Hoy." In *Legal Hermeneutics: History, Theory, and Practice*, edited by Gregory Leyh, 187–99. Berkeley: University of California Press, 1992.

Lahoud, Nelly. *Political Thought in Islam: A Study of Intellectual Boundaries*. London: Routledge Curzon, 2005.

Lakatos, Imre. "Falsification and the Methodology of Scientific Research Programmes." In *Criticism and the Growth of Knowledge*, edited by Imre Lakatos and Alan Musgrave, 91–195. Cambridge: Cambridge University Press, 1970.

Leaman, Oliver. *Islamic Aesthetics: An Introduction*. Notre Dame, IN: University of Notre Dame Press, 2004.

Levinson, Bernard. *Legal Revision and Religious Renewal in Ancient Israel*. Cambridge: Cambridge University Press, 2008.

Lutfi, Huda. "Manners and Customs of Fourteenth-Century Cairene Women." In *Women in Middle Eastern History: Shifting Boundaries in Sex and Gender*, edited by Nikki Keddie and Beth Baron, 99–121. New Haven: Yale University Press, 1991.

Madelung, Wilferd. *Religious Trends in Early Islamic Iran*. Albany, NY: Persian Heritage Foundation, 1988.

Maḥmūd, ʿAbd al-Majīd. *Al-Madrasa al-fiqhiyya li-al-muḥaddithīn*. Cairo: Maktabat al-Shabāb, 1972.

Melchert, Christopher. *The Formation of the Sunnī Schools of Law, 9th-10th Centuries C.E.* Leiden: E. J. Brill, 1997.

"The Early History of Islamic Law." In *Method and Theory in the Study of Islamic Origins*, edited by Herbert Berg, 293–324. Leiden: E. J. Brill, 2003.

"Whether to Keep Women out of the Mosque: A Survey of Medieval Islamic Law." In *Authority, Privacy and Public Order in Islam*, edited by Michalak-Pikulska and A. Pikulski, 59–70. Leuven: Peeters, 2006.

Modarressi, Hossein. *Kharāj in Islamic Law*. London: Anchor Press, 1983.

Motzki, Harald. *The Origins of Islamic Jurisprudence*. Trans. Marion Katz. Leiden: E. J. Brill, 2002.

"The Author and His Work in Islamic Literature of the First Centuries: The Case of ʿAbd al-Razzāq's *Muṣannaf*." *Jerusalem Studies in Arabic and Islam* 28 (2003): 171–201.

Nicolet Boekhoff-van der Voort, and Sean W. Anthony. *Analysing Muslim Traditions: Studies in Legal, Exegetical and Maghazi Hadith*. Leiden: E. J. Brill, 2010.

Musallam, Basim. *Sex and Society in Islam: Birth Control before the Nineteenth Century*. Cambridge: Cambridge University Press, 1983.

Naqīb, Aḥmad b. Muḥammad Naṣīr al-Dīn al-. *Al-Madhhab al-Ḥanafī: marāḥiluh wa-ṭabaqātuh, ḍawābiṭuh wa-muṣṭalaḥātuh, khaṣāʾiṣuh wa-muʾallafātuh*. Riyadh: Maktabat al-Rushd, 2001.

Pelikan, Jaroslav. *Interpreting the Bible and the Constitution*. New Haven and London: Yale University Press, 2004.

Popper, Karl. *The Logic of Scientific Discovery*. London: Hutchinson, 1959.

Rawls, John. "The Idea of Public Reason Revisited." *The University of Chicago Law Review* 64.3 (Summer 1997): 765–807.

Political Liberalism. Expanded ed. Columbia University Press: New York, 2005.

Reinhart, Kevin. "When Women Went to Mosques." In *Islamic Legal Interpretation: Muftis and their Fatwas*, edited by Muhammad Khalid Masud, Brinkley Messick, and David Powers, 116–27. Cambridge: Harvard University Press, 1996.

Robinson, Chase. "Reconstructing Early Islam: Truth and Consequences." In *Method and Theory in the Study of Islamic Origins*, edited by Herbert Berg, 101–34. Leiden: E. J. Brill, 2003.

Sadeghi, Behnam. "The Traveling Tradition Test: A Method for Dating Traditions." *Der Islam* 85.1: 203–42.

Sanders, Paula. "Gendering the Ungendered Body: Hermaphrodites in Medieval Islamic Law." In *Women in Middle Eastern History: Shifting Boundaries in Sex and Gender*, edited by Nikki Keddie and Beth Baron, 74–95. New Haven: Yale University Press, 1991.

Schacht, Joseph. "Pre-Islamic Background and Early Development of Jurisprudence." In *Law in the Middle East*, edited by Majid Khadduri and Herbert J. Liebesny, 28–56. Washington, D.C.: The Middle East Institute, 1955.

Introduction to Islamic Law. Oxford: Clarendon Press, 1966.

The Origins of Muhammadan Jurisprudence. Oxford: Clarendon Press, 1967.

Schoeler, Gregor. *Charakter und Authentie der muslimischen Überlieferung über das Leben Mohammeds*. Berlin: de Gruyter, 1996.

Sezgin, Fuat. *Geschichte des arabischen Schrifttums*. Leiden: E. J. Brill, 1967-.

Shamsy, Ahmed El. "The First Shāfiʿī: The Traditionalist Legal Thought of Abū Yaʿqūb al-Buwayṭī (d. 231/846)." *Islamic Law and Society* 14 (Nov. 2007): 301–41.

Watson, Alan. *Legal Origins and Legal Change*. London: Hambledon Press, 1991.

The Nature of Law. Edinburgh: Edinburgh University Press, 1977.

The Evolution of Law. Baltimore: John Hopkins University Press, 1985.

Ancient Law and Modern Understanding. Athens, Georgia: University of Georgia Press, 1998.

Society and Legal Change. 2nd ed. Philadelphia: Temple University Press, 2001.

Weiss, Bernard. *The Search for God's Law*. Salt Lake City: University of Utah Press, 1992.

The Spirit of Islamic Law. Athens, Georgia: University of Georgia Press, 2006.

Wheeler, Brannon. *Applying the Canon in Islam: The Authorization and Maintenance of Interpretive Reasoning in Ḥanafī Scholarship*. Albany: State University of New York Press, 1996.

Zaman, Iftikhar. "The Evolution of a Hadith: Transmission, Growth, and the Science of *Rijal* in a Hadith of Sa'd b. Abi Waqqas." PhD diss., University of Chicago, 1991.

"The Science of *Rijāl* as a Method in the Study of Hadiths." *Journal of Islamic Studies* 5.1 (1994): 1–34.

Ziriklī, Khayr al-Dīn. *Al-A'lām*. 5th ed. Beirut: Dār al-'Ilm li-al-Malāyīn, 1980.

Zysow, Aron. "The Economy of Certainty: An Introduction to the Typology of Islamic Legal Theory." PhD diss., Harvard University, 1984.

Index

Titles in the series *(continued from page iii)*

Popular Culture in Medieval Cairo, Boaz Shoshan

Early Philosophical Shiism: The Ismaili Neoplatonism of Abu Ya'qub Al-Sijistani, Paul E. Walker

Indian Merchants in Eurasian Trade, 1600–1750, Stephen Frederic Dale

Palestinian Peasants and Ottoman Officials: Rural Administration Around Sixteenth-Century Jerusalem, Amy Singer

Arabic Historical Thought in the Classical Period, Tarif Khalidi

Mongols and Mamluks: The Mamluk–Ilkhanid War, 1260–1281, Reuven Amitai-Preiss

Hierarchy and Egalitarianism in Islamic Thought, Louise Marlow

The Politics of Households in Ottoman Egypt: The Rise of the Qazdağlis, Jane Hathaway

Commodity and Exchange in the Mongol Empire: A Cultural History of Islamic Textiles, Thomas T. Allsen

State and Provincial Society in the Ottoman Empire: Mosul, 1540–1834, Dina Rizk Khoury

The Mamluks in Egyptian Politics and Society, Thomas Philipp and Ulrich Haarmann (eds.)

The Delhi Sultanate: A Political and Military History, Peter Jackson

European and Islamic Trade in the Early Ottoman State: The Merchants of Genoa and Turkey, Kate Fleet

Reinterpreting Islamic Historiography: Harun Al-Rashid and the Narrative of the 'Abbasid Caliphate, Tayeb El-Hibri

The Ottoman City Between East and West: Aleppo, Izmir, and Istanbul, Edhem Eldem, Daniel Goffman, and Bruce Masters

A Monetary History of the Ottoman Empire, Sevket Pamuk

The Politics of Trade in Safavid Iran: Silk for Silver, 1600–1730, Rudolph P. Matthee

The Idea of Idolatry and the Emergence of Islam: From Polemic to History, G. R. Hawting

Classical Arabic Biography: The Heirs of the Prophets in the Age of Al-Ma'mun, Michael Cooperson

Empire and Elites After the Muslim Conquest: The Transformation of Northern Mesopotamia, Chase F. Robinson

Poverty and Charity in Medieval Islam: Mamluk Egypt, 1250–1517, Adam Sabra

Christians and Jews in the Ottoman Arab World: The Roots of Sectarianism, Bruce Masters

Culture and Conquest in Mongol Eurasia, Thomas T. Allsen

Revival and Reform in Islam: The Legacy of Muhammad Al-Shawkani, Bernard Haykel

Tolerance and Coercion in Islam: Interfaith Relations in the Muslim Tradition, Yohanan Friedmann

Guns for the Sultan: Military Power and the Weapons Industry in the Ottoman Empire, Gábor Ágoston

Marriage, Money and Divorce in Medieval Islamic Society, Yossef Rapoport

The Empire of the Qara Khitai in Eurasian History: Between China and the Islamic World, Michal Biran

Domesticity and Power in the Early Mughal World, Ruby Lal

Power, Politics and Religion in Timurid Iran, Beatrice Forbes Manz

Postal Systems in the Pre-Modern Islamic World, Adam J. Silverstein

Kingship and Ideology in the Islamic and Mongol Worlds, Anne F. Broadbridge

Justice, Punishment, and the Medieval Muslim Imagination, Christian Lange

The Shiites of Lebanon Under Ottoman Rule, Stefan Winter

Women and Slavery in the Late Ottoman Empire, Madeline Zilfi

The Second Ottoman Empire: Political and Social Transformation in the Early Modern World, Baki Tezcan

Non-Muslims in the Early Islamic Empire: From Surrender to Coexistence, Milka Levy-Rubin

The Legendary Biographies of Tamerlane: Islam and Heroic Apocrypha in Central Asia, Ron Sela

Ritual and Piety in Medieval Islamic Law, Megan Reid

The Origins of the Shi'a: Identity, Ritual, and Sacred Space in Eighth-Century Kufa, Najam Haider

Politics, Law and Reason in Islamic Thought: The Taymiyyan Moment, Ovamir Anjum

The Power of Oratory in the Medieval Muslim World, Linda G. Jones

Animals in the Qur'an, Sarra Tlili

The Logic of Law Making in Islam: Women and Prayer in the Legal Tradition, Behnam Sadeghi